D0153094

Alcoholism and Clinical Psychiatry

Alcoholism and Clinical Psychiatry

Edited by
Joel Solomon
Downstate Medical Center
Brooklyn, New York

Plenum Medical Book Company
New York and London

Library of Congress Cataloging in Publication Data

Main entry under title:

Alcoholism and clinical psychiatry.

  Bibliography: p.
  Includes index.
  1. Alcoholism—Addresses, essays, lectures. 2. Psychiatry—Addresses, essays,
lectures. 3. Psychology, Pathological—Addresses, essays, lectures. I. Solomon,
Joel. [DNLM: 1. Alcoholism—Complications. 2. Alcoholism—Therapy. 3. Mental
disorders—Complications. WM 274 A3548]

| RC565.A44533 | 616.86′1 | 81-22701 |
| ISBN 0-306-40794-9 | | AACR2 |

© 1982 Plenum Publishing Corporation
233 Spring Street, New York, N.Y. 10013
Plenum Medical Book Company is an imprint of Plenum Publishing Corporation

All rights reserved

No part of this book may be reproduced, stored in a retrieval system, or transmitted,
in any form or by any means, electronic, mechanical, photocopying, microfilming,
recording, or otherwise, without written permission from the Publisher

Printed in the United States of America

OLSON LIBRARY
NORTHERN MICHIGAN UNIVERSITY
MARQUETTE, MICHIGAN 49855

Contributors

Malcolm Beaudett, BS   Third-Year Medical Student, State University of New York, Downstate Medical Center, Brooklyn, New York

Sheila B. Blume, MD   Director, New York State Division of Alcoholism and Alcohol Abuse, Clinical Associate Professor, Department of Psychiatry, Albany Medical College, Albany, New York

Marc Galanter, MD   Director, Division of Alcoholism and Drug Abuse, Associate Professor, Department of Psychiatry, Albert Einstein College of Medicine, Bronx, New York

Donald M. Gallant, MD   Professor, Department of Psychiatry, Adjunct Professor of Pharmacology, Tulane University School of Medicine, New Orleans, Louisiana

Donald W. Goodwin, MD   Professor and Chairman, Department of Psychiatry, University of Kansas Medical Center, Kansas City, Kansas

Meredith Hanson, MSW   Clinical Instructor, Division of Alcoholism, State University of New York, Downstate Medical Center, Brooklyn, New York

Martin S. Kesselman, MD   Professor, Department of Clinical Psychiatry, State University of New York, Downstate Medical Center, Director of Psychiatry, Kings County Hospital Center, Brooklyn, New York

Elizabeth T. Khuri, MD   Clinical Associate Professor of Public Health, Cornell University Medical College, New York, New York

Benjamin Kissin, MD   Associate Chairman and Professor, Department of

Psychiatry, State University of New York, Downstate Medical Center, Brooklyn, New York

Gerald L. Klerman, MD Professor of Psychiatry, Psychiatric Service, Harvard Medical School, Massachusetts General Hospital, Boston, Massachusetts

Robert B. Millman, MD Clinical Professor of Public Health, Associate Professor of Clinical Psychiatry, Cornell University Medical College, New York, New York

Frederic M. Quitkin, MD Director, Depression Evaluation Service, New York State Psychiatric Institute; Associate Professor of Clinical Psychiatry, Columbia University College of Physicians and Surgeons, New York, New York

Judith G. Rabkin, PhD Research Scientist, New York State Psychiatric Institute; Adjunct Assistant Professor of Public Health in Psychiatry, Columbia University College of Physicians and Surgeons, New York, New York

Austin Silber, MD Clinical Professor of Psychiatry, Training and Supervising Analyst, The Psychoanalytic Institute at the New York University Medical Center, New York, New York

Joel Solomon, MD Clinical Associate Professor, Director, Division of Alcoholism and Drug Dependence, Department of Psychiatry, State University of New York, Downstate Medical Center, Brooklyn, New York

Barbara Thornton, RN Unit Chief, Kingsboro Psychiatric Center, Clinical Instructor, State University of New York, Downstate Medical Center, Brooklyn, New York

Joseph Westermeyer, MD, PhD Professor, Department of Psychiatry, University of Minnesota, Minneapolis, Minnesota

Sheldon Zimberg, MD Director of Psychiatry, Joint Diseases, North General Hospital, New York, New York

Foreword

It is well known that alcoholism continues to be one of this country's major public health problems. This issue is carefully documented by Dr. Gerald Klerman, Chief of ADAMHA, in the second chapter of this volume. In spite of the major role that alcohol plays in the health care issues of internal medicine, neurology, and psychiatry, the subject continues to fall between the cracks of the various disciplines. For this reason, it has become almost a discipline of its own; yet there are no academic departments of alcoholism because academic departments are unidisciplinary and alcoholism is clearly a multidisciplinary field within medicine.

In spite of the many disciplines involved in the study and treatment of alcoholism, psychiatry continues to have a special, albeit often neglected, relationship to alcoholism, and it is the articulation of that relationship which prompted the Department of Psychiatry at the Downstate Medical Center to organize the conference upon which many chapters in this volume are based. Particular emphasis in selecting the topics to be covered was placed on the interface between alcoholism and clinical psychiatry, including affective disorders, schizophrenia, suicide, adolescence, the special problems of women, and psychotherapy, to mention only some of them.

The realization that psychiatric disorders cause as well as result from alcoholism has prompted the Residency Review Committee of the American Psychiatric Association to call increasing attention to the need for more training in alcoholism in psychiatric training programs. We hope that this volume will serve as a resource for trainees, clinicians, and other students of this area of medicine and health care.

EUGENE FEIGELSON, MD
Chairman, Department of Psychiatry

State University of New York
Downstate Medical Center
Brooklyn, New York

Preface

This book is composed largely of papers delivered at a conference held on October 24 and 25, 1980 at the New York Academy of Medicine. The decision to develop this conference and subsequent book was based on several events presently occurring in the fields of alcoholism and psychiatry.

Alcoholism or alcohol dependence is now generally accepted as a psychiatric disorder and during the acute phase, alcoholism can manifest a wide range of psychiatric symptomatology. The course of alcoholism is acknowledged to be progressive and varied and psychiatric factors may be present at all points along the alcoholic pathway. Psychiatric symptoms may preexist the alcoholism and play a role in its development, may arise as a complication of chronic alcoholism, may be part of any phase of acute alcoholism, or may occur as an independent event in an alcoholic. Until recently, psychiatrists generally ignored the alcoholic or viewed him as morally weak, with a bad habit symptomatic of severe underlying psychopathology which was substantiated by labeling it with psychoanalytic terminology.

From the other perspective, the alcoholic community has been wary of psychiatry and its labels as well as the ability of psychiatrists to treat this population. Medication was often inappropriately prescribed, groups such as AA were perceived as threatening, and patients spent years on the couch drinking their way through interpretations of preoedipal conflicts rather than directly addressing the problem.

The rapprochement has been slow, but has been taking place nevertheless. There seems to be general agreement that psychiatric impairment is not the same in all alcoholics. Many, perhaps even most alcoholics can be treated without psychiatric involvement because their primary problem is alcohol and the medical and social complications which arise as a result. Other alcoholics clearly need the assistance of psychiatric intervention and withholding it may be ignoring a factor which perpetuates the alcoholism.

The relationships between the various psychiatric disorders and alcoholism need clear delineation. It is hoped that this volume is of assistance in developing a better understanding of both conditions and, most important, their effective treatment.

JOEL SOLOMON, MD

Contents

CHAPTER 1

The Bio-psycho-social Perspective in Alcoholism

BENJAMIN KISSIN, MD, and MEREDITH HANSON, MSW

In the past several decades, a bio-psycho-social perspective has become very popular in psychiatry, most particularly in the field of psychosomatic medicine but elsewhere as well.[1-4] There is general agreement that certain behavioral disorders may involve several pathogenetic mechanisms at one level or another; however, in any given syndrome, there is wide disagreement as to the relative impact of these mechanisms. Thus, for schizophrenia, biological psychiatry stresses aberration in biogenic amine metabolism, psychoanalysis emphasizes defective ego structures and traumatic early experience, and social psychiatry describes pathological family constellations. Although each discipline tends to acknowledge the existence of the others and the legitimacy of their findings, little attempt is made to investigate possible interactions among pathogenetic mechanisms at different levels. Rather, each discipline tends to see its own explanations as paramount, with other influences either adding or substracting (in a purely arithmetic and linear fashion) to the critical mass necessary to achieve clinical pathology. This viewpoint tends to dominate psychiatry, which, like its parent discipline, medicine, recognizes that multiple explanations frequently signify only that the real etiology has not yet been discovered.

In the field of alcoholism the situation is further complicated by the fact that many conflicting theories—often associated with different academic disciplines—exist side by side with only minimal efforts to integrate them into a unified approach to the study of alcoholism. Each of these theories is highly

BENJAMIN KISSIN • Associate Chairman and Professor, Department of Psychiatry, State University of New York, Downstate Medical Center, Brooklyn, New York 11203. **MEREDITH HANSON** • Clinical Instructor, Division of Alcoholism, State University of New York, Downstate Medical Center, Brooklyn, New York, 11203.

resilient in the face of competing evidence. According to Golüke et al, there is good reason for this resilience:

> They all are necessary but insufficient, decriptions of reality. There is always some alcoholic whose crucial enzyme is missing, always someone who drinks to experience delusions of power, . . . and always one who has an oral fixation. Unfortunately, however, the reverse is also true.[5(p11–12)]

Given this wealth of contradictory information, the typical reseacher and practitioner follow a pattern similar to the one described by Pearson:

> Commonly all the busy practitioner can do is forget it and "get on with the job," and commonly all the researcher or academic can do is recognize that the conclusion of someone else's study is not his own conclusion. . . . All conclusions embody theories and ideologies, and no amount of conclusive evidence can sway a reader from a theory or ideology which he finds persuasive. . . . Men choose from theories what they find useful, and they ditch what they cannot use or what discomforts them.[6(x–xi)]

It is highly probable that most syndromes are multiply determined and that they require a combination of biological, psychological, and social factors for their development. It is our contention that alcoholism represents a prototypical bio-psycho-social syndrome with influences operating at all three levels in the pathogenesis of the condition. As the alcoholic dynamic emerges, mechanisms at all three levels appear to operate sequentially and simultaneously so as to influence the development and course of the syndrome, its perpetuation, and its interruption.

Before expanding on this concept, however, it is necessary to define the terms in the title of this paper. The word "biological" as used here is certainly a misnomer; it should probably be replaced by the term "physiological" since all behavior—physiological, psychological, and social—is in some respects biological. Nevertheless, we shall continue to use the original term in its more popular sense. "Psychological" behavior, in turn, is reciprocally determined by physiological (metabolic), experiential (psychological), and social influences so that its interpretation must also be qualified. Finally, "social" refers to the contextual and situational factors, such as culture, class, normative standards, and physical setting, which impinge on and influence the actions of individuals.

The term "alcoholism" is equally indeterminate. As used here, alcoholism is best conceptualized as the last stage in a continuum of drinking which extends from social drinking to heavy drinking to problem drinking to alcoholism, where each population represents a subcategory of the one preceding it (Fig 1). Heavy drinkers, as defined here, are social drinkers who, often because of social influences, drink more than the average person. Problem drinkers are heavy drinkers who have developed significant psychological dependence on alcohol. Alcoholics are those who have

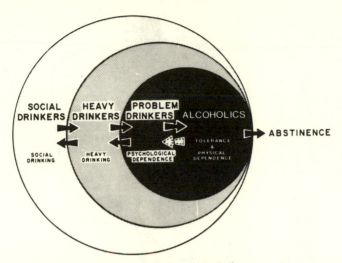

Fig 1. Progression of alcoholism.

developed both significant psychological and physical dependence. It should be noted that according to this thesis, heavy drinking and problem drinking are frequently reversible, but alcoholism is probably not. Therefore, problem drinkers may revert to the heavy drinking or even social drinking conditions, but such a recourse may or may not be possible for true alcoholics.

The relationships hypothesized in Figure 1 are based upon clinical experience, sociological findings, and laboratory data. This model suggests that the alcoholism syndrome typically is an interactive phenomenon, realized in multiple forms and under the influence of multiple variables operating sequentially and simultaneously in its development. Although each of these factors—the sociological, psychological, and biological variables—may be more or less critical for different persons at different points in time and in different settings, an understanding of each factor is necessary for an accurate assessment of the condition.

The sequence illustrated in Figure 1 may also be viewed as the interaction over time of a more or less susceptible individual with the psychopharmacological agent, ethanol, in a variety of social contexts. This paradigm is illustrated in Figure 2. At each point in the emergence of alcoholism, the individual's reactions are reciprocally determined by biological, psychological, and social influences which lead to increased or decreased alcohol ingestion. At some point in this sequence (different for different persons), however, an "addictive cycle" develops, in which the person becomes physically dependent on alcohol. The emergence of physical dependence has major implications for the assessment and treatment of the alcohol condition.

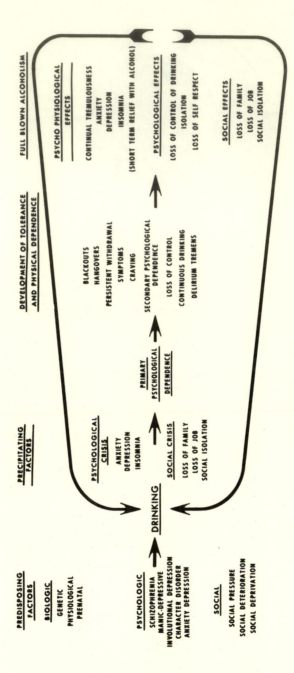

Fig 2. The addictive cycle in alcoholism.

At the point when physical dependence has been established the syndrome "alcoholism" may be said to have developed.

Before discussing the variables lised in Figure 2 a final point must be made about the use of the bio-psycho-social conceptualization. This approach is more accurately viewed as an organizing framework or perspective from which to view the multiple factors which determine whether or not a particular person develops an alcohol problem or condition. Such a viewpoint insures that the professional will address equally those biological, psychological, and social factors which impinge on the alcoholic, helping him to avoid premature closure on any one factor.

To follow Minahan's distinction between perspectives and theories, a theory is "a coherent set of general propositions that are related or connected to each other in a way that *explains* phenomena." A perspective, on the other hand, does *not* explain phenomena;

> Perspectives are ways to think about and visualize situations. . . . Before applying *theories* to situations, we need to use a *perspective* for looking at situations of concern. . . . [The] perspective [we use] needs to be broad enough to help us identify and view all [the] pertinent interaction.[7]

Given these distinctions, the bio-psycho-social view presented here is a perspective within which we can organize our knowledge about alcoholism. It is *not* a comprehensive, explanatory theory.

The influences which contribute to individual susceptibility are listed in Figure 2 under the heading "Predisposing Factors." They may be biological, psychological, and/or social. These mechanisms are reviewed in depth elsewhere[8] but will be touched upon here. The widely quoted study of Goodwin *et al*[9] uncovered an increased incidence of alcoholism in the children of alcoholic parents even though they had been adopted shortly after birth by nonalcoholic foster parents. This study provided statistical evidence for the role of genetic factors in the development of alcoholism. Equally interesting was the finding in the Goodwin study that heavy drinking in the offspring correlated more highly with such drinking in the foster parents than with the drinking habits of the biological parents.

The Goodwin study has been criticized for a number of methodological reasons,[10] and it is well recognized that statistical significance alone does not guarantee that a study's findings will have clinical relevance and utility. Nevertheless, Goodwin's results which suggest that the level of heavy drinking is strongly influenced by social factors (a finding supported by the work of Robins, Bates, and O'Neal[11]), while the emergence of alcoholism may have a stronger biological basis,[12] reinforce the perspective presented in this paper.

The putative role of psychological factors in the etiology of alcoholism has been one of the most controversial issues in the field. The early psychoanalytic writings of Knight,[13] Simmel,[14] and Rado[15] stressed the "alcoholic personality" as the most significant predisposing factor in the development of alcoholism: the emotionally immature, passive–dependent, impulsive personality disorder characterized by low frustration tolerance and latent homosexual tendencies. Recent evidence suggests that some of the characteristics of the "alcoholic personality" may actually be the product of prolonged alcoholism rather than the cause. For example, it has been demonstrated that alcohol-related brain damage may produce personality changes similar to those found in chronic alcoholics and that prolonged alcoholism of more than ten years in duration is almost always associated with significant brain damage sufficient to cause such personality changes.[16] On the other hand, the report of Morrison and Stewart[17] that hyperactive children are subject to a significantly higher incidence of alcoholism in adulthood than average supports the thesis that at least certain types of personality disorders predispose to the development of alcoholism.

The entire question of the alcoholic personality has been admirably reviewed by Barnes.[18-20] His reviews and studies suggest that the concept of "clinical alcoholic personality" as a consequence of prolonged alcoholism is demonstrably valid: "This personality pattern exists, no doubt, as a cumulative result of a prealcoholic personality and the effects of a person's drinking history on that personality pattern."[18(622-623)] On the other hand, although some evidence supports the notion of a prealcoholic personality.[21-22] he concludes that it appears that not all alcoholics show such tendencies prior to the onset of drinking.

The role of psychosis in the etiology of alcoholism appears to be equally unclear. A significant number of persons suffering from schizophrenia and affective psychoses use alcohol, frequently during periods of agitation. Further, psychoses and alcoholism have several symptoms, such as hallucinations, social alienation, and depression, in common. However, no unifying principal or simple relationship connecting the two conditions has been clearly established.[23] In a review of 24 studies on alcoholism and schizoprenia, Freed[24] found that the range of alcoholic patients with schizophrenic diagnoses varied from 1% to 33%, and the range of schizophrenics who abused alcohol varied from 3% to 63% in the studies. These findings led him to conclude "that a not insignificant proportion of schizophrenics are intemperate and that many alcoholics suffer an underlying schizophrenia."[24(p865)] Although other authors have estimated that between 10% and 15% of all alcoholics fall within several major psychotic diagnostic categories, including schizophrenia, endogenous depressions, and manic-depressive psychoses,[25-27] and there has been speculation that alcohol may be used as an antipsychotic tranquilizer by some persons,[28] more empirical evidence about the points of convergence and divergence among the two conditions is needed before definitive conclusions can be drawn.[29]

The critical role of social factors in determining the level of drinking which exists in a given setting as suggested by the research of Robins,[11] Goodwin,[9,30] and Cahalan[31-33] has influenced many investigators in the field of alcoholism toward the position that social factors may be the most important of all in the etiology of alcoholism. Since alcoholism does not develop except after a significant period of heavy drinking (Fig 1) and since level of drinking appears to be most strongly determined by social influences, this position appears eminently rational. However, as Goodwin's research has demonstrated, there is by no means a one-to-one correlation between heavy drinking and the ultimate development of alcoholism; certain individuals appear to have resistance to the development of alcoholism while others, with a significantly lower level of intake, will develop both psychological and physical dependence on alcohol.

Another type of interaction which correlates with the bio-psycho-social orientation has been described under the rubric of the "psycho-social equation."[8] This concept hypothesizes that there is an inverse relationship between the acceptability of certain forms of drug use in a given subculture and the level of psychopathology exhibited by those subculture members who become alcoholics or drug addicts. For example, Kaufman[34] reported that heroin addicts in the ghetto showed a low level of psychopathology, those coming from a blue-collar subculture showed moderate levels of psychopathology, and those from an upper middle-class suburban society showed high levels. Similarly, studies in the field of alcoholism report that female alcoholics characteristically show either more or different patterns of psychopathology than male alcoholics,[35-37] that black American women drinkers have a higher proportion of heavy escape drinkers (a measure of psychological involvement with alcohol) than do white American women drinkers,[33,38] and that Jewish alcoholics might be more "psychologically vulnerable" to alcohol than are alcoholics from other ethnic groups.[39]

It is interesting to note that in discussing their results several of the investigators in the aforementioned studies allude to processes that are consistent with those hypothesized in the psycho-social equation. For example, Cahalan and Cisin, noting that black women have higher proportions of both abstainers and heavy escape drinkers that do white women, speculate that the higher level of abstention might reflect the life style and religious beliefs of this group, while the higher proportion of heavy escape drinkers might indicate (among other possibilities) a greater sense of alienation and/or unhappiness among members of this subgroup.[38] Similarly, in discussing their review of the clinical records of 29 Jewish alcoholics Schmidt and Popham[39] refer to Jellinek's acceptance—vulnerability hypothesis,[40] which postulates that in societies where there are social sanctions against consumption of large daily quantities of alcohol the risk of addiction is higher for persons who, because of high psychological vulnerability, will be likely to go against the sociocultural sanctions discouraging heavy drinking and drunkenness.

Although the psycho-social equation may explain the development of alcoholism by some individuals, in other populations cultural influences appear to be most important in determining the development of alcoholism. The age at which social drinking begins and the customary level of intake are most generally determined by the particular subculture in which the individual lives. The operating influences include nationality, ethnicity, race, religion, sex, socioeconomic status, peer group, occupational group, and a variety of other social factors. These influences are sometimes so conductive to the development of alcoholism as to override all other considerations. For example, in certain ghetto subcultures like the black inner cities early heavy drinking is so much a way of life for males that no special biological or psychological predisposition may be necessary for alcoholism to develop in its most virulent form.

Robins' investigations[41-43] of heroin addiction among Vietnam veterans is especially informative for the insights they provide into the interaction of setting and predisposition in the emergence of an addiction. In her studies she found not only that a higher than expected number of servicemen became addicted to heroin in Vietnam, but also that virtually all of them were able to discontinue addictive drug use upon their return to the United States. However, she also found that, although the majority of returning veterans were able to give up their heroin addiction upon returning home, (1) there was a significant correlation between the level of behavioral difficulties prior to entering the service and subsequent addiction and (2) there was a positive relationship between these factors and the persistence of addiction patterns after returning from Vietnam.[41]

In a related paper Robins notes that four predictor scales—parent behavior, preservice deviance, demography, and preservice drug use— "together explained 6% of the variance in post-Vietnam addiction, with the Drug Use scale alone explaining slightly over 2%"[42(p30)] In a third paper she clarifies her position to indicate that predisposing factors alone are not primary in predicting subsequent addition; rather, it is the role of the setting (social context) in interaction with predisposition that is predictive of drug use and addiction:

> We found that in a setting [ie, Vietnam] greatly facilitating narcotic use, pre-existing differences in narcotic use were more fully expressed than they had been in a more inhibitory environment . . . . Rather than equalizing the drug experience of men from different social and behavioral backgrounds, easy access to narcotics seemed to increase their pre-existing differences.[43(p195)]

Despite the interaction of setting and norms and despite the existence of drinking norms which "demand" a certain level of drinking in various situational contexts,[44, 45] some individuals in each group tend to drink at either higher or lower levels than average. Apart from specific situational influences (eg, family pressure) and biological reactivities (eg, intolerance to alcohol), it seems likely that psychological responses to the effects of alcohol also play a major role in setting the individual level of intake. Each episode of alcohol abuse is associated both with elements of gratification (eg, euphoria, distinction, relief or anxiety, and depression) and with elements of discomfort (eg, nausea and vomiting, hangovers, etc). The susceptible individual apparently is willing to suffer the many discomforts (usually delayed) associated with problem drinking to achieve the more immediate gratification he gains from drinking. Some investigators have hypothesized that alcoholics may suffer fewer of the discomforts associated with drinking than do nonalcoholics; neither clinical nor experimental evidence appears to support this position. It appears rather that the alcoholism-prone individual achieves greater gratification than do others—either directly euphoric, or through the relief or some psychic discomfort (anxiety, tension, or depression), or in a transcendental need to escape reality.

With continued drinking, for whatever reasons, a pattern emerges in which the person's drinking behavior is constantly reinforced through the repeated gratification of the "need to drink," and a feedback loop develops in which the more one drinks the more one needs to drink. This mechanism, primary psychological dependence, is one of several feedback loops that develop in the course of alcoholism. Neither the physiology nor the dynamics of the phenomenon are well understood but it is a well-established behavioral phenomenon.

With the establishment of primary psychological dependence—a dependence which is appropriately described as a socially acquired and learned pattern "maintained by numerous antecedent cues and consequent reinforcers that may be of a psychological, sociological, or physiological nature"[46(p5)]— the tempo of drinking increases and the stage is set for the development of a second major feedback loop, that of increased tolerance and physical dependence. As these physiological reactivities increase in severity, the alcoholic finds that he needs more and more alcohol to obtain less and less gratification, while each drinking episode is followed by increasingly severe withdrawal symptomatology. The emergence of increased tolerance, decreased gratification, and increased withdrawal symptomatology is illustrated graphically for heroin addiction in Figure 3; the picture in alcoholism, although somewhat less dramatic, would be essentially similar. After a sufficient period of drug-taking, the physically dependent individual is taking larger doses, yet obtaining very little gratification, except for relief from the withdrawal symptoms produced by the last dose. At this point, the alcoholic drinks both to relieve signs of withdrawal and to prevent withdrawal symptomatology. These physiological and psychological mechanisms are

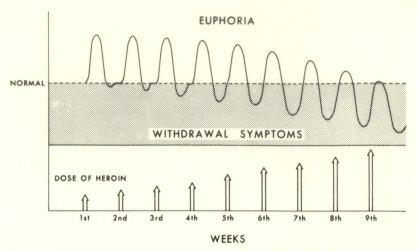

Fig 3. Tolerance, physical dependence, and the addictive cycle.

translated into the clinical symptomatology of craving, loss of control, and inability to abstain, and interact with social contextual mechanisms to produce the full blown picture of alcoholism (Fig. 2).

The effect of high tolerance and physical dependence may be manifested either in a severe acute form as in the acute alcohol withdrawl syndrome (eg, delirium tremens) or in the low-grade chronic form of the "protracted abstinence syndrome." This latter syndrome consisting of tremulousness, anxiety, depression, and sleep disturbances, frequently follows an acute withdrawl episode and may persist at a gradually diminishing level for six months or more of abstinence. However, it may occur in the absence of an acute withdrawl episode during the regular course of chronic alcoholism, recurring each morning in the form of "morning shakes." In either case, it is associated with craving for alcohol and a relative inability to abstain from drinking. These low grade subclinical symptoms of withdrawl perpetuate drinking behavior when they are due to actual chemical withdrawl from alcohol (Fig 2) or as Ludwig[47] has pointed out, even when they are simulated in episodes of anxiety.

Still another type of physiological feedback mechanism which develops during the course of alcoholism is activated through brain damage. Neuropsychological testing and radiographic studies have demonstrated that the majority of alcoholics who have drunk heavily and steadily for at least ten years, show evidence of significant brain damage.[48,49] It is still not clear whether such damage is due primarily to the toxic effects of alcohol, to the malnutrition typically associated with alcoholism, or to a combination of both effects; in any event, there is clear evidence of both anatomical and functional impairment. The kinds of neuropsychological deficits found in alcoholics correlate highly with the functional pathology of the parts of the brain involved, namely the frontal and parietal lobes and the limbic system. In fact, there is at least the possibility that many of the personality variables characteristic of the "alcoholic personality" may be the behavioral correlates of the specific pattern of brain damage found in chronic alcoholics. These neuropsychological defects include impaired memory, impairment of spatial orientation, perseveration, and difficulty in planning ahead. Such reactivities, particularly perseveration and the inability to plan for the future, probably contribute to the perpetuation of drinking.

Associated with these several physiological feedback loops are similar feedback cycles of psychological and social origin. At the most obvious level, the alcoholic's preoccupation with drinking leads to a deterioration in his personal and social relationships, as a result of which his problems increase while his overall ability to cope with them steadily diminishes. The loss of family support, friends, and job are associated with a loss of self-esteem for which a quick remedy is alcohol. Thus, the psychological and social consequences of alcoholism increase the need for alcohol and perpetuate alcohol-seeking behavior.

The role of social-psychological factors in the maintenance of the addictive cycle is illustrated by several studies. Jackson's early work on the reactions of family members to a husband's alcoholism describes how the family system reorganizes itself as the husband's condition deteriorates. This may actually serve to deter the husband in his efforts to reenter the family, thus perpetuating his drinking cycle.[50] In a clinical study of two pairs of alcoholic brothers, Steinglass *et al* found that the brothers' drinking served system-maintenance functions: "Alcohol allowed for a controlled release of aggression by engineering a role reversal [between two of the brothers, and] . . . the end result was the stabilization of a dyadic system which might otherwise be expected to have been characterized by chaos."[51(p408)]

Ray's investigation of the cycle of abstinence and relapse among heroin addicts suggests that a loose system of organizational and cultural elements in the addict's social world can act to perpetuate the addition cycle. The addict, having gained status and identity among his addict peers, is quite ambivalent about how he stands with addict and nonaddict groups in the early stages of abstinence. The tendency toward relapse, therefore, can develop "out of the meanings of the abstainer's experience in social situations when he develops an image of himself as socially different from non-addicts. . . . Relapse occurs when he redefines himself as an addict."[52(p170)] As the abstainer reenters the social world of addiction, that world "places demands and restraints upon his interactions and the meaningfulness of his experience. . . . It demands participation in the old ways of organizing conduct and experience and, as a consequence, the readoption of the secondary status characteristics of addiction."[52(p173)]

Viewing alcoholism (and addiction in general) as a condition in which increasingly severe feedback mechanisms develop is important to the understanding of the new "disease concept of alcoholism." In the old disease concept of alcoholism as promulgated Jellinek[40] and expanded upon by both psychoanalysis and Alcoholics Anonymous, the alcoholic was seen as more or less preordained to become alcoholic and then to remain quintessentially alcoholic even after he became abstinent. The main difference in the two viewpoints was that psychoanalysis defined the stigma in psychological terms whereas Alcoholics Anonymous defined it in physical ones. With the entry of sociologists into the field, the thesis was presented that anyone could become alcoholic if social pressures were sufficient. Since, under those conditions, neither physical nor psychological susceptibility is obligatory, the old disease concept of alcoholism has largely been discarded.

In the new approach to the disease concept a variety of influences—physiological, psychological, and social—are seen as contributing to the development of problem drinking, a condition which emerges as an adaptive response (see Davis et al[53]) to pressures from one or another of these influences. With the development of alcohol addiction/physical dependence (characterized by significant tissue tolerance, craving, and withdrawl symptoms), the syndrome takes on a more monolithic character and assumes the nature of a specific disease; that is, physiological factors assume an increasingly important role in establishing the parameters of the condition. Furthermore, as illustrated in Figure 1, at this point the process tends to become irreversible, as evidenced by the questionable success which gamma alcoholics have in becoming social drinkers.

The various feedback mechanisms described in Figure 2—physiological, psychological, and social—do not operate independently one from the other, but are all interrelated in a complex functional matrix. These intricate interactions would be impossible to follow more than superficially in a clinical setting, but they do lend themselves to computer modeling. Recently, Golüke et al[5] have developed a computer model which attempts to take into account, in a mathematical way, the multiple physiological and social influences which are operative in the initiation and perpetuation of alcoholism (Fig 4).

The central theme upon which the model is based is taken from the following quote from Kissin:

> It is truism that alcoholics cannot cope. They cannot deal with the normal frustrations and irritations of the external world nor can they deal with the anxiety, depression and sense of inadequacy which swells from within. Accordingly they drink, and by drinking they are able to ignore (although they do not reduce) their external problems. Thus alcohol becomes their method of coping with the problems of life.[8(p31–32)]

Golüke translates this paradigm into the central feedback loop of Figure 4, where alcohol consumption suppresses information (awareness of prob-

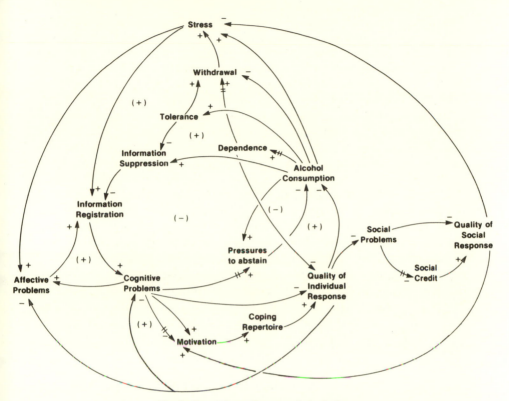

Fig 4. Causal loop diagram of alcoholism.

lems), thus reducing the level of recognized problems and, in the absence of adequate coping skills, permitting the individual to maintain psychological homostasis. This sequence constitutes a negative feedback loop since it supports homostasis by decreasing the level of perceived problems and to that extent is essentially self-limiting. However, the long-term effects of heavy drinking bring about specific changes in the physiological, psychological, and social spheres, each of which serves to increase the need for more alcohol. Such mechanisms are called positive feedback loops (also known as vicious cycles) and are characterized by exponential growth or collapse of the process under consideration. In Figure 4 the four positive feedback loops are in the areas of tolerance and dependence, affective problems, coping skills, and social stability. Each of these is intimately related not only to the critical variable alcohol consumption but to all of the other bio-psycho-social functions as well.

The various feedback loops in Figure 4 ultimately merge on two behavioral parameters, quality of social response and quality of individual response, which determine the dependent variable alcohol consumption. The computer program developed by Golüke and his colleagues permits the entry of a variety of hypothetical stresses into the life history of a hypothetical subject; the computer then prints out what the qualities of social and individual response and the level of alcohol consumption will be over a period of 40 years. In these hypothetical cases, given a subject with normal ability to cope and with the usual stresses of adolescence and early adulthood, the computer print-out indicates a high quality of social and individual responses and a low level of alcohol consumption, that is, social drinking. On the other hand, given the same social and personal stresses in an individual who has 70% of the normal ability to cope, the computer print-out indicates a low level of "quality of social and individual response" and a level of sustained alcohol consumption 15 to 20 times higher than in the previous case. Tolerance and physical dependence develop and the individual is designated as alcoholic. With the development of alcoholism in the hypothetical subject, the introduction of a two-year treatment regimen with disulfiram (Antabuse) results in a temporary cessation of alcohol consumption but with only slight improvement in the quality of social and individual response. In this case, according to the computer, with the cessation of disulfiram treatment, alcoholic drinking resumes. On the other hand, if disulfiram therapy is accompanied by individual or group psychotherapy, Alcoholics Anonymous attendance, family therapy and social supports, the individual will continue to do well even after disulfiram therapy has been discontinued.

The potential clinical and experimental value of this computer model of alcoholism is apparent. At present this model is functional only at a theoretical level because it can predict the drinking patterns only of hypothetical subjects either prior to or subsequent to the development of alcoholism. It is still necessary to develop the critical software before the model will be applicable to actual clinical cases.

The computer model does, however, illustrate the conceptual value of a bio-psycho-social perspective on alcoholism, although as yet it has no immediate practical application. On the other hand, implicit in the computer model is the concept that in different individuals mechanisms at one physiological or social level or another may predominate and produce clinically different pictures. Such indeed proves to be the case, as illustrated in Figure 5. On the three-dimensional matrix of social, psychological, and physiological influences, it becomes possible to distinguish among the various categories of alcoholics designated by Jellinek.[40] The alpha alcoholic is psychologically impaired but relatively intact socially and physically, whereas the gamma alcoholic is physically impaired but relatively intact socially and psychologically. Similar differential descriptions can be given for the problem drinker, the ghetto alcoholic, the skid row alcoholic, and the delta alcoholic.

A bio-psycho-social perspective in alcoholism not only offers a convenient method of describing alcoholics in their situational context but also

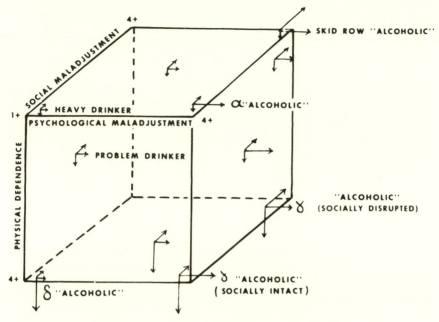

Fig 5. The bio-psycho-social dimensions of alcoholism.

has therapeutic implications as well. If a given individual's problems are identified as being a function of the interaction of physiological, psychological, and social variables, then it would seem reasonable to postulate that the assessment process should consider each of these areas and that major therapeutic interventions should be directed at the areas of greatest disruption. Figure 6 illustrates this general principal. A core therapy, applicable to all patients, attempts to deal with what has been defined as the core problem, that is, the use of alcohol as the instrument of choice for dealing with problems. The special therapies are designed to deal differentially with the special problems of specific alcoholic subpopulations—the medically ill, the alcoholic in withdrawl, the alcoholic with severe psychopathology, the indigent alcoholic, and the alcoholic with family problems. The emphasis in Figure 6 is of course not on the superiority of any one treatment over another but rather on the importance of tailoring therapy to the special needs of each individual patient.

In summary, a bio-psycho-social perspective on alcoholism is presented not as a purely theoretical concept but as a clinically significant paradigm which has descriptive and therapeutic validity. It may be that one day alcoholism will be demonstrated to be caused by some esoteric enzyme deficiency, but in the meantime, a bio-psycho-social approach appears to be most valid for an holistic understanding of the pathogenesis of this syndrome.

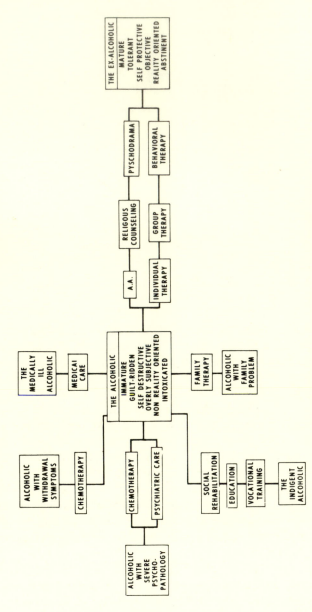

Fig 6. Core and special therapies of chronic alcoholism.

The perspective offers a valuable organizing framework which not only is broad enough to insure that all the factors involved in the emergence of alcoholism are considered in assessing the condition but also is specific enough to encourage the depth of analysis necessary to evaluate each variable.

References

1. Dubos R: *The Mirage of Health*. New York, Harper & Row, 1959.
2. Mechanic D: The concept of illness behavior. *J Chron Disease* 15:189–194, 1962.
3. Fabrega H Jr: Disease and illness from a biocultural standpoint, in Ahmed PI, Coelho GV (eds): *Toward New Definition of Health: Psychosocial Dimensions*. New York, Plenum Press, 1979, pp 23–51.
4. Leigh H, Reiser MF: *The Patient: Biological, Psychological, and Social Dimensions of Medical Practice*. New York, Plenum Press, 1980.
5. Golùke U, Landeen R, Meadows D: A physio-psycho-social computer model of the pathogenesis of alcoholism, in Kissin B, Begleiter H (eds): *The Biology of Alcoholism*, vol 7, 1982 (in press).
6. Pearson G: *The Deviant Imagination*. New York, Holmes and Meier, 1975.
7. Minahan, A: Theories and perspectives for social work. *Social Work* 25:435, 1980.
8. Kissin B: Theory and practice in the treatment of alcoholism, in Kissin B, Begleiter H (eds): *The Biology of Alcoholism*, vol 5:*Treatment and Rehabilitation of the Chronic Alcoholic*. New York, Plenum Press, 1977, pp 1–52.
9. Goodwin DW, Schulsinger F. Hermansen L, *et al*: Alcohol problems in adoptees raised apart from alcoholic biological parents. *Arch Gen Psychiatry* 28:238–243, 1973.
10. Tolor A, Tamerin J: The question of a genetic basis for alcoholism. *Q J Stud Alcohol* 34:1341–1345, 1973.
11. Robins LN, Bates WM, O'Neal P: Adult drinking patterns of former problem children, in Pittman DJ, Snyder CR (eds): *Society, Culture, and Drinking Patterns*. New York, John Wiley and Sons, 1962, pp 395–412.
12. Schuckit MA, Rayses V: Ethanol ingestion: Differences in blood acetaldehyde concentrations in relatives of alcoholics and controls. *Science* 203:54–55, 1979.
13. Knight RP: The psychodynamics of chronic alcoholism. *J Nerv Ment Dis* 86:538–548, 1937.
14. Simmel E: Alcoholism and addiction. *Psychoanal Q* 17:6–31, 1948.
15. Rado S: Psychoanalysis of pharmacothymia. *Psychoanal Q* 2:1–23, 1933.
16. Ryan C, Butters N: Cognitive deficits in alcoholics, in Kissin B, Begleiter H (eds): *The Biology of Alcoholism*, vol 7, 1981 (in press).
17. Morrison JR, Stewart MA: Evidence for polygenetic inheritance in the hyperactive child syndrome. *Am J Psychiatry* 130:791–792, 1973.
18. Barnes GE: The alcoholic personality: A reanalysis of the literature. *J Stud Alcohol* 40:571–634, 1979.
19. Barnes GE: Characteristics of the clinical alcoholic personality. *J Stud Alcohol* 41:894–910, 1980.
20. Barnes, GE: Psychological mechanisms in alcoholism, in Kissin B, Begleiter H (eds): *The Biology of Alcoholism*, vol 7, 1982 (in press).
21. Loper RG, Kammeier ML, Hoffmann H: MMPI characteristics of college freshman males who later become alcoholics. *J Abnorm Psychol* 82:159–162, 1973.
22. Hoffmann H, Loper RG, Kammeier ML: Identifying future alcoholics with MMPI alcoholism scales. *Q J Stud Alcohol* 35:490–498, 1974.

23. Solomon J: Psychiatric characteristics of alcoholics, in Kissin B, Begleiter H (eds): *The Biology of Alcoholism*, vol 7, 1981 (in press).
24. Freed EX: Alcoholism and schizophrenia: The search for a perspective. *J Stud Alcohol* 36:853–881, 1975.
25. Panepinto WC, Higgins MJ, Keane-Dawes WY, *et al*: Underlying psychiatric diagnosis as an indicator of participation in treatment. *Q J Stud Alcohol* 31:950–956, 1970.
26. Sherfey MJ: Psychopathology and character structure in chronic alcoholism, in Diethelm O (ed): *Etiology of Chronic Alcoholism*. Springfield, Illinois, Charles C Thomas, 1955, pp 16–42.
27. Zwerling I: Psychiatric findings in an interdisciplinary study of forty-six alcoholic patients. *Q J Stud Alcohol* 20:543–554, 1959.
28. Irwin S: A rational approach to drug abuse prevention. *Contemporary Drug Problems* 2:3–46, 1973.
29. Kesselman M: Alcoholism and schizophrenia, in Solomon J (ed): *Alcoholism and Clinical Psychiatry*. New York, 1981 (in press).
30. Goodwin DW: Family and adoption studies in alcoholism, in Mednick S, Christiensen KO (eds): *Biosocial Bases of Criminal Behavior*. New York, Gardner Press, 1977, pp 143–157.
31. Cahalan D, Room R: *Problem Drinking Among American Men*, monograph No 7. New Brunswick, Rutgers Center of Alcohol Studies, 1974.
32. Cahalan D: *Problem Drinkers*. San Francisco, Jossey-Bass Inc. 1970.
33. Cahalan D, Cisin IH, Crossley HM: *American Drinking Practices*, monograph No. 6 New Brunswick, Rutgers Center of Alcohol Studies, 1969.
34. Kaufman E: The psychodynamics of opiate dependence: A new look. *Am J Drug and Alcohol Abuse* 1:349–370, 1974.
35. Rathod H, Thomas IG: Women alcoholics. *Q J Stud Alcohol* 32:45–46, 1971.
36. Beckman LJ: Alcoholism problems and women: An overview, in Greenblatt M, Schuckit MA (eds): *Alcoholism Problems in Women and Children*. New York, Grune & Stratton, 1976, pp 65–96.
37. Sclare AB: Alcohol problems in women, in Madden JS, Walker R, Kenyon WH (eds): *Alcoholism and Drug Dependence: A Multidisciplinary Approach*. New York, Plenum Press, 1977, pp 181–187.
38. Cahalan D, Cisin I: American drinking practices: Summary of findings from a national probability sample. I. Extent of drinking by population subgroups. *Q J Stud Alcohol* 29:130–151, 1968.
39. Schmidt W, Popham RE: Impressions of Jewish alcoholics. *J Stud Alcohol* 37:931–939, 1976.
40. Jellinek EM: *The Disease Concept of Alcoholism*. New Haven, College and University Press, 1960.
41. Robins LN, Helzer JE, Hesselbrock M, *et al*: Vietnam veterans three years after Vietnam: How our study changed our view of heroin, in Harris L (ed): *Problems of Drug Dependence*. Proceedings of the Committee on Drug Dependence. Cambridge, Mass, 1977, pp 24–40.
42. Robins LN: Estimating addiction rates and locating target populations, in Rittenhouse JD (ed): *The Epidemiology of Heroin and Other Narcotics*, NIDA Research Monograph 16. Washington, DC, US Government Printing Office, 1977, pp 25–39.
43. Robins LN: The interaction of setting and predisposition in explaining novel behavior: Drug initiation before, in, and after Vietnam, in Kandel DB (ed): *Longitudinal Research on Drug Use*. New York, Halsted Press, 1978, pp 179–196.
44. Room R. Sociocultural aspects of alcohol use and problems: A normative perspective. Paper presented at the Addiction Research Foundation, Clinical Institute Lecture Series on the Sociology of Drug Dependence. Toronto, October 3, 1974 (mimeographed).
45. Cosper R: Drinking as conformity. *J Stud Alcohol* 40:868–891, 1979.
46. Miller PM, Eisler RM: Alcohol and drug abuse, in Craighead WE, Kazdin AE, Mahoney MJ

(eds): *Behavioral Modification: Principles, Issues, and Applications*. Boston, Houghton-Mifflin, 1975.

47. Ludwig A: Why do alcoholics drink?—Experimental evidence, in Kissin B, Begleiter H (eds): *The Biology of Alcoholism*, vol 7, 1981 (in press).

48. Porjesz B, Begleiter H: Visual evoked potentials and brain dysfunction in chronic alcoholics, in Begleiter H (ed): *Evoked Brain Potentials and Behavior*. New York, Plenum Press, 1979, pp 227–302.

49. Lusins J, Zimberg S, Smokler H, *et al*: Alcoholism and cerebral atrophy: A study of 50 patients with CT scan and psychologic testing. *Alcoholism: Clinical and Experimental Research* 4:406–411, 1980.

50. Jackson JK: The adjustment of the family to the crisis of alcoholism. *Q J Stud Alcohol* 15:562–586, 1954.

51. Steinglass P, Weiner S, Mendelson JH: A systems approach to alcoholism. *Arch Gen Psychiatry* 24:401–408, 1971.

52. Ray MB: The cycle of abstinence and relapse among heroin addicts, in Becker HS (ed): *The Other Side*. New York, The Free Press, 1964, pp 163–177.

53. Davis DI, Berenson D, Steinglass P, *et al*: The adaptive consequences of drinking. *Psychiatry* 34:209–215, 1974.

CHAPTER 2

Prevention of Alcoholism

GERALD L. KLERMAN, MD

The Scope of the Problem

For many years, alcoholism was viewed as a moral defect. The problem was seen in drunkenness and not in drinking, in alcoholism and not alcohol. The focus was firmly entrenched on the individual. In spite of new research on the alcoholic personality and the probability that genetics determines thresholds of alcohol tolerance, alcoholism can no longer be viewed only in terms of the individual. Unfortunately, there has been a great reluctance to look at the broader economic and social issues.

In recent years, however, there has been an impressive accumulation of data on economic and social factors as they affect alcoholism. I believe that it is within this sphere that our best hopes for prevention may lie.

Ten million adult Americans—7% of those 18 years or older—are estimated to be alcoholics or problem drinkers. Alcoholism is now recognized as a serious public health concern. It has direct health consequences for the individual, and the social and economic burdens associated with it are enormous.

Health Consequences for the Individual

Alcohol abuse is responsible for a substantial amount of premature death, illness, and disability in the United States. It is estimated that alcohol and its related problems are associated with more than 200,000 deaths—or more than 10% of all deaths in the United States each year. Alcohol is implicated in half of all traffic deaths, many of which involve teenagers. Cirrhosis, which is among the ten leading causes of death, is largely due to alcohol consumption, and there is evidence now that liver cancer is

GERALD L. KLERMAN • Professor of Psychiatry, Psychiatric Service, Harvard Medical School, Massachusetts General Hospital, Boston, Massachusetts 02114.

attributable almost exclusively to alcohol consumption and that people who drink and also smoke have greater increases in esophageal cancer rates.

Less is known about the levels of alcohol intake associated with neuropsychiatric disorders, psychosis, and brain damage among alcoholics. But it is clearly documented that severe birth defects, including mental retardation, can develop among infants born to pregnant women who drink excessively. This has become known as fetal alcohol syndrome.

Consequences for the Family

Those who abuse drinking affect not only themselves but also their family members—some 40 million people—and the local community as well. From police, social service, and hospital reports we know that repercussions of alcohol abuse include family disruption, domestic violence, child and spouse abuse, crime, property damage, homicide, and suicide.

Children can be particularly affected by having a problem-drinker parent or parents. Some of the possible problems they face are neglect, difficulties with normal development, trouble in school, juvenile delinquency, and juvenile drinking.

The community at large is affected by the obnoxious and violent behavior of problem drinkers. They are also the victims of drinker-caused accidents, especially automobile accidents.

Consequences for the Nation

We must also consider the cost of alcohol abuse and alcoholism to the national economy. No exact figures can be extrapolated, of course, but we do know that alcohol abuse and alcoholism have a major impact which includes lost production of goods and services, motor vehicle accidents, violent crime, and losses from fire, among other factors.

The economic costs of alcohol-related problems are manifested in two general ways. First, because problem drinking often makes people less effectively functional, society loses a part of the economic value of their normal production. Second, because certain goods and services such as health and social service resources and police and fire protection must be increased to cope with some of the consequences of alcohol abuse, the added costs are paid for by the general public.

A National Institute on Alcohol Abuse and Alcoholism (NIAAA) report estimated that in 1975 alcohol abuse and alcoholism cost the United States nearly $43 billion (Table I).

The nearly $13 billion spent on health care for alcohol-related problems accounted for more than 12% of all adult health expenditures. Moreover, most of the health costs associated with alcoholism were for hospital care and accounted for almost 20% of all hospital care costs in the country (Table II).

TABLE I. Economic Costs of Alcohol Misuse and Alcoholism in the United States, 1975[a]

Effect	Cost (billion $)
Lost production	$19.64
Health and medical	12.74
Motor vehicle accidents	5.14
Violent crime	2.86
Social responses	1.94
Fire losses	0.43
Total	$42.75

[a]Third Report to Congress, US Public Health Service, Department of Health and Human Services, 1979.

TABLE II. Estimated U.S. National Health Expenditures for Alcohol-Related Problems in 1975, According to Type of Expenditures[a]

Type of expenditure	Total adult population health expenditures	Expenditures resulting from alcohol abuse (billion $)	Expenditures resulting from alcohol abuse as a percentage of total expenditures (%)
Health service and supplies			
Hospital care	$ 42.3	$ 8.40	19.9
Physician's services	17.9	1.30	7.3
Dentist's services	6.2	—	—
Other professional services	1.7	0.12	7.3
Drugs and drug sundries	8.9	0.28	3.2
Eyeglasses and appliances	2.0	—	—
Nursing home care	8.8	0.19	2.2
Expenses for prepayment and administration	3.9	0.78	19.9
Government public health activities	3.0	0.33	13.1
Other health services	2.5	0.39	13.1
Research and medical facilities construction	6.1	0.78	13.1
Training and education	2.3	0.17	7.3
Total	$105.6	$12.74	12.1

[a] Third report to Congress, US Public Health Service, Department of Health and Human Services, 1979.

Regardless of whether these estimates are too high or too low, the point is that alcohol abuse produces a highly costly series of chain reactions throughout our society.

Public Health Approaches to Prevention of Alcoholism

Given the magnitude of the problem of alcoholism, we must develop prevention strategies to deal with it. Classic public health thinking distinguishes among three kinds of prevention:

1. Primary prevention includes actions or interventions designed to prevent or reduce a health problem.
2. Secondary prevention is concerned with the early detection and treatment of the health problem.
3. Tertiary prevention is aimed at rehabilitation.

In terms of alcohol-related problems, we have had considerable success on the secondary and tertiary levels.

On the tertiary level we have seen progress in rehabilitation efforts aimed at ameliorating the seriousness of alcohol-related problems and in reducing subsequent disability and dependence. Some indications of success with tertiary prevention programs are the decrease in the number of chronic inebriates in jail and in public mental hospitals and the reduction of chronic disability among alcoholics.

We have also expanded efforts at preventing violent behavior among alcoholic drinkers, particularly relating to incidents of alcohol-related child abuse.

On the secondary level, most people have been alerted by public education campaigns to the warning signs of alcoholism in an individual. This has resulted in increased numbers of people coming into the health care system for early treatment. Moreover, there is a greater awareness of the need for early detection and treatment among health providers such as physicians, nurses, people working in emergency rooms, and social workers. The successes of these early interventions are reflected in the decrease of deaths due to cirrhosis, alcohol coma, and withdrawals from delirium tremens.

As an example, until a few years ago the death rate in this country from cirrhosis of the liver had been increasing steadily for over 40 years. Now the data indicate that there has been a turning around of the curve and the death rate is down (Fig 1).

We have reason to be optimistic about alcohol prevention on the secondary and tertiary levels.

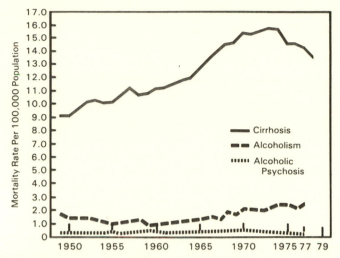

Fig 1. Trends in selected mortality rates in the US, 1949–1978 (from National Center for Health Statistics).

Primary Prevention

Primary prevention—or the attempt to reduce incidence, that is, new cases of alcoholism—remains a problem area. Since alcoholism is a public health problem, the traditional public health model—host, agent, and environment— provides a useful framework for understanding and organizing primary prevention programs. Using this model for alcohol-related problems, the host is the individual and his or her drinking behavior; the agent is the alcohol—its content, distribution, and availability; and the environment is the community or setting in which drinking occurs (Fig 2).

Traditionally, alcoholism has been viewed as a moral defect within the host. But now it is known that there are predispositions and vulnerabilities within the individual based on personality, genetic, and personal defects that are associated with alcoholism. Nevertheless, a prevention program that deals only with the host and not the agent and the environment is doomed to failure.

Interventions focusing on these three factors need not be in conflict. In fact, they often overlap or complement work directed at the others.

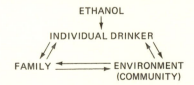

Fig 2. Alcohol-related problems: Interactions.

OLSON LIBRARY
NORTHERN MICHIGAN UNIVERSITY
MARQUETTE, MICHIGAN 49855

Host. One of the priorities in prevention dealing with the host is identifying high-risk groups such as women and youth. There is evidence of an increase in alcohol consumption among these two groups. Among women there is concern about the harmful consequences of the fetal alcohol syndrome and about the fact that the stigma of alcoholism may keep women from entering the treatment systems as readily as they should. Among youth, we are concerned especially about the dangers of automobile accidents and the unfortunate toll that abusive drinking takes on personal and family adjustment.

Environment. Another component of a prevention program is intervention in the environment setting, particularly in occupation settings. As many as 80% of individuals identified within occupation settings who come into employee assistance programs experience significant reduction in their alcoholism problem and improvement in their family and work adaptation. Early recognition and treatment of alcoholism must also take place within the general health care setting. If the health care system diagnoses alcoholism early, tragic and serious consequences can be prevented.

Agent. The third component of any prevention plan is the agent, or the consumption of alcoholic beverages. Any comprehensive prevention policy should address the issues of consumption. To look at consumption does not mean that we are neoprohibitionist and advocate prohibiting the use of alcohol. But some attention must be paid to identifying the relationship of patterns of use to public health policy and possible preventive efforts.

Relationship of Intake and Health Hazards for the Individual

Alcohol has a pervasive effect on the body from its point of entry through the gastrointestinal tract, the liver, and the blood stream. The brain, nervous system, heart muscles, and endocrine system are also affected. There is general agreement and a good deal of research which indicates that consequences such as domestic violence and home and auto accidents are more likely to occur when an adult's blood alcohol level exceeds 0.10 ml%. In a 150-pound person, for example, this point is reached with the intake of four drinks, each containing one half ounce of ethanol, consumed in one hour.

There may well be different health consequences for different individuals and an upper limit of alcohol that can be taken in by each person. Some studies indicate that alcohol used in moderation—under 2 ounces a day—may actually decrease the risk of coronary disease. But this is not definitive data, and it should be weighed against the possible risk of other documented adverse effects. For example, it is known that alcohol is associated with the heart muscle disease cardiomyopathy, and diseases of the coronary arteries such as angina pectoris and myocardial infarction. Mental impairment, too, is a concomitant of alcoholism, and a high percentage of alcoholics are in psychiatric hospitals for brain damage.

The relationship between daily consumption, or doses of ethanol, and medical complications has been figured out for several diseases. The risk for serious liver damage begins at 80 to 100 gm of daily ethanol intake—or three 2-ounce shots of whisky. Above 150 gm a day—or five 2-ounce shots—the risk rises rapidly. It has also been found that alcohol is implicated in chronic relapsing pancreatitis: Most patients with the condition have consumed 150 gm of ethanol daily over a long period of time.

The withdrawal syndrome has been documented at daily intakes of 200 to 400 gm. Less is known concerning the levels of alcohol intake associated with neuropsychiatric disorders, psychosis, and brain damage.

Relationship of Intake and Health Factors for the Population

According to many recent studies, aggregate health problems associated with alcoholism are closely related to per capita consumption of alcohol. The data have been worked out most thoroughly for cirrhosis of the liver; researchers consistently find a very high correlation between per capita consumption and cirrhosis.

There are two methods of looking at this relationship: cross-culturally and longitudinally.

Cross-culturally, we can look at the data across different nations. In countries where per capita consumption is low, cirrhosis mortality is also low; in countries where per capita consumption is high, death from cirrhosis is also high (Table III).

In Norway, for example, the per drinker consumption is 5.9 liters, and the death rate from liver cirrhosis per 100,000 population is 4.7. In the United States, where per drinker consumption is 12 liters, the death rate from cirrhosis per 100,000 is 18.4. And in France, the country reporting the highest

TABLE III. Annual Consumption of Alcohol and Rates of Death from Liver Cirrhosis by Nation (Random Selection)

Country	Per drinker consumption (liters)	Rate of death from liver cirrhosis per 100,000 population
France	25.9	45.3
Portugal	19.5	42.7
West Germany/West Berlin	16.0	26.7
Luxembourg	12.5	34.2
USA	12.0	18.4
USSR	11.4	13.1
England and Wales	10.9	3.7
Netherlands	7.7	4.9
Norway	5.9	4.7

annual consumption of alcohol, the drinker consumption is 25.9 liters, and the death rate from cirrhosis per 100,000 is 45.3. Looking at the data longitudinally, we also can see fluctuations that occur within a country, as this graph of alcohol consumption over two and a half centuries in England shows (Fig 3).

A sharp decline in average consumption in a country also usually means a sharp decline in the nation's cirrhosis rates. This correlation held true in France during the extreme shortage of wine because of rationing during both world wars and in the United States during prohibition. Prohibition in the United States was a public health success. Not only was there a decline in cirrhosis, but also there was a decline in auto accidents and hospitalization from alcohol-related problems in general. But prohibition failed because of its adverse effects on the country, such as the undermining of the law enforcement system.

Data from Finland provide a more recent example. In 1972, a strike of retail clerks closed the state alcohol stores for more than one month. These stores account for almost one half of all alcoholic beverage sales in Finland. What happened in Finland, when the availability of alcohol was drastically restricted, is indeed striking. There was a marked decrease in arrests for public drunkenness and in alcohol-related visits to hospitals, particularly visits

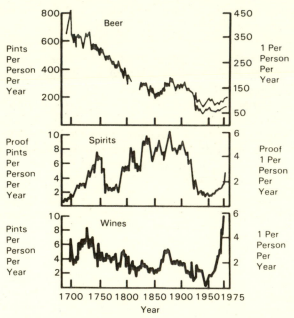

Fig 3. Alcoholic beverages available per person in the United Kingdom, 1700–1975 (from *Nature*, vol 270, December 1977).

relating to injuries from accidents for fights. The effect of the strike on drunk driving were also noticeable, but not very remarkable. Researchers speculated that driving was likely to be highly correlated with drinking in restaurants, and, since these establishments were not affected by the strike, the low impact on drunk driving was predictable.

The Finnish findings dramatically illustrate the impact of fluctuations in the general consumption of alcohol on alcohol-related problems.

Availability and Price

We have determined that per capita consumption is related to health hazards on individual and aggregate levels. But what determines consumption? We do not know all the factors, but two of the important factors are availability and price. Regulations have been relaxed concerning hours of sales and types of establishments selling alcohol products, and some states have lowered the drinking age from 21 to 18 years of age.

The problems of access and availability are highlighted by statistics concerning drinking among college and high school students—and even among junior high school students. According to the report of the Surgeon General's on health promotion and disease prevention,[1] about 80% of 12 to 17 years olds report having had a drink; more than half drink at least once a month, and nearly 3% drink daily. In a recent study of drinking among college students in New England, it was found that fewer than 5% of college men and women abstained from alcohol. Moreover, both men and women drink more frequently as they progress through their four years of college.

A controversy over lowering the drinking age emerged not because of drinking per se, but because of drinking and driving. There is a considerable body of research suggesting that the increase in availability of alcohol in the 18- to 20-year age group contributed to an increase in the alcohol-related crash and fatality rate. Some of these findings have been challenged, and it is argued that changes in police methods of recording crashes created an artificial rise in recorded crashes. Clearly, the issue of legal drinking age needs further study since it could have serious implications for consumption levels and the related social and health consequences of problem drinking.

The price of alcohol is another controversial determinant of consumption. It has been argued that one of the reasons why per capita alcohol consumption has not fallen—indeed, has increased among young people—is that the true cost of alcohol has dropped in the past 20 years relative to inflation and taxes have not increased proportionally.

It is not clear why per capita consumption of alcohol is not influenced to a greater degree by price. Perhaps heavy drinkers are less susceptible to changing their habits because of price alone. There are three commodities for which we are attempting to change behavior through pricing: tobacco, gasoline, and alcohol. In none of these areas, do we have as much evidence as we would like, but there is some suggested evidence that when price goes up, consumption of tobacco, gasoline, and alcohol goes down. Over the past decade, many international researchers have come to the conclusion that price and disposable income—or some measure that combines the two—seem to have some bearing on levels of total alcohol consumption in a society.

While these findings are potentially important for public policy, they are very controversial. Nevertheless, psychiatrists working with alcoholic patients should be aware of the relationship of economic and social factors to consumption. We are not advocating a return to prohibition. But the alternative to prohibition is not necessarily unrestricted availability. However, as I have noted, recent trends have been more in the direction of increasing the availability of alcohol than in restricting it.

Demographics of Consumption

In the 1950s a French demographer, Sully Ledermann, published a study of the distribution of consumption among various Western nations. His findings were surprising. Normally, patterns within a community are represented by a bell curve, with the largest number of people representing the average, and fewer people representing the highs and lows—as with the standard bell curve for height, weight, or IQ. But Ledermann noted that drinking within a community follows a log-normal curve with one peak positively skewed. This means that consumption is distributed among a very large group who drink very little or seldom, a much smaller group who drink regularly but in moderation, and a very small group who drink heavily and compulsively. The distribution of alcoholic purchases, according to this curve, would show the largest number of purchasers buying small quantities, a smaller group buying somewhat larger but still moderate amounts, and a very small group purchasing still more (Fig 4).

Ledermann's thesis has been confirmed in numerous general population studies. In the United States, for example, about 10% of the population accounts for more than half of the alcohol consumed. It is this minority who are most prone to health problems and who contribute to the major portion of social and health costs related to alcohol problems.

Floyd Allport's model of conforming behavior, developed in the early 1930s, followed a similar log-normal curve. It was heavily skewed toward conformance. Allport found that the great majority of people conformed rather closely to a rule—stopped at a stop sign, arrived at work on time—while a smaller group committed minor deviations, and a very small group barely conformed or flagrantly ignored the rules. But when compliance was monitored—for example, by stationing a policeman at the intersection—the rate of conformity increased and the rate of nonconformity and violation declined.

The implications of this for altering the consumption patterns of the

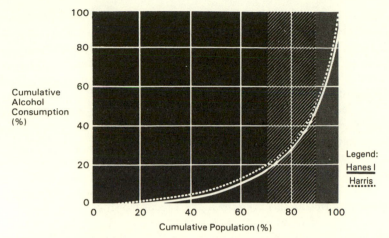

Fig 4. Cumulative distribution of alcohol consumption. Drinkers only, aggregated from several US national surveys, 1971–1975 (from Hanes I, 1971–1974 Medical History Questionnaire Microdata tape and Louis Harris and Associates, Inc, 1972–1974 [4 pooled surveys]).

small monitoring of problem drinkers in this country are very controversial. Some people believe that in order to reach even that small population of heavy drinkers all members of the population will have to be reached. Others believe that it is possible to target efforts at the heavy drinkers in an attempt to identify them and to modify their behavior. The Alcohol, Drug Abuse, and Mental Health Administration has prevention programs that are aimed at the heavy drinkers but is also committed to helping the large majority of Americans who are light or moderate drinkers from becoming members of the minority of heavy drinkers. Either way, the per capita consumption should be affected.

It is hoped that public education programs will help reduce the incidence and prevalence of alcoholism. Public education campaigns, so far, have been aimed at secondary and tertiary prevention—attempting to get people into treatment early and to reduce some of the adverse consequences of alcoholism. Primary prevention is more difficult. However, one of the best ways to prevent new cases is by identifying the population of heavy drinkers who are not yet suffering from the consequences of alcoholism or to reach high-risk groups such as youth and pregnant women and persuade them to reduce their levels of consumption.

Conclusions

Alcoholism is not just a problem of the individual. The social and economic determinants of consumption discussed above must be considered in an integrated manner in order to ensure the success of prevention programs.

The analyses of data concerning consumption are controversial, and, although more research is needed to confirm findings, it is likely that the controversy will continue, much like the debate over smoking and health data.

There has been progress in tertiary and secondary prevention of problems associated with alcoholism, and we in the public health field are heartened that our efforts are meeting with some success.

The death rate in the United States from cirrhosis of the liver has decreased over the past few years for the first time in over 40 years. There is some indication that the combined efforts of prevention, early intervention, treatment, and public understanding are influencing this outcome of the late stage of the illness.

Trends on consumption are less encouraging. Since 1971 per capita alcohol consumption has been the highest recorded since 1850, ranging from 2.63 to 2.69 gal of absolute ethanol per person 14 years or older (Fig 5). And although there has been no significant change in the relative proportion of abstainers and heavier drinkers, heavier drinking has increased for males and women are showing a significant trend to increase their levels of moderate drinking. Statistics concerning the drinking levels of young people are also cause for concern: although they may drink less regularly than older people, they tend to consume larger quantities when they drink and are more likely to become intoxicated.

Psychiatrists working with patients suffering from alcoholism—particularly psychiatrists who work in institutions—have seen some success with treatment and rehabilitation programs at the secondary and tertiary levels of

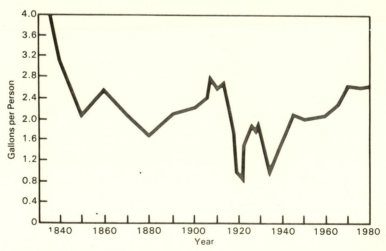

Fig 5. Long-term trend of apparent US per capita ethanol consumption, drinking age population, 1830–1977 (from Keller & Gurioli, 1976; Gravin–Jobsen Associates, 1978; Warburton, 1932).

prevention. But the involvement of psychiatrists in primary prevention must be through participation in matters of public policy.

There is much to be done in the field of alcoholism prevention. Psychiatrists must be aware of both the health and public policy aspects of alcohol-related problems. It is clear that a broad consensus involving both the public and private sectors is necessary to meet the challenges presented by a public health problem of such broad and potentially tragic consequences. But through cooperation and collaboration we hope to reduce the individual health and social consequences of the many alcohol-related problems in our country today.

Reference

1. *Healthy People: The Surgeon General's Report on Health Promotion and Disease Prevention*, US Department of Health, Education, and Welfare, Public Health Service, 1979.

CHAPTER 3

Alcoholism and Psychiatry

A Cross-cultural Perspective

JOSEPH WESTERMEYER, MD, PhD

What is Culture?

Culture, a complex and highly abstract concept, does not have the same direct basis in reality as does a rock, a cloud, or sound. It is based upon a myriad of notions which are often in themselves abstract or even vague, such as norms and attitudes. Researchers concerned with cultural matters often expand or contract the meaning of culture to fit their own methods and purposes, just as psychiatrists and "alcohologists" do in the study of psychiatric disorder and alcoholism.

In its broadest sense, culture includes the technology of a people: their modes of transportation, architectural forms, food supply, tools, fuel, and clothes. All people have social units and institutions, which can be as simple as the nuclear family, clan, and village or band, yet can also include larger and more complex units such as the church, education system, guilds, industrial corporations, or nation-states. Culture as a concept is intimately bound to a people's mode of communications: their language, nonverbal behavior, clothing and grooming styles, their notions about behavioral conformity and deviance. And finally, culture includes numerous behavioral and psychosocial elements: world view, beliefs, values, attitudes, ideal norms, actual norms, role, prestige, ritual ceremony, symbol, ideas about recreation and "time out."[1-4]

"Ethnic group" and "subcultural group" are two more recent concepts which have particular relevance for North America. They often refer to people who are distinctive from others within a population by virtue of race, national origin, religion, or language.[5,6]

JOSEPH WESTERMEYER • Professor, Department of Psychiatry, University of Minnesota, Minneapolis, Minnesota 55455.

Contributions of Cultural Studies to Theories About Alcoholism

Pathoplasticity Between Alcoholism and Neurosis

Family studies have pointed strongly toward a link between alcoholism and affective disorder.[7-12] More recently, relatives of patients with anxiety neurosis have also been shown to be at higher risk to alcoholism.[13] Cross-cultural data similarly point toward a link between alcoholism and neurotic disorders, including depression. In a clinical study done almost three decades ago,[14] Irish-American patients were observed to present most often with alcohol-related problems, but none of them came with psychoneurotic disorders. Conversely, Jewish patients came frequently for psychoneurotic disturbances, but never for alcohol-related problems. Intermediate mixing of alcoholism and psychoneurosis was seen among the American patients of eastern and northwestern European extraction. My own experience with approximately 100 American Indian patients over the last dozen years parallels these early observations among the first and second generation American Irish. Of approximately 90 Indian patients with nonpsychotic disorders, only one woman did not have alcohol dependence as part of her problem (she had a severe phobic neurosis). All of the remainder had alcohol-related problems, usually admixed with various personality, neurotic, and organic components.

Epidemiologic studies also point towards an inverse correlation between alcoholism and neurosis. In areas of Africa and North America where prevalence of alcoholism is low among adults (ie., under 5%) Leighton found prevalence rates of moderate to severe psychoneurosis which ranged around one half of the population in large samples.[15] Where rates of alcoholism are high, there is a concomitant drop in rates of psychoneurosis. In a North American Indian community, Shore et al[16] found 31 primary diagnoses of alcoholism and 18 diagnoses of psychoneurosis among 100 people—a combined rate of 49 per 100 people. My own clinical and research work among the Hmong in Asia, a poppy-producing people, indicates a similar relationship. In Asia, where the addiction prevalence among Hmong adults ranges up to 20%,[17] neurotic disorders were present but less frequent than addiction. Here in the United States, where the Hmong have no access to opium, depression and neurotic disorders account for 90% and substance abuse accounts for about 1% of mental health problems in a clinical setting.

Another finding pointing toward a link between alcoholism and affective disorder is the high rate of affective symptoms among alcoholics in ethnic groups with high rates of alcoholism. Kelleher has remarked on this finding among Irish in comparison to London and New York patients[18] this is similar to my own observations among two groups with high rates of substance abuse (American Indian alcoholics in Minnesota and opium addicts in Laos).

This perspective suggests the presence of premorbid factors which are in part genetic and constitutional but which can be modified by childhood and current adult experiences. If alcohol use is well controlled by a society, its "members-at-risk-to-alcoholism-or-neurosis"—call them "dysphoria-prone" people—may manifest their dysphoria as neurotic disorders. If alcohol abuse is widespread in the society, alcoholism replaces neurosis among many (but not all) dysphoria-prone people. In societies between two extremes, it appears likely that the more impulsive, antiauthoritarian, extroverted, and nonintrospective dysphoria-prone individuals in the society develop alcoholism. The more compulsive, conforming, introverted, and introspective dysphoria-prone individuals develop a neurotic disorder. (This hypothetical dysphoria-prone condition would probably not be an all-or-none phenomenon, but rather one that exists along a continuum and is sensitive to environmental events.)

Rapid Culture Change and Alcoholism

The usual stereotype about alcoholism and culture is that societies without traditional alcohol use are at risk to alcoholism, while societies with traditional alcohol use are immune to alcoholism. Considerable data to support this view do exist.[19,20] However, the situation is becoming more complex.

Rapid sociocultural change around the world in recent decades has been associated with increased incidence and prevalence of substance abuse. In some places, drug abuse increases rather than alcohol abuse. For example, the Moslem Malays have continued to observe their traditional stricture against alcohol use, while their rates of opiate addiction have increased markedly within the last decade.[21] In another Moslem society, Kuwait, alcohol abuse has far exceeded drug use in recent years despite stringent antialcohol laws.[22] Many other groups which traditionally have had nonproblematic alcohol use have developed increasing rates of problem drinking and alcoholism. These include the following: ethnic Chinese,[23] Apache,[24] and Jewish people[25] in North America; Melanesians[26,27] and Polynesians[28] in the Pacific Islands; the Spanish,[29] Italian,[30] and Israeli[32] peoples around the Mediterranean; and the Japanese[33] in Asia.

Migration and rapid culture change are often associated with a variety of increased mental health and social problems besides alcoholism. Increased rates of psychiatric disorder,[34,35] drug abuse,[36,22] juvenile delinquency,[37] social dislocation and disruption,[38,39] and psychophysiological disorders[40] have been reported in association with cultural change. These sequelae of rapid change have been variously ascribed to such factors as the role of growing literacy in breaking down traditional beliefs and social control,[41] industrialization with concentrated populations and the undermining of tradition,[42] growing adherence to secular or so-called Western attitudes and values,[43] a widening gap between ideal norms and actual norms,[44] weakening of family and community ties,[45] and grief and mourning at the loss of previous identities, purposes, and lifeways.[46] One author has argued that stress is directly correlated with the rate of change,[47] whereas another believes that relationship between change and stress is highly complex and case-specific.[48]

In the midst of rapid change and identity confusion, alcohol intoxication can be a symbol of new values or of opposition to new values. This symbolic use of alcohol has been suggested in various settings: for the Bougainvillians, who emulate their Australian plantation bosses[27]; for Chippewa drinkers as a means of rejecting white society while entering an all-Indian social context[49]; and as "retaliation drinking" for the vengeful person who "exploits the incapacitating power of alcohol in order to make himself a passenger on the system."[50] This modern day symbolic use of alcohol is not extraordinary because in many cultures over the centuries alcohol has frequently assumed symbolic importance similar to that of blood.[51]

Blackout in Various Cultures

"Blackouts" (amnesia for behavior while drinking) have been carefully studied in a North American group of alcoholics.[52] This work suggests that there is a spectrum of blackouts, from those which are primary organic (especially where amnesia is complete for a certain period of time) to those which are more functional (especially where the amnesia is incomplete or fluctuating over time).

The cross-cultural data suggest that ethnicity can influence the rate of blackouts. Negrete in Canada[53] found that Franco-Catholics had the lowest rate (45%, n=29), Anglo-Protestants were intermediate (74%, n=34), and Anglo-Catholics had the highest rate of blackout (86%, n=28). Rimmer *et al* in St Louis[54] observed that, while alcoholic men and women varied in their rate of reported blackouts, black and white alcoholics did not differ in this regard, especially within the same social class. In my own experience with Chippewa alcoholics (among whom intoxication and blackout comprise acceptable excuses for un-Chippewayan behavior), virtually all report having experienced blackout. It appears that blackout is more common among people who accept drinking as an excuse of deviant, antisocial, or problematic behavior.

Effects of Alcoholism on Ethnicity

Change in Attitudes, Values, and Behavioral Norms

Certain values and attitudes are almost universal among ethnic groups, at least toward other members of the group. These include responsibilities to the group, care of children and sick, respect for others and their personal belongings, participation in certain social or religious rituals, and adherence to cultural norms. Increasing time spent in an intoxicated state and increasing economic resources devoted to alcohol (and to alcohol-related problems) conflict with these values and attitudes by reducing the time and resources available for culturally sanctioned activities.

Over time, the alcoholic person begins to place higher priority on the alcohol experience than on commitment to family or group. Less time is spent in the service of others and in ethnically related ritual or ceremony. For example, Chippewa alcoholics in Minneapolis spend less time visiting relatives, return to the reservation less frequently, gradually cease ethnic activities (such as powwows, hunting, fishing, wild ricing), and often sell their traditional Indian dress.[55] Similar events take place in the majority society. Substance abusers break ties with their families, have progressively fewer friends, stop attending church (if they have previously attended), and transgress both the informal taboos and the formal laws of their society.[56-58]

Alcoholism Subcultures

Many alcoholic people remain as social isolates. Physicians, housewives, teachers, and dentists are typical examples. However, many alcoholic people join together into bottle gangs, tavern culture, and cocktail lounge groups. These have been well described for various areas, races, and social classes[59-62] and for other drugs.[63,64]

The ethnic differences which alcoholic people bring to these subcultures begin to blur as they spend more of their lives intoxicated and more of their time with each other. There develops the classical description of the alcoholic seen in many texts on abnormal psychology. These include hostile dependency, lying, failure to keep commitments, narcissism, and self-injuring or self-destructive behavior.

By the same token, the social dynamics of these alcoholic subcultures often resemble those of other natural groups. Affiliation may be marked by special jargon, dress, and behaviors. Members may be expected to reciprocate in certain ways, such as buying drinks for each other, exchanging information (such as about jobs, treatment resources, police policies toward alcoholics), and supporting each other emotionally through crises.

In many respects these groups tend to be rather fragile. They are more like a group of business people or fellow workers who share a specific common interest with narrow circumscribed commitments. Once a member becomes a liability to the group (ie, can no longer reciprocate in a symmetric fashion), loyalty rapidly disappears. Weaker members may be liable to parasitism by the needy strong. Consequently, alcoholic subcultures tend not to have the resources of persistence of extended families, stable neighborhoods, or ethnic groups.

Within some alcoholic subcultures there is considerable interethnic mixing. For example, Chippewa in Minneapolis who are heavy drinkers but still employed drink in a largely Indian neighborhood. Those with advanced alcohol addiction migrate to a Skid Row area inhabited by other racial and ethnic groups.

Symbols and Ideal Norms

Previous ethnic values and attitudes are not totally forgotten or irrevocably abandoned. Indeed, the ideal ethnic norms often persist, leading to remorse and shame at one's inability to behave in "the proper way." This is often symbolized in some fashion. For example, a Navaho woman had completely abandoned contact with her reservation, had stopped attending powwows, and spent most of her time with people from non-Indian backgrounds. However, she refused to sell or pawn some very valuable silver and turquoise jewelry which her grandmother had given her. Similarly, a Chippewa Catholic alcoholic had abandoned contacts with his family, church, and tribe but continued to wear a holy medal around his neck and to carry rosary beads in his pocket. These symbols can often be a guide to the therapist regarding fruitful strategies for treatment and rehabilitation.

Social Networks

Most adults can name about 1,500 acquaintances. Asked to report the people who are currently important to them, however, most normal people name 20 to 30 individuals.[65–68] These people can be categorized into four or five subgroups or "plexus" based on such common features as the household, relatives, friends, coworkers, hobby group, or church association. Any one member of the network usually knows 60 to 80% of the other members.

People in the midst of neurotic disorders or active alcoholism report around 10 to 19 people, divided into three or four plexus groups. Often they report a solitary friend or coworker who does not know anyone else in the network. Hostile-dependent interactions mark their relationships with their household and relatives. Their one-to-one relationships with friends, co-workers, and others tend to be short-lived, tenuous or relatively inactive. They may name a person whom they have not seen for years, someone who is dead, or a pet.

Psychotic individuals or those in advanced stages of alcoholism tend to have fewer than 10 people in their network, with only one or two plexus groups. Instead of the symmetric reciprocity which prevails in the other networks, the individual primarily receives while returning very little.

Role of Ethnicity in Treatment

Anomie During Treatment

In abandoning the familiar values, attitudes, and behaviors of the alcoholic lifestyle, the individual becomes enmeshed in a condition known as "anomie." This is a state of both psychological and social disorientation, with lack of reference regarding what is right or wrong, desirable or undesirable. The person struggling to maintain abstinence is faced with new social situations in which alcohol-related norms no longer apply. Confusion and depression commonly ensue, and sometimes even "anomic suicide."[69] MacIver describes anomie as "the state of mind of one who has been pulled up by his moral roots, who has no longer any standards but only disconnected urges, who has no longer any sense of continuity, of folk, of obligation."[70]

Recovery from alcoholism involves not only abstinence from alcohol or phychological resolution of dependency strivings. It also hinges on the evolution of values, attitudes, and behaviors which do not center on the alcohol experience. This may come about by reversion to a prior ethnicity or a move to a new ethnicity or, as probably occurs most often, some combination of these two.

Ethnicity in Recovery

Most recovering alcoholics gradually resume values, attitudes, and behaviors abandoned during their past. They may show even greater enthusiasm for their group's lifeways than they did in the past. For example, Euramerican alcoholics often become active with a club at church, coach sports activities among the young, or pursue philanthropic activities of benefit to the community. Recovering Chippewa alcoholics resume bead work or make a traditional costume, attend powwows, join a drum group, teach the Chippewa language to youth in schools, and/or become active in Indian religious, social, or political organizations. Recovering people of all ethnic backgrounds begin again to attend rituals related to birth, marriage, and death, participate in annual ceremonies, and become interested in social and political matters.

A few people (perhaps one in twenty) do not resume their earlier ethnicity. They may never have been enculturated into their own group, either because their alcohol and drug abuse began during childhood or adolescence or because their families did not provide an enculturation learning experience (perhaps due to parental neurosis or alcoholism). A few have such negative feelings about their own ethnic group that they do not wish to resume their ethnic affiliations. Development of new ethnic behaviors and affiliations is not a brief or easy process. As experience with therapeutic communities has shown, it requires a few to several years.

There is, of course, a spectrum between these two extremes, so that some people resume aspects of their previous lifeways at the same time that they adopt new behaviors and outlooks.

Social Network Reconstruction

Recovering alcoholics can be helped in bringing about the social engineering of a supportive network. They must be prepared to accept rejection, either because of past problems or because other people have full networks and cannot add to them. (There appear to be reciprocal inhibitions to enlarging the intimate social network beyond a certain maximum,[71] probably because the burden of reciprocity becomes too large.) Simply taking a history of past and current ethnic affiliations can help recovering alcoholics to assess their current status and set goals for themselves.

Membership in Alcoholics Anonymous (AA) can facilitate network regeneration in two ways. First, attendance at AA meetings can temporarily substitute for more natural group affiliations in the community at large. It is not unusual for AA members early in their recovery to attend two to five different AA meetings each week. Secondly, four of the AA Twelve Steps can involve social network reconstruction. These are as follows:

Step 5. Admitted to God, to ourselves, and to another human being the exact nature of our ways.

Step 8. Made a list of all persons we had harmed, and became willing to make amends to them all.

Step 9. Made direct amends to such people where possible, except when to do so would injure them or others.

Step 12. Having had a spiritual experience as a result of these steps, we tried to carry this message to alcoholics, and to practice these principles in all our affairs.

Role of Ethnicity in Treatment Programs

Ethnicity strongly influences access to treatment. In a Massachusetts study, white drivers were more apt to be reached by drinking driver programs than were black drivers.[72] Alcoholics having minority status, including Hispanic, black, and Indian alcoholics, have been less likely to enter white-run treatment programs.[73–78] Location of treatment facilities can also influence access to alcoholism treatment, either by virtue of distance[79,80] or geographic placement outside of an ethnic enclave.[81] Ethnic community attitudes may also influence treatment-seeking. It has been suggested that the great stigma against alcoholism in Jewish communities[25] and the continued support for heavy drinking in some black communities[74] may inveigh against entry into treatment.

For those minority individuals admitted to treatment in a white-run program, the treatment outcome appears to be good. In one white-run program, the treatment outcome among black and white patients at six months was the same.[74] Analysis of treatment modalities, length of stay, and post-discharge referral have not shown ethnic bias.[74,75,82,83] Despite favorable outcomes and absence of demonstrated bias during treatment, many ethnic minorities still choose not to enter majority facilities.

This reluctance to enter treatment has been overcome to a considerable extent by establishing minority-run treatment programs, to which minority alcoholics come in large numbers.[81,84] Indigenous or "folk" treatment modalities are sometimes included in such programs (such as sweat baths among Plains Indians). While long-term, careful, independent evaluations of these programs have not yet been widely done, early findings indicate that outcomes are comparable to those of majority-run programs.[85] The advantage of ethnically oriented programs appears not so much that something particularly efficacious happens in treatment, but rather that the attraction to treatment is greater when one can join peers in a familiar setting.

In the context of cross-cultural treatment, both transference and countertransference issues loom more important than with intracultural treatment. Minority patients often categorize the physician along with teachers, social workers, bosses, police, or judges at whose hands they have received unfair treatment. In the same way, the physician may label resistance as a character disorder although the patient's life experience may suggest that it is foolish to trust or be open with an authority figure from the majority society. In order to understand what transpires in this particular doctor–patient relationship, the physician may be aided by attending to what anthropologists call the "emic" perspective: that is, seeking to understand the problem from the patient's point of view. This involves gaining some comprehension of the patient's world view, his or her attitudes toward alcohol, and the day-to-day problems and decisions which the patient must face.

Culture and Primary Prevention

Genetic and childhood loss studies on alcoholism have contributed greatly to our understanding regarding the etiology of alcoholism. But they have done little for prevention. Given the high prevalence of alcohol and neurotic disorders and their incomplete penetrance (ie, the influence of environmental factors over them), family planning or genetic engineering do not appear to be likely alternatives. Moreover, since virtually all people may be prone to at least transient neurotic or alcoholic disorders at some time in their lives, genetic tinkering would not seem a panacea.

What about cultural tinkering? Over history, two social strategies have proven successful in reducing or eliminating alcohol abuse. One of these is the abstinence model, as practiced by the Moslems and certain other religious groups. The other is the social learning model, as practiced by many para-Mediterranean, Asian and African peoples. This includes the following: early family ensocialization into drinking during childhood or preteen years; drinking in a context of ritual or ceremony, with both sexes and multiple generations present; drinking while sitting and eating; taboos against solitary drinking and use of alcohol for self medication (eg, for "nerves," insomnia, colds); absence of facilities established primarily or solely for drinking (eg., taverns, bars, cocktail lounges). In recent years both the abstinence and the learning models have become progressively less effective in preventing alcoholism as secular values replace religious values and as people have more opportunity (especially with occupational and geographic mobility) to leave their original ethnic group and live among other peoples.

Investigation of families with an alcoholic parent suggests that identity, taboo, and ritual can significantly influence the transmission of alcoholism.[86] They have found that families which abandon their rituals or passively accept interference in family rituals by an alcoholic family member are more apt to produce alcoholic children. The reverse is true in families which persist in ritual activities (eg., evening meals, celebrating holidays), actively limit the drinking or interference of ritual by the alcoholic member, have visitors, maintain discipline, take vacations and otherwise maintain continuity and identity as a family despite the alcoholism. These data may have preventive implications. As family members seek to deal with their disturbed and disturbing member, they may be able to adopt strategies which avoid the all too common repetition of this disorder in subsequent generations.

References

1. Boas F: Anthropology, *Encyclopedia of the Social Sciences.* New York, Macmillan, 1930, p 79.
2. Linton R: *The Study of Man.* New York, Appleton Century, 1936.
3. Krocher AL, Kluckhohn C: Culture: A critical review of concepts and definitions. Papers of the Peabody Museum of American Archeology and Ethnology, vol 47, 1952.
4. Levi-Straus C: Social structure, in Krocher AL (ed): *Anthropology Today.* Chicago, University of Chicago Press, 1953.
5. Montagu MFA: *Man's Most Dangerous Myth.* New York, Columbia University Press, 1942.
6. Glazer N, Moynihan DP: *Beyond the Melting Pot.* Cambridge, Mass, Massachusetts Institute of Technology Press, 1963.

7. Pitts FN, Winokur G: Affective disorder. VIII. Alcoholism and affective disorder. *J Psychiatric Res* 4:37–50, 1966.
8. Winokur G, Clayton PJ: Family history studies. II. Sex differences and alcoholism in primary affective illness. *Br J Psychiatry* 113: 973–979, 1967.
9. Freed EX: Alcoholism and manic depressive disorders: Some perspectives. *Q J Stud Alcohol* 31:62–89, 1970.
10. Winokur G, Cadoret R, Dorzab J: Depressive disease: A genetic study. *Arch Gen Psychiatry* 24:135–144, 1971.
11. Taylor M, Abrams R: Manic states: A genetic study of early and late onset of affective disorders. *Arch Gen Psychiatry* 28:656–658, 1973.
12. Morrison JR: The family histories of manic-depressive patients with and without alcoholism. *J Nerv Ment Dis* 160:227–229, 1975.
13. Noyes R, Clancy J, Crowe R, *et al*: The familial prevalence of anxiety neurosis. *Arch Gen Psychiatry* 35:1057–1059, 1978.
14. Roberts B, Meyers J: Religion, national origin, immigration, and mental illness. *Am J Psychiatry* 110:759–764, 1954.
15. Leighton AH: A comparative study of psychiatric disorder in Nigeria and rural North America, in Plog SC, Edgerton RB (eds): *Changing Perspectives in Mental Illness*. New York, Holt Rinehart & Winston, 1969, pp 179–199.
16. Shore J, Kinzie JD, Hampson JL, *et al*: Psychiatric epidemiology in an Indian village. *Psychiatry* 36:70–81, 1973.
17. Westermeyer J: Influence of opium availability on addiction rates in Laos. *Am J Epidemiology* 109:550–562, 1971.
18. Kelleher MJ: Alcohol and affective disorder in Irish mental hospital admissions. *J Irish Med Assoc* 69:140–143, 1976.
19. Everett MW, Waddell JO, Heath DB, (eds): *Cross Cultural Approaches to the Study of Alcohol*. The Hague, Mouton Publ., 1976.
20. Marshall M (ed): *Beliefs, Behaviors, and Alcoholic Beverages: A Cross Cultural Survey*. Ann Arbor, University of Michigan Press, 1979.
21. Spencer C, Navaratnam V: Patterns of drug use amongst Malaysian secondary school children. *Drug Alcohol Dependence* 5:379–391, 1980.
22. Saleh SM, Demerdash AM: A retrospective study of a selected population of drug dependent subjects in Kuwait. *Br J Addictions* 73:89–92, 1978.
23. Wang RP: A study of alcoholism in Chinatown. *Int J Soc Psychiatry* 14:260–267, 1968.
24. Levy JE, Kunitz SJ: Notes on White American Apache social pathologies. *Plateau* 42:11–19, 1969.
25. Zimberg S: Sociopsychiatric perspectives on Jewish alcohol abuse: Implications for the prevention of alcoholism. *Am J Drug Alcohol Abuse* 4:571–579, 1977.
26. Hocking RB: Problems arising from alcohol in the New Hebrides. *Med J Australia* 2:908–910, 1970.
27. Ogan E: Drinking behavior and race relations. *Amer Anthropologist* 68:182–188, 1966.
28. Lemert EM: Forms and pathology of drinking in three Polynesian societies. *Am Anthropol* 66:361–374, 1964.
29. Fernandez FA: The state of alcoholism in Spain covering its epidemiological and aetiological aspects. *Br J Addiction* 71:235–242, 1976.
30. Bonfiglio G, Falli S, Pacini A: Alcoholism in Italy: An outline highlighting some special features. *Br J Addiction* 72:3–12, 1977.
31. Hartocollis P: Alcoholism in contemporary Greece. *Q J Stud Alcohol* 27:721–727, 1966.
32. Hes JP: Drinking in a Yemenite rural settlement in Israel. *Br J Addiction* 65:293–296, 1970.
33. Moore R: Alcoholism in Japan. *Q J Stud Alcohol* 25:142–150, 1964.
34. Duff DF, Arthur RJ: Between two worlds: Filipinos in the U.S. Navy. *Am J Psychiatry* 123:836–843, 1967.

35. Odegaard O: Emigration and insanity. *Acta Psychiatr et Neurol Scand,* Suppl IV, 1932.
36. Robertson A, Cochrane R: Deviance and culture change. *Int J Soc Psychiatry* 22:79–84, 1976.
37. Pecheco e Silva AC: Infanto-juvenile criminality in Brazil. *Internatl J Soc Psychiatry* 6:190–194, 1960.
38. Rosen DH, Voorhees-Rosen D: The Shetland Islands: The effects of social and ecological change on mental health. *Culture, Medicine and Psychiatry* 2:41–64, 1978.
39. Keyes CF: Millennialism, Theravada Buddhism, and Thai society. *J Asian Studies* 36:283–302, 1977.
40. Ginsberg GL, Frosch WA, Shapiro T: The new impotence. *Arch Gen Psychiatry* 26:218–220, 1972.
41. Howe J: The effects of writing on the Cuna political system. *Ethnology* 18:1–16, 1979.
42. Brody EB: Psychiatric implications of industrialization and rapid social change. *J Nerv Ment Dis* 156:300–305, 1973.
43. Bourne P: The Chinese student: Acculturation and mental illness. *Psychiatry* 38:269–277, 1975.
44. Klausner SZ: Inferential visibility and sex norms in the Middle East. *J Soc Psychol* 63:1–29, 1964.
45. Bruhn JG, Philips BU, Wolf S: Social readjustment and illness patterns: Comparisons between first, second and third generation Italian-Americans living in the same community. *J Psychosom Res* 16:387–394, 1972.
46. Garza-Guerrero AC: Culture shock: Its mourning and the vicissitudes of identity. *Am Psychoanal Assoc J* 22:408–429, 1974.
47. Lauer RM: Rate of change and stress: A test of the "Future Shock" thesis. *Social Forces* 52:510–514, 1974.
48. Barger WK: Culture change and psychosocial adjustment. *Am Ethnologist* 4:471–495, 1977.
49. Westermeyer J: Options regarding alcohol usage among the Chippewa. *Am J Orthopsychiatry* 42:398–403, 1972.
50. Fallding H: The source and burden of civilization illustrated in the use of alcohol. *Q J Stud Alcohol* 25:714–724, 1964.
51. Klausner SZ: Sacred and profane meanings of blood and alcohol. *J Soc Psychol* 64:27–43, 1964.
52. Goodwin DW, Crane JB, Guze SR: Alcoholic "blackouts": Review and clinical study of 100 alcoholics. *Am J Psychiatry* 126:191–198, 1969.
53. Negrete JC: Cultural influences on social performance of alcoholics: A comparative study. *Q J Stud Alcohol* 34:905–916, 1973.
54. Rimmer J, Pitts FN, Reich T, *et al*: Alcoholism. II. Sex, socioeconomic status and race in two hospitalized samples. *Q J Stud Alcohol* 32:942–952, 1971.
55. Westermeyer J: *Alcohol related problems among Ojibway people in Minnesota.* Doctoral thesis, University of Minnesota, 1970.
56. Westermeyer J, Walzer V: Drug use and sociopathy among young psychiatric inpatients. *Dis Nerv Syst* 36:673–677, 1975.
57. Westermeyer J, Walzer V: Drug abuse: An alternative to religion? *Dis Nerv Syst* 36:492–495, 1975.
58. Westermeyer J: Studying drug abuse in psychiatric populations: A reanalysis and review, in Pickens R, Heston L (eds): *Psychiatry and Drug Abuse.* New York, Grune & Stratton, 1979, pp 47–66.
59. Hertz E, Hutheesing O: On the edge of society: The nominal culture of urban hotel isolates. *Urban Anthropology* 4:317–332, 1975.
60. Kuttner R, Lorincz A: Alcoholism and addiction in urbanized Sioux Indians. *Mental Hygiene* 51:530–542, 1967.

61. Dumont MP: Tavern culture: The sustenance of homeless men. *Am J Anthropology* 37:938–945, 1967.
62. Cavan S: *Social interaction in drinking places.* Doctoral dissertation, University of California at Berkeley, 1965.
63. Finestone M: Cats, kicks, and colors. *Social Problems* 5:3–13, 1957.
64. Westermeyer J: Opium dens: A social resource for addicts in Laos. *Arch Gen Psychiatry* 31:237–240, 1974.
65. Pattison EM: Psychosocial systems therapy, in Hirschowitz RG, Levy B (eds): *The Changing Mental Scene.* New York, Spectrum, 1976.
66. Pattison EM: A theoretical-empirical base for social systems therapy, in Foulks E, Wintrob R, Westermeyer J, Favazza A (eds): *Current Perspectives in Cultural Psychiatry,* New York, Spectrum, 1977.
67. Pattison EM, Llamas R, Hurd G: Social network medication of anxiety. *Psychiatric Ann* 9:56–67, 1979.
68. Westermeyer J, Pattison EM: Social networks and mental illness in a peasant society. *Schizophr Bull* 7:125–134, 1981.
69. Durkheim E: *Suicide.* London, Routledge and Kegan Paul, republished in 1952.
70. MacIver RM: *The Ramparts We Guard.* New York, Macmillan, 1950.
71. Westermeyer J, Bush J, Wintrob R: A review of the relationship between dysphoria, pleasure, and human bonding. *Dis Nerv Syst* 39:415–424, 1978.
72. Ageriou M: Reaching problem drinking Blacks: The unheralded potential of the drinking driver programs. *Int J Addictions* 13:443–459, 1978.
73. Nathan PE, Lipson AG, Vettraino AP, *et al*: The social ecology of an urban clinic for alcoholism: Racial differences in treatment entry and outcome. *Int J Addictions* 3:55–63, 1968.
74. Lowe GD, Hodges HE: Race and the treatment of alcoholism in a southern state. *Social Problems* 20:240–252, 1972.
75. Lowe GD, Alston JP: An analysis of racial differences in services to alcoholics in a southern clinic. *Hosp Community Psychiatry* 24:547–551, 1973.
76. Westermeyer J: Chippewa and majority alcoholism in the Twin Cities: A comparison. *J Nerv Ment Dis* 155:322–327, 1972.
77. Westermeyer J, Lang G: Ethnic differences in use of alcoholism facilities. *Int J Addict* 10:513–520, 1974.
78. Paine HJ: Attitudes and patterns of alcohol use among Mexican Americans: Implications for service delivery. *J Stud Alc* 38:544–553, 1977.
79. Hoffman H: County characteristics and admission to state hospital for treatment of alcoholism and psychiatric disorders. *Psychol Rep* 35:1275–1277, 1974.
80. Mellsop GW: The effects of distance in determining hospital admission rates. *Med J Australia* 2:814–817, 1969.
81. Kane G: *Inner City Alcoholism: An Ecological and Cross Cultural Study.* New York, Human Sciences Press, 1981.
82. Chegwidden M, Flaherty BJ: Aboriginal versus non-Aboriginal alcoholics in an alcohol withdrawal unit. *Med J Austral* 1:699–703, 1977.
83. Hoffman H, Noem AA: Adjustment of Chippewa Indian alcoholics to a predominantly White treatment program. *Psychol Rep* 37:1284–1286, 1975.
84. Shore JH, Von Fumetti B: Three alcohol programs for American Indians. *Am J Psychiatry* 128:1450–1454, 1972.
85. Wilson LG, Shore JH: Evaluation of a regional Indian alcohol program. *Am J Psychiatry* 132:255–258, 1975.
86. Bennett LA, Wolin SJ, Noonan DL: Family identity and intergenerational occurrence of alcoholism. Alcoholism 13:100–108, 1977.

CHAPTER 4

Altered Use of Social Intoxicants After Religious Conversion

MARC GALANTER, MD

A patient's positive attitude and his commitment to therapy goals are of central importance to the treatment of alcoholism. Denial of the illness, on the other hand, leads many alcoholics to drop out of treatment. It is, therefore, important to improve the means by which we may achieve a successful transformation in the alcoholic's attitudes. This chapter reviews material from a number of studies[1-6] conducted in two religious sects. It examines the marked transformations reported by sect members regarding social intoxicant use, as achieved through religious conversion. These findings are then related to the social psychology of altering patterns of intoxicant use.

A number of new religious sects have arisen in recent years which appeal primarily to late adolescents and young adults. Many of these groups offer a life style which is closely organized around group norms and is relatively austere. Most discourage the use of drugs among their members. In order to gain some understanding of the role that large, cohesive groups such as these can play in altering drug use patterns, levels of drug use among sect members were examined on the basis of systematic self-reports.

This work was conducted over the course of five years. Extensive interviews within two sects, the Divine Light Mission (DLM) and the Unification Church (UC), were used as a basis for developing self-report research instruments, which were then applied to large cohorts of members and potential members. Our initial report on this work[1-3] dealt with the effects of membership on an individual's psychological and social adjustment. In addition, however, these studies were also directed at patterns of social intoxicant use, that is, alcohol and marijuana. The following experimental subject groups were studied: long-standing members of the Divine Light

MARC GALANTER • Director, Division of Alcoholism and Drug Abuse, Associate Professor, Department of Psychiatry, Albert Einstein College of Medicine, Bronx, New York 10461.

Mission and the Unification Church and persons undergoing recruitment into the Unification Church.

Members of the Divine Light Mission, the first sect studied, are followers of the Guru Maharaj Ji. The Guru arrived in the United States in 1971, at the age of 13. His father had been a religious leader in India, and he was first accorded a position of respect and leadership shortly after his father's death; at that time the boy was only six. Upon coming to the United States, he soon developed a sizeable following.

Americans in the sect employed many of the public relations techniques which have been developed in the West. For example, they soon produced a mass-circulation magazine and undertook extensive media publicity to bring out a large showing at one of their religious gatherings at the Houston Astrodome in 1974. Commitment to such organizing techniques set the DLM apart from certain smaller groups which also drew their ritual origins from India and which emphasized relative isolation and exclusiveness. The DLM, however, like such smaller groups, did place strong emphasis on meditation. Most members also maintained communal residences, with some living in Ashrams under the more strict religious regulations.

At the time of the study, the DLM was philosophically opposed to drug use, but strict constraints were applied only to the minority of members who lived in Ashrams. The remainder were encouraged to understand the value of achieving spiritual enlightenment through meditation and religious experience, rather than through the use of external agents.

The Unification Church, the second sect studied, is better known as the "Moonies." This religious group is organized around modifications of traditional Christian theology. The Reverend Sun Myung Moon is believed by members of this group to have a divine mission.

Virtually all full members of the UC in the United States lived in close-knit communal residences which place strong emphasis on extramarital sexual abstinence and abstinence from illicit drugs, as well as on conformity to behavioral norms and work assignments. The latter involve solicitation of charitable contributions and charitable sales, as well as recruitment for the sect. In addition, a certain number participate in small industries and sales operations run by sect members, and most spend some portion of their time in maintenance of the physical plant of church-owned buildings and in cooking or office work. Many of the new members are brought into the sect through organized workshops which have been established throughout the country.

The subject groups were studied by means of interviews with members, conducted by the author with colleagues, followed by questionnaire administration. The studies were undertaken with agreement of the respective national organizations which conduct administrative matters for each of the sects. Because of this, assistance was available during administration from members, who were trained and supervised by the author. Respondents were specifically instructed by the assistants to answer frankly and factually. Because of the willingness of members to cooperate with officially sanctioned activities, questionnaires were carefully filled out and items which were unclear were individually reviewed.

Members of the DLM were surveyed at a national religious festival in Florida in 1975. A sample of 119 initiated members were selected in a random fashion at the time of registration for the festival. In 1977, 227 American-born UC members were studied in large church residences in the New York area. Because of the residential policies of the UC, these members originally came from all parts of the United States. The third population studied consisted of 104 nonmembers who in 1978 began three-week residential workshop sequences which can lead to joining the UC.

As indicated in the reports cited; members of both sects had a mean age in the mid-twenties and were predominantly white, with a majority of males. A majority had attended college, and of these about half had been graduated. The mean duration of membership was 21 months for the DLM and 34 months for the UC members. The UC members had been introduced to the Unification Church at about the same age as had those in the sample of current workshop registrants.

Questionnaire items addressed a number of demographic, psychological, and social issues. Subjects were also asked to assess their level of drug use during different two-month periods, along a five-point quantity–frequency scale ("not at all" to "more than once on most days") as indicated in Table I. The drug categories which will be discussed here are marijuana (or hashish) and alcohol (wine, liquor or beer). The four two-month periods addressed were: "the most you ever took this drug during a two-month period before first contact with the sect," "the two months right before first contact," "the two months right after joining," and "the last two months [right before administration of the survey instrument]."

TABLE I. Heaviest Use During Any Two-Month Period Before Joining the Sect: Divine Light Mission (DLM) Members, Unification Church (UC) Members, and UC Workshop Participants (UCW)

		Reponse distribution (%)						
	Sect	None	1–3 times	1–2/ week	Daily	>1 per day	x^2	P
Marijuana	DLM	8	8	20	21	44 ⎫	36.13	<.001
	UC	21	22	23	12	22 ⎬		
	UCW	13	9	15	12	39 ⎭	19.75	<.001
Alcohol	DLM	14	22	47	9	8 ⎫	2.51	ns
	UC	10	27	46	11	6 ⎬		
	UCW	8	16	30	14	18 ⎭	19.60	<.001

The long-standing members were also asked to respond to a series of eight items which reflected their feelings of social affiliation toward different groups of people inside and outside the religious sect. These were derived from items originally developed by Schultz[7] for studying feelings of group cohesiveness. Responses were given on a five-point scale ("not at all" to "very much"). Typical items were (a) "They care for me," (b) "They are suspicious of me (scored in reverse)," and (c) "I like being part of their activities." The three groups which they were asked to evaluate with these items were (a) "the ten members you see most (in the sect)," (b) "all members (of the sect) the world over," and (c) "the ten (non-sect members) whom you see most." The differential responses on these items for each of the three target groups were examined to ascertain differences in affiliative feelings toward the respective groups.

As indicated, long-standing members in both groups were asked to report on the two-month periods prior to contact with the sect during which they consumed the most alcohol and the most marijuana. Their responses are listed in Table I. Members of the DLM and UC workshop members reported higher levels of marijuana use than did their UC counterparts. For alcohol consumption, however, DLM and UC members had similar levels of use, and the workshop respondents had higher levels than the long-standing UC members.

The incidence of any use at all of alcohol and marijuana among members of the DLM was calculated for each of four two-month periods to ascertain the effects of membership on social intoxicant use, and a decline in incidence was found, as indicated in Table II. This decline persisted up to the time of questionnaire administration. A similar decline was observed in "moderate to heavy" drug use.

Affiliative feelings toward the sect were considered in relation to the decline in use of alcohol and marijuana. First, reported levels were examined in the DLM for the two two-month periods immediately *before* introduction

TABLE II.   Social Intoxicant Use Relative to Joining the Divine Light Mission

		Respondents using drugs (%)				
		Most before joining	Right before joining	Right after joining	Last two months	Q Value[a]
Marijuana	ever used	92	82	44	42	129.7
	daily use	65	45	0	7	154.2
Alcohol	ever used	86	71	29	33	140.9
	daily use	17	13	1	0	47.7

[a] Cochran Q Test, all comparisons significant $P < .001$

to the sect and immediately *after* joining. Using the quantity–frequency rating scale given in Table I, the mean decline in scores on this scale was 43% for marijuana and 32% for alcohol. Second, responses on the social affiliation scale were then examined to demonstrate relative affiliative ties of members both inside and outside the sect. Members' mean responses to affiliation scale items reflected closer ties toward both the members they saw most often (mean 4.31) and the membership overall (4.07) than toward the nonmembers they saw most often (3.31). These comparisons of group means were highly significant ($P < .001$). Finally, the declines in scores on the alcohol and marijuana scales were used as dependent variables in two stepwise multiple regression analyses. The cohesiveness items served as independent (predictor) variables. The resulting multiple correlations showed that cohesiveness items were significant predictors of decline in alcohol and marijuana use (accounting for 15% and 14% of the variance, respectively).

With regard to contemporaneous use, UC members were also polled for marijuana and alcohol consumption at the time of the study. A small number used some marijuana or alchol during the most recent two-month period, and each of the two drugs was used on a daily basis by only one (0.4%) of the UC members during the most recent two-month period.

It is possible to compare the DLM and UC for relative decline in intoxicant use. The ubiquitous incidence of any marijuana use at all among the DLM members declined by a half from 92% to 42%, after joining. The decline among UC members, however, was more precipitous (79% to 3%), probably reflecting a more restrictive attitude in the UC toward the use of an illicit drug, albeit a social intoxicant.

Use of alcohol, a licit intoxicant, is less restricted among UC members than use of marijuana. The incidence of alcohol use for the same periods did not decline as precipitously (from 90% to 13%) as did marijuana use. In addition, daily use of marijuana continued for a significant portion (7%) of DLM respondents, although daily use among UC members virtually disappeared (0.4%). Relative to the UC, the DLM is somewhat more permissive with marijuana, a drug closely associated with the counterculture, and perhaps more compatible with the group's accepting attitude at that time toward positive aspects of altered states of consciousness, as expressed in the sect's openness toward transcendental experiences during meditation. It would appear that the nature of atypical or deviant drug use in the sects, as well as normative patterns of use, is also colored by informal social norms.

Let us now consider some implications of these findings. The mechanisms by which society exercises control over social intoxicants may be divided into two types: formal social controls, which reflect explicit social regulation and legal codes, and informal social controls, which operate by consensus and by the pressure inherent in social relations. In our own society examples of formal controls include laws against unlicensed liquor production, legal restraints on the sale of marijuana, and codes involving physicians' prescribing of certain drugs subject to abuse. Informal controls include parental pressure on teenage children, disapproval by strangers of public drunkenness, and pressure from coreligionists to conform to codes for proper behavior. Significantly, the second group are generally conceded to carry the principal weight of the regulation of drug use.[8] In a setting in which religion is influential, religious norms may then assume a primary role in the network of informal social controls.

A cross-cultural perspective on this issue is useful here. DeRios and Smith[9] reviewed patterns of drug use in nonindustrial societies. They conclude that drug use is generally a means to a socially approved end, such as contacting the supernatural. They observe that drugs are used to reconfirm the values of the culture. In most cases, drug use is controlled by rituals rather than by legal means.

It is interesting to note that even when rigidly applied formal controls are the principal means of regulation, the components of an informal network are still important. An interesting example of this existed among the pre-Columbian Aztecs, where multiple offenses of drunkeness comprised a capital offense, part of the system of formal social controls in that punitive society. Concomitantly, however, the Aztec culture had a mythology which described alcohol as a potentially dangerous drug and had specific myths involving the difficulties experienced by Aztec gods in relation to excessive drinking.[10] These components of the informal control systems served to support the formally defined behavioral norms.

Alcohol, because of its ubiquity, also offers the opportunity for study in a large number of cultures. Horton was able to study the incidence of drunkenness in primitive societies and ascertained that it "is determined less by the level of fear in society, than by the absence of corporate kin groups with stability, permanence, formal structure, and well-defined functions."[11] We therefore find that the interplay between drug use and the informal social structure may have to be understood as an interaction between behavioral phenomena with complex cultural antecedents. Either one may affect the form which the other takes.

The large-group phenomena described here apparently exerted considerable influence in altering members' behavioral norms. A related model may provide assistance in gaining a better understanding of the considerable potency and cost-effectiveness of Alcoholics Anonymous (AA). Given the observations reported here, the following traits of large-group therapy for the alcoholic may apply both to self-help groups and religious sects: large-group size vs. small therapy-group size (such as large chapter meetings); high level of social cohesiveness and a shared support system; intense, nonrational or antirational belief system; members' psychological well-being correlated with cohesiveness and a consensual belief system[5]; major behavioral norms, such as those for drinking, determined by the group; and an explicit system of rituals (such as the Twelve Steps of AA).

Some of these traits have already been studied in relation to large-group phenomena which contribute to diminished drinking. For example, the development of cohesive social relations within the AA membership has been emphasized by Trice and Roman for its importance in stabilizing membership and conformity to group norms.[12] In addition, ascription to the norms of traditional religious groups has also afforded changes in attitude toward alcohol consumption. Examples range from Christian conversion experiences[13] to peyote ceremonies of the Native American Church.[14]

Our understanding of the psychological forces which lead to behavior and attitude changes in charismatic religious groups may therefore have wider application. Perhaps professional approaches to group treatment of the alcoholic may in time incorporate some of these large-group principles.

References

1. Galanter M: The "relief effect": A sociobiologic model for neurotic distress and large-group therapy. *Am J Psychiatry* 135:588–591, 1978.
2. Galanter M, Buckley P: Evangelical religion and meditation: Psychotherapeutic effects. *J Nerv Ment Dis* 166:685–691, 1978.
3. Galanter M, Rabkin R, Rabkin J, Deutsch A: The "Moonies": A psychological study. *Am J Psychiatry* 136:165–170, 1979.
4. Galanter M: Psychological induction into the large group: Findings from a contemporary religious sect. *Am J Psychiatry* 137(12): 1980.
5. Galanter M: Sociobiology and informal social controls on alcohol consumption: Findings from two charismatic sects. *J Stud Alcohol* 42:64–79, 1981.
6. Galanter M, Buckley P, Deutsch A, Rabkin J, Rabkin R: Large-group influence for decreased drug use. *Am J Alcohol and Drug Abuse* 7(3): 1980.
7. Schutz WC: *The Interpersonal Underworld*. Palo Alto, Calif, Science and Behavior Books Inc, 1966.
8. Amar AM: Social control as a factor in non-medical drug use. *Symposium of the World Health Organization,* Toronto, 1977, pp 113–139.
9. DeRios MD, Smith DE: Drug use and abuse in cross cultural perspective. *Human Org* 36:14–21, 1977.
10. Paredes A: Social control of drinking among the Aztec Indians of Mesoamerica. *J Stud Alcohol* 36:1139–1153, 1975.
11. Horton DJ: The functions of alcohol in primitive societies: A cross-cultural study. *Q J Stud Alcohol* 4:199–320, 1943, p 223.
12. Trice HM, Roman PM: Sociopsychological predictors of affiliation with Alcoholics Anonymous: A longitudinal study of "treatment success." *Social Psychiatry* 5:51–59, 1970.
13. James W: The Varieties of Religious Experience. New York, Modern Library, 1929 (original publ. 1902), p 247.
14. Bergman RL: Navajo peyote use: Its apparent safety. *Am J Psychiatry* 128:695–699, 1971.

CHAPTER 5

Alcoholism and Clinical Psychiatry

JOEL SOLOMON, MD

The association between alcoholism and psychiatric disorders has been the subject of many studies, reviews, and myths. Alcohol has been implicated as the agent responsible for a variety of psychiatric disturbances, and psychiatric factors have frequently been described as underlying all cases of alcoholism.

Various descriptions of the behavioral effects of alcohol abuse have changed over time. This was probably a function of the various cultural climates in which the effects occurred and their acceptance or rejection in that culture. In some ways the history of alcoholism is not unlike that of psychiatry; at times the alcoholic lunatic was accepted as a pathetic yet tolerated part of society and at other times was banished to the fringes or asylums. Our understanding of the relationship between alcoholism and psychiatry has advanced slowly, partly because of the moral issues which have so heavily permeated both fields and have frequently been thought to be responsible for excessive drinking and the problems which arose as a result of it, particularly the behavioral ones.

It was a psychiatrist, Dr. Benjamin Rush, who in 1786 first defined alcoholism as a disease. Rush, the founder of modern psychiatry, contributed in several ways toward developing an understanding of alcoholism.

> First, he identified the causal agent—spirituous liquors; second, he clearly described the drunkard's condition as loss of control over drinking behavior—as compulsive activity; third, he declared the condition a disease; and fourth, he prescribed total abstinence as the only way to cure the drunkard.[1]

As might be expected, he also strongly supported the temperance movement which saw the alcoholic as a weak-willed sinner and degenerate who did not possess the inner strength to abstain from intoxicating beverages—an early expression of the ambivalence toward the alcoholic by the psychiatric

JOEL SOLOMON • Clinical Associate Professor, Director, Division of Alcoholism and Drug Dependence, Department of Psychiatry, State University of New York, Downstate Medical Center, Brooklyn, New York, 11203.

community. In fact, many of Rush's writings about alcohol were concerned with the harmful effects of alcohol, including "insanity."[2]

Until only recently, psychiatric problems in alcoholics were thought to result almost exclusively from the excessive use of alcohol on either an acute or chronic basis, and there was little attempt at evaluating any other kind of relationship. Among the acute changes were those first described by Krafft-Ebbing (quoted in Banay[3]) as a pathological alcohol reaction, later called acute alcohol insanity and finally pathological intoxication.

As an example of the chronic effects of excessive alcohol use, Bowman and Jellinek[4] described a variety of psychiatric syndromes which resulted from the chronic ingestion of alcohol. Many of them, as we know today, are mostly neurologic in origin, but, since they become manifest behaviorally, they were classified as psychiatric. In Bowman and Jellinek's historical review, many of the acute and chronic psychoses occurring in the alcoholic are described.

The historical relationship between alcoholism and psychiatry is an interesting one. Unfortunately, many aspects of this relationship were used for purposes not entirely scientific and probably led to much of the confusion that currently exists, since both alcoholism and mental illness have been ascribed to a variety of negative attitudes, values, and social stigmata. For example, many apocryphal stories regarding the acute and chronic behavioral effects of alcohol were used by the fundamentalist groups to support their moralistic position concerning alcohol and the people who consumed it.

Much of the so-called scientific literature of the time attempted to prove that most cases of insanity were the direct result of alcohol use and that if alcohol were banished insanity would disappear as well. It is clear that this type of prohibitionist-era thinking was successful in retarding research concerning the abuse of alcohol and psychiatric illness. Unfortunately, some of these moral attitudes vis-à-vis alcoholics have not fully disappeared from our current thinking in spite of repeal of the Eighteenth Amendment. However, with time, the sin and vice that were alcoholism became replaced with the disease, which, although more socially acceptable, nevertheless carried many of the stigmata of other social diseases.

As the movement toward prohibition continued, the recognition that alcoholism represented a serious health problem was also taking place. At the urging of social organizations, a number of public institutions for the treatment of alcoholics were established. The first such institution, The New York State Inebriate Asylum, was opened in 1858.[5] This effort, however, was short lived, and in 1879 this institution was converted into an insane asylum. Other facilities that had been established for alcoholics also closed and the residents were placed in these converted insane asylums or almshouses. The general level of care and understanding of alcoholism is described by Rothman:

> Since local officials institutionalized not only the needy but the drunks and public
> nuisances as well, and since these structures did not permit any degree of
> classification, a motley assortment of people mingled about. No one regulated the
> daily routine of these institutions. There was little attempt to keep inmates at work,
> except perhaps for the occasional superintendent who held out the reward of liquor
> to those who would labor.[6]

Although Rush's primary concern was that of abstinence, his concept of alcoholism as a disease continued to flourish and develop into a combination of medical, moral, and social attitudes and responses towards alcoholism.

As the prohibitionist movement was gaining strength in the United States, another movement which was also to have an effect on our understanding of alcoholism was beginning to develop in Europe. In some ways equally orthodox, this movement, psychoanalysis, did not try to prohibit alcoholism and its psychiatric sequelae, nor assign moral value to it. It attempted, rather, to understand it from a particular perspective. Although relatively little about alcoholism was known from the psychoanalytic perspective, there were a number of analysts who did take an interest in it, such as Fenichel[7] and Rado.[8] Knight,[9] for one, felt that the small number of articles on psychoanalysis was due to the few alcoholics who were seen in treatment. On the other hand, this may be due to the reluctance of psychoanalysts to identify alcoholics. From Knight's perspective,

> Alcohol addiction is a symptom rather than a disease—because the excessive
> drinking is the outstanding presenting complaint. In spite of the conviction of most
> alcoholics that they would be quite normal if only they could stop drinking, one
> never finds an alcoholic who is a psychologically healthy person when sober. There
> is always an underlying personality disorder evidenced by obvious maladjustment,
> neurotic character traits, emotional immaturity or infantilism and often by other
> neurotic symptoms. In some cases, if not in all, thinly veiled psychotic trends—
> especially paranoid and schizoid features—are discovered. In symptoms of
> excessive drinking, one sees both the regressive acting out of unconscious libidinal
> and sadistic drives and the progressive attempt at solution or cure of the conflict by
> means of ingestion of a pharmacologically potent substance, which is thus
> exploited both as a means of obtaining forbidden gratifications and carrying out of
> otherwise repressed hostilities (ego-alien impulses) and a dissolver of inhibitions
> and anxieties (ego-protective impulses).[8]

Rather than addressing the acute or chronic psychiatric complications of alcoholism, the psychoanalysts looked for causes. They generally agreed that psychiatric problems which occurred in alcoholics were not necessarily moral shortcomings, but rather oral ones. This psychoanalytic perspective continued to be developed, but in a somewhat different context. As will be described, it was Winokur and his group who attempted to classify alcoholics according to whether there was an underlying primary psychiatric disorder or whether the alcoholism itself was primary.[10]

This psychoanalytic position, whereby all alcoholics were thought to be on a regressive flight from reality through alcohol, was balanced by yet another group who saw the problem in neither moral nor oral terms but rather felt the problem of alcoholics was alcohol. Alcoholics Anonymous, founded in 1934, took the position that not all alcoholics were psychiatrically disturbed and that once the alcoholic achieved sobriety he could once more become a responsible member of society. They felt that sobriety could be achieved not through lengthy psychoanalysis for the oral problems, but rather through reorganization of one's life-style with help from the fellowship to exclude alcohol from the individual's psychosocial system.

A variety of models of alcoholism have been developed to explain the etiology and pathogenesis of alcoholism and to justify how the alcoholic patient has been treated. More recently, there have been attempts not to search for the cause of alcoholism in disturbed morals, frustrating mothers, or uniquely in the drug (alcohol) itself, but rather to view alcoholism as a common behavioral pathway in a process that may have several origins—one of which may be psychiatric in nature.

Although the diagnosis of alcoholism as a psychiatric disorder and the generalization of all alcoholics having severe psychopathology have been the subjects of much controversy, recently a more enlightened psychiatric position has begun to emerge. This position was concretized with the publication of the *Diagnostic and Statistical Manual of Mental Disorders* (Third Edition).[11] The position acknowledged the normal and appropriate use of alcohol under recreational circumstances. From this point of nonpathological use, changes associated with pathological patterns of use and impaired social or occupational functioning of at least one month's duration were designated as alcohol abuse (see Table I). If tolerance and withdrawal upon cessation occurred, the diagnosis then became alcohol dependence (see Table

TABLE I. Diagnostic Criteria for Alcohol Abuse[a]

A. Pattern of pathological alcohol use: need for daily use of alcohol for adequate functioning; inability to cut down or stop drinking; repeated efforts to control or reduce excess drinking by "going on the wagon" (periods of temporary abstinence) or restricting drinking to certain times of the day; binges (remaining intoxicated throughout the day for at least two days); occasional consumption of a fifth of spirits (or its equivalent in wine or beer); amnesic periods for events occurring while intoxicated (blackouts); continuation of drinking despite a serious physical disorder that the individual knows is exacerbated by alcohol use; drinking of nonbeverage alcohol.

B. Impairment in social or occupational functioning due to alcohol use: eg, violence while intoxicated, absence from work, loss of job, legal difficulties (eg, arrest for intoxicated behavior, traffic accidents while intoxicated), arguments or difficulties with family or friends because of excessive alcohol use.

C. Duration of disturbance of at least one month.

[a]Source: American Psychiatric Association (DSM–III), 1980.

TABLE II. Diagnostic Criteria for Alcohol Dependence[a]

A.   Either a pattern of pathological alcohol use or impairment in social or occupational functioning due to alcohol use:

Pattern of pathological alcohol use: need for daily use of alcohol for adequate functioning; inability to cut down or stop drinking; repeated efforts to control or reduce excess drinking by "going on the wagon" (periods of temporary abstinence) or restricting drinking to certain times of the day; binges (remaining intoxicated throughout the day for at least two days); occasional consumption of a fifth of spirits (or its equivalent in wine or beer); amnesic periods for events occurring while intoxicated (blackouts); continuation of drinking despite a serious physical disorder that the individual knows is exacerbated by alcohol use; drinking of nonbeverage alcohol.

Impairment in social or occupational functioning due to alcohol use: eg, violence while intoxicated, absence from work, loss of job, legal difficulties (eg, arrest for intoxicated behavior, traffic accidents while intoxicated), arguments or difficulties with family or friends because of excessive alcohol use.

B.   Either tolerance or withdrawal:

Tolerance: need for markedly increased amounts of alcohol to achieve the desired effect, or markedly diminished effect with regular use of the same amount.

Withdrawal: development of alcohol withdrawal (eg, morning "shakes" and malaise relieved by drinking) after cessation of or reduction in drinking.

---

[a]Source: American Psychiatric Association (DSM–III), 1980.

II). By definition, alcohol abuse and dependence were now psychiatric disorders. It is important to note that issues of predisposition, social implications, and the temporal process of alcoholism were also addressed. Psychiatry was finally beginning to pay attention to the complex nature of alcoholism.

Psychiatric symptomatology may be present in many ways and at many points in time along the alcoholic pathway. It is, therefore, obviously essential to evaluate any symptoms in the context of the entire dynamic process. For example, the questions that could be asked when evaluating a hallucinating alcoholic patient might be: Are these hallucinations those of a schizophrenic patient and unrelated to any drinking? Are they hallucinations of alcohol withdrawal, or acute intoxication, or an organic brain syndrome? Hallucinations are but one of many symptoms common to alcoholism and a variety of other psychiatric disorders. As with any psychiatric patient, attempts to evaluate the alcoholism on the basis of one symptom is bound to be misleading at best. There may be psychiatric factors which predispose some individuals to develop alcoholism and, conversely, alcohol may play a role in the development of psychiatric disorders. Just as psychiatric symptoms may arise as a result of both the acute and chronic effects of alcohol, any psychiatric disorder may independently coexist in a person with alcoholism; and just as there are psychiatric patients who never develop alcoholism, there are also alcoholics whose psychopathology is basically alcoholism.

Many alcoholic patients have concurrent psychiatric illness, and many psychiatric patients are also afflicted with alcoholism. The association between these two conditions has been well documented by many authors in a variety of clinical and research settings. Crowley et al[12] looked at problems of alcohol and drug abuse in 50 consecutive admissions to an adult psychiatric inpatient ward and found that alcohol contributed to over one fourth of the admissions. Fowler,[13] at a Veterans Administration Hospital, found that 53% of admissions to the psychiatric inpatient service met the diagnostic criteria for alcoholism. In this group of alcoholic patients, 33% were diagnosed as only having alcoholism, while 67% had another psychiatric diagnosis in addition to alcoholism.

Alcoholic patients are also overrepresented in psychiatric emergency rooms and clinics. Idestrom,[14] in an extensive study carried out at the Karolinska Hospital Psychiatric Emergency Service, found 35% of the patients seen there to be alcoholic.

In another study of alcoholics who arrived at a psychiatric emergency room, Schwarz and Feld[15] found that during an eight-week period, of the 305 patients who were diagnosable as alcoholic, 116 were admitted to the hospital; alcoholic psychosis was diagnosed in 28%, personality disorder in 54%, and chronic brain syndrome in 35%.

In a similar type of study, of 4,086 outpatients seen in several psychiatric clinics during a one-year period, 435 or 10% were also diagnosed as excessive drinkers. The psychiatric diagnosis for these excessive drinkers ranged from 40% who had personality disorders, 18% with either mental deficiency or organic brain syndromes, 15% with no mental disorder or undiagnosed, 9% with a diagnosis of psychosis, and 6% with a diagnosis of neurosis.[16]

From the other perspective, Tyndal[17] found that 100% of 1,000 patients who were hospitalized for alcoholism could be psychiatrically diagnosed according to criteria in the *Diagnostic and Statistical Manual of Mental Disorders* (Second Edition). The psychiatric diagnosis for these patients who were hospitalized primarily for alcoholism were: 58% neurotic, 6% psychotic, 36% personality disorders, 4.2% affective psychosis, 1.3% schizophrenia, and 0.5% paranoia.

Other authors have also looked at groups of alcohol patients, and, although a diagnosis was not applicable to all patients as Tyndal found, it was present in many. For example, Halikas et al[18] recently reported on the results of structured psychiatric interviews in 71 women alcoholics. Among their findings was that 56% fulfilled the criteria for a psychiatric diagnosis in addition to alcoholism.

Other authors have looked at the familial associations between alcoholism and psychiatric disorders. Pitts and Winokur[19] interviewed 748 consecutive patients admitted to a psychiatric service and found there was significantly more alcoholism among the immediate male relatives of the entire psychiatric patient group as well as the affective disorder, schizophrenic, neurotic and alcoholic subgroups, than in a control population.

From these reports and others, there is little doubt that alcoholism and psychiatric disorders coexist in many patients, and there are many studies in which demographic, epidemiological, and diagnostic data are reported upon. There are, however, very few reports which examine the interaction of these two conditions and the particular relationships which may exist between them. The fact that a specific psychiatric disorder occurs more frequently in alcoholic patients and vice-versa, although important to recognize, sheds little light on whether it predisposed the individual to alcoholism; predated the alcoholism, but yet was independent to its development; or arose as a result of an individual's alcoholism.

As mentioned previously, Winokur and his co-workers[10] were particularly interested in this question of the temporal relationship between alcoholism and psychiatric disorders. In a study of 259 alcoholic patients, they found that they were able to group them on the basis of the primacy of the alcoholism or of the psychiatric disorder. For example, an individual who by history fulfilled the diagnostic criteria for affective illness and who recently began drinking in an alcoholic fashion would be considered to have a primary affective disorder with secondary alcoholism. On the other hand, a patient who has for many years had several areas of his life complicated by the effects of alcohol and who has recently developed a depression would be considered as having primary alcoholism with a secondary affective disorder. The authors found they were able to delineate three major groups of alcoholics: (1) primary alcoholics, (2) depression alcoholics, and (3) sociopathy alcoholics. Males tended to predominate in the first and third group while women were more common in the second. They also found that in first-degree relatives, alcoholism was seen more frequently in primary alcoholics, depression in the depression alcoholics, and sociopathy in the sociopathic alcoholics.

Rimmer et al[20] followed up on this concept of diagnostic differences among alcoholics based on history to see if there were any clinical differences among these groups. They did indeed find significant differences in both alcoholism histories and demographic variables. Additionally, they hypothesized that the failure to establish a diagnosis and then base treatment upon it may be responsible for much of the ambiguity and conflict in the literature concerning treatment. Obviously, the making of a psychiatric diagnosis in an alcoholic patient should have more than just theoretical value.

In 1970, Kissin et al[21] postulated that the overall efficiency of alcoholism treatment was related to three major patterns of patient characteristics: (1) general prognostic factors—those patients who are socially stable, intellectually superior, psychologically intact, and well motivated will tend to do better regardless of the treatment to which they are assigned; (2) patterns related to acceptability—although this seems rather obvious, no matter how appropriate a modality may be considered for particular patients, they must accept the treatment in order for it to be considered effective; (3) specific prognostic factors—that is, the array of patient characteristics which make them most appropriate for a given treatment modality and consequently most likely to succeed in it.

With this outline serving as a hypothesis, 405 patients were randomly assigned to one of three different treatment modalities: (1) a medical model, (2) a psychological model, and (3) a social model. Patients were followed for one year after intake and evaluated on a 4-point scale of improvement. Those patients who could not be contacted for follow-up were considered as treatment failures. Success was determined by abstinence or near abstinence plus significant social and vocational adjustment during the six months prior to evaluation.

Based upon the results of this study, three groups of patients were identified and matched to three specific treatment modalities. One of these groups was found to be those patients who carried in addition to alcoholism a psychiatric diagnosis. When assigned to a treatment modality specifically designed to address the psychiatric problem, these patients did significantly better than a similar group of patients who were offered other types of treatment or nonpsychiatric patients who were offered this type of treatment.

Not only can psychiatric diagnosis act as a prognostic factor; Panepinto et al[22] showed how it might also act as an indication of participation in treatment, if indeed the treatment was based upon it. They found that patients who were diagnosed as schizophrenic and put into treatment employing primarily a medical model had more doctor visits over a longer period of time than did patients with various personality disorders. Clearly, the defining of psychiatric characteristics of alcoholic patients, and developing a treatment based upon them, is an approach which can affect the outcome in a positive way and which should obviously be explored further.

In addition to primacy of the alcoholism or the psychiatric disorder, there have been several attempts to develop a typology of alcoholism based upon psychopathology and early familial history of alcoholism. For example, a recent report by Frances et al[23] found that among a large group of men admitted to the naval residential alcohol treatment program those who reported at least one family member with a possible drinking problem also showed more antisocial behavior and worse academic, social, and employment performance. This group might be related to the "essential" alcoholic as described by Knight,[9] who thought it to be more severe and, therefore, more difficult to treat. He likened this form of alcoholism to process schizophrenia and thought both had a generally poor prognosis. Tartar et al[24] hypothesized that there was a subgroup of alcoholics who as children displayed symptoms of minimal brain dysfunction and as young adults began to consume excessive quantities of alcohol. They did not, however, reveal the presence of other major psychiatric disturbance. These patients were described as primary alcoholics. They also raised the possibility that the secondary alcoholics were normal children who as adults became psychiatrically disturbed and turned to alcohol for symptomatic relief.

Another area if interest is the recent discovery of a variety of neuro-transmitters which are thought to play a role in the development of mental illness.[25] Several of these neurotransmitters may also be of importance in the field of alcoholism, since they have shown alterations with chronic alcohol consumption which might account for some of the psychiatric syndromes seen with prolonged alcohol use. The question has also been raised as to whether the lack of or excess of a particular transmitter may predispose an individual to develop alcoholism.[26] The endorphins are thought to interact in particular with a dopaminergic neurotransmitter system, and although their role in the actual development or perpetuation of psychosis is unclear, the dopamine system was also found to be altered by the chronic exposure to alcohol.[27] The whole field of neurotransmitter pharmacology has been moving extremely rapidly and may soon offer new insights into alcoholic subgroups and drinking behavior.

The issues of subgroups of alcoholics is particularly important in terms of treatment. Now that alcoholism is being more clearly defined and understood, we are seeing that different groups of people may develop alcoholism at different rates and in different patterns—patterns which may or may not include a psychiatric disorder. The specific psychiatric disorders are covered in depth in each of the subsequent chapters and consequently will not be discussed here.

There is no evidence to substantiate a general theory of alcoholism and psychiatric disorders. Alcoholism can mask, mimic, precipitate, or independently coexist with the gamut of psychiatric disorders. These psychiatric symptoms or syndromes may predate the alcoholism and play a role in its etiology. They may result from the acute effects of alcohol such as intoxication and withdrawal, or they may develop as a consequence of longstanding, chronic, compulsive alcohol abuse. They may also independently coexist in the same patient with no causal relationship but may in some way influence the course of the other condition.

Treatment for alcoholism is no longer only the treatment of the underlying pre-oedipal causes as described by Knight,[9] since we now understand that psychiatric of psychological factors are not the only ones that may precipitate and propagate alcoholism. In some patients, however, they may play a role which requires equally careful attention, since they may be causal in the development of alcoholism. On the other hand, they may develop as the result of chronic alcoholism and in this case, too, will need careful evaluation and attention.

Psychiatry and alcoholism have a long and confusing history. This history is replete with moral, religious, legal, medical, and psychiatric nuances which have made clarification of the relationship ambiguous and frequently difficult. Consequently, the role of the psychiatrist has also been unclear. Better understanding of this relationship will begin to shed light on some of the most confusing yet potentially important aspects of both conditions.

References

1. Levin HG: The discovery of addiction. *J Stud Alcohol* 39:143–174, 1978.
2. Rush B: An enquiry into the effects of ardent spirits upon the human body and mind. *Q J Stud Alcohol* 4:321–341, 1943.
3. Banay RS: Pathological reaction to alcohol I. Review of the literature and original case reports. *Q J Stud Alcohol* 4:580–605, 1944.
4. Bowman KM, Jellinek EM: Alcoholic mental disorders. *Q J Stud Alcohol* 2:312–390, 1941.
5. Pollack H: Alcoholism, in *Social Work Yearbook,* vol 1. New York, Russell Sage Foundation, 1929.
6. Rothman D: *The Discovery of the Asylum.* Boston, Little Brown & Co, 1971.
7. Fenichel O: *The Psychoanalytic Theory of Neurosis,* New York, W W Norton & Co, 1945.
8. Rado S: Psychoanalysis of pharmacothymia. *Psychoanal Quart* 2:1–23, 1933.
9. Knight RP: The dynamics and treatment of chronic alcohol addiction. *Bull Menninger Clinic* 1:233–250, 1937.
10. Winokur G, Rimmer J, Reich I: Alcoholism IV: Is there more than one type of alcoholism? *Br J Psychiatry* 118:525–531, 1971.
11. *Diagnostic and Statistical Manual of Mental Disorders,* ed 3 (DSM-III). Washington, DC, American Psychiatric Association, 1980.
12. Crowley, TJ, Chesluck D, Dilts S, Hard R: Drug and alcohol abuse among psychiatric admissions. *Arch Gen Psychiatry* 30:13–20, 1974.
13. Fowler RC, Liskow BL, Tanna VL, Van Valkenburg C: Psychiatric illness and alcoholism. *Alcoholism: Clinical and Experimental Research* 1(2):125–128, 1977.
14. Idestrom CM: Psychiatric emergency service. *Acta Psychiatr Scand* 50:636–647, 1974.
15. Schwarz L, Feld SP: The alcoholic patient in the psychiatric emergency room. *Q J Stud Alcohol* 30:104–111, 1969.
16. Bahn AK, Chandler CA: Alcoholism in psychiatric clinic patients. *Q J Stud Alcohol* 22(3):411–417, 1961.
17. Tyndal M: Psychiatric study of one thousand alcoholic patients. *Can Psychiatr Assoc J* 19:21–24, 1974.
18. Halikas JA, Herzog MA, Mirassou MM, Lyttle MD: Psychiatric diagnosis among female alcoholics, in Galanter M (ed): *Currents in Alcoholism,* vol 8. New York, Grune & Stratton, 1981.
19. Pitts F, Winokur G: Affective disorder. VII: Alcoholism and affective disorder. *J Psychiatr Res* 4:37–50, 1966.
20. Rimmer J, Reich T, Winokur G: Alcoholism V. Diagnosis and clinical variation among alcoholics. *Q J Stud Alcohol* 33:658–666, 1972.
21. Kissin B: Patient characteristics and treatment specifically in alcoholics, in *Recent Advances in the Study of Alcoholism,* Proceedings of the First International Magnus Huss Symposium, Stockholm, Sept. 2-3, 1976. Amsterdam, Excerpta Medica, 1977, pp 110–122.

22. Panepinto WC, Higgins MJ, Keane-Dawes WY, Smith D: Underlying psychiatric diagnosis as an indicator of participation in alcoholism therapy. *Q J Stud Alcohol* 31(4):950–956, 1970.

23. Frances R, Timms S, Bucky S: Studies of familial and non-familial alcoholism. I: Demographic studies. *Arch Gen Psychiatry* 37:564–566, 1980.

24. Tarter RE, McBride H, Bounpane N, Schneider DU: Differentiation of alcoholics: Childhood history of minimal brain dysfunction, family history and drinking patterns. *Arch Gen Psychiatry* 34:761–768, 1977.

25. Verby K, Volavka J, Clouet DH: Endorphins in psychiatry: An overview and a hypothesis. *Arch Gen Psychiatry* 35:877–888, 1978.

26. Verbey K, Blum K: Alcohol euphoria: Possible mediation via endorphinergic mechanisms. *J Psychedelic Drugs* 11:305–311, 1979.

27. Tabakoff B, Hoffman PL, Ritzmann RF: Dopamine receptor function after chronic ingestion of ethanol. *Life Sciences* 23:643–648, 1978.

CHAPTER 6

Alcoholism and Schizophrenia

MARTIN S. KESSELMAN, MD, JOEL SOLOMON, MD, MALCOLM BEAUDETT, BS, and BARBARA THORNTON, RN

Clinical experience indicates that the concurrence of alcoholism and schizophrenia in the same individual is a far from unusual circumstance. Clinicians generally attribute a poor prognosis and stormy course to the combination and it is not uncommon to find alcohol treatment programs which reject patients with the stigmata of functional psychosis, or so-called schizophrenia treatment units which prematurely discharge or refuse to accept patients with a history of serious alcohol abuse.

In view of the commonplace and vexatious nature of the problem, one would expect to find an ample literature on this subpopulation. One would like to know, for instance, how their clinical course differs from patients with the separate diagnoses of alcoholism or schizophrenia. Would treatment for schizophrenia or alcoholism alone sufficiently ameliorate the level of pathology so that the need to treat the other diagnosis is affected? Or, if not, should the alcoholism or the schizophrenia be treated first, or should both be treated concurrently? How does treatment outcome for this group differ from that for patients with alcoholism or schizophrenia alone? Unfortunately, the published literature on this subject is scanty. For example, there are no joint citations in the index of the most recent three-volume edition of the *Comprehensive Textbook of Psychiatry*.[1] Similarly, the five-volume comprehensive review of alcoholism by Kissin and Begleiter[2] contains only a single

MARTIN S. KESSELMAN • Professor, Department of Clinical Psychiatry, State University of New York, Downstate Medical Center, Director of Psychiatry, Kings County Hospital Center, Brooklyn, New York 11203.   **JOEL SOLOMON** • Clinical Associate Professor, Director, Division of Alcoholism and Drug Dependence, Department of Psychiatry, State University of New York, Downstate Medical Center, Brooklyn, New York 11203.   **MALCOLM BEAUDETT** • Third-Year Medical Student, State University of New York. Downstate Medical Center, Brooklyn, New York 11203.   **BARBARA THORNTON** • Unit Chief, Kingsboro Psychiatric Center, Clinical Instructor, State University of New York, Downstate Medical Center, Brooklyn, New York 11203.

page on the topic. It is clear, therefore, that a major area of clinical investigation remains to be explored. Confronted with what were apparently large numbers of patients in the category of this combined diagnosis, the Department of Psychiatry at the State University of New York Downstate Medical Center has sampled a small group of about 40 patients from both inpatient and outpatient services with combined and separate diagnoses. (In the course of this paper the phrase "combined diagnosis" refers to patients who bear the diagnosis of both schizophrenia and alcoholism.) This group has served solely as a "benchmark" against which to measure some of the impressions gleaned from the literature and to generate several hypotheses of our own. Clearly the group is too small and uncontrolled to serve as the basis for firm conclusions. It is important to note, however, that the patients were assessed in terms of the diagnostic criteria of the Diagnostic and Statistical Manual of Mental Disorders—III (DSM–III), and therefore we are provided with a major advantage in diagnostic stringency over earlier reports. (See, for example, Freed, who felt that a methodological flaw in many studies was based upon flexible diagnositc criteria.[3]) Patients in all our groups were drawn from an inner city ghetto population in which the diagnoses of chronic alcoholism and schizophrenia of all types is heavily represented.

Incidence

It has been argued that in some cases alcohol abuse may characterize the behavior of patients in the elated phase of a bipolar psychosis. If a parallel situation should exist in the case of schizophrenia, one might expect a higher incidence of alcoholism among schizophrenics than among the population group from which they are drawn. Similarly, if alcoholism serves as a defense in some patients against further devolution into the psychotic process, one might expect a lower than anticipated incidence of schizophrenia among alcoholics. Psychotic patients whose drinking is deeply enmeshed in their disordered behavior are not uncommon, and the development of a schizophrenic picture during alcohol withdrawal has also been described.[2] It would be hoped, therefore, that population studies might help to elucidate some of the assumptions which underlie our understanding of these illnesses.

Unfortunately, a comprehensive historical review of prevalence studies in both the alcoholism and schizophrenia literatures fails to clarify this issue. Freed's paper[3] is a major contribution to this field. It is clear from his extensive review that there is a wide range in the reported incidence; for schizophrenia among alcoholics, for example, figures range from 1% among 797 inpatients in a short-term alcoholism treatment unit to 33% of 1,171 patients in a VA Hospital. From the other perspective, the prevalence of schizophrenic patients abusing alcohol varies between 3% and 63%. On the state hospital ward from which we drew our experience, approximately 33% of the patients admitted with a diagnosis of schizophrenia are identified as alcohol abusers. Clearly, it is impossible to interpret these figures without knowing the prevalence of alcohol abuse in the population from which our schizophrenics were drawn, data which we do not have at this time.

Some studies have been published which investigate the prevalence of alcoholism in the *families* of schizophrenics. As one might expect, it appears that the families of schizophrenic probands will display higher rates of alcoholism if the family members themselves come from populations afflicted by that disease. For example, in his comprehensive review of the schizophrenic disorders,[4] Manfred Bleuler cited three large studies which report the prevalence of alcoholism among the fathers of a combined sample of 408 schizophrenics. His figures range from 3.2% to 24.2%. In these studies, it was clear that this range reflected the provenance of the sample rather the effect of the schizophrenic diagnosis.

A recent study of Rimmer and Jacobsen[5] used a more sophisticated design. They compared schizophrenic adoptees and their biological relatives with control adoptees and their biological relatives. They concluded that "neither schizophrenics nor their relatives had higher rates of alcoholism than did controls."

In our own sample, the alcoholic/schizophrenic group lay between pure alcoholics and pure schizophrenics in giving a positive family history of drinking. Sixty-two percent of the patients with the combined diagnosis and 100% of the patients with alcoholism gave such a history. None of the nonalcoholic schizophrenics did. Although we do not fully understand the determinants of drinking behavior, it appears likely that schizophrenics learn to drink the same way nonschizophrenics do.

The data, therefore, fail to support the implication that schizophrenia and alcoholism are anything but unrelated entities, although with the possible exception of the Rimmer and Jacobsen study, the published studies may be faulted on the basis of diagnostic adequacy or methodological design. This does *not* mean that the clinician treating a patient with the combined diagnosis can afford to ignore the presence of both diagnoses or their effect on each other.

Interaction of Alcoholism and Schizophrenia

The ways in which patients with the combined diagnoses may present a more complicated treatment picture may arise from several issues: the diagnosis may be confused at least temporarily because the two clinical pictures may consist of similar symptoms; the patients' drinking behavior may modify the patient's schizophrenic course or vice versa; the long-term prognosis may be affected by the concurrent illness; one may have to modify one's psychopharmacological treatment regimen to take the other diagnosis into account; one may have to modify the nonpharmacological aspects of treatment; and finally, the high incidence of medical complications in alcoholism may significantly affect one's treatment plan for the patient's schizophrenia. The foregoing considerations serve as a basis for review of several salient points in the diagnosis and treatment of this population.

Diagnostic Issues

It is likely that some of the conflicting impressions concerning the combined occurrence of alcoholism and schizophrenia have their source in the shifting diagnostic criteria which have been adopted in these conditions. The third edition of the *Diagnostic and Statistical Manual of Mental Disorders* (DSM–III),[6] utilizes more objectifiable and reliable bases for diagnosis. Borderline conditions, schizophreniform disorder, and schizoaffective schizophrenia have been more precisely defined. There is some evidence that these conditions overlap the affective disorders.[7] In light of recent evidence linking alcoholism and affective disorder,[8,9] one might expect that if these speculations are sustained, patients with these less typical schizophrenia-like disorders may resemble patients with affective disorders in their patterns of alcohol use. Certainly, among patients with borderline disorders who evince transient psychoses, a history of alcohol or drug abuse is quite common. In our clinical experience, it is not uncommon to find a similar history of alcohol abuse in patients in the excited phase of schizoaffective schizophrenia.

It has long been common experience that chronic schizophrenic patients may show deterioration and a general failure of self-care, salient features of which may be an increase in impulsivity and alcohol abuse. These patients, however, seldom present diagnostic difficulties, since their psychosis will have antedated the heavy drinking and classic schizophrenic symptoms will have been well documented.

The most vexing diagnostic problems are presented by the nondeteriorated patient who presents with the acute (or subacute) onset of hallucinations and delusions. Writing in 1911, Bleuler commented:

> The differentiation between delirium tremens and the agitated state of schizophrenia is so simple that it is hard to understand how it is possible that so many schizophrenics are referred to institutions with a diagnosis of delirium tremens.[10]

A psychiatrist working in a contemporary emergency room or consultation service must be equally impressed by how many patients with alcohol withdrawal psychoses are referred with the diagnosis of schizophrenia.

The symptoms of schizophrenia are prominent but not very discriminating. Hallucinations and delusions, which often provide the most striking features in the clinical picture, occur across many psychiatric illnesses; yet, when marked clouding of the sensorium is not present, hallucinating patients are almost automatically diagnosed as schizophrenic. Gross and his colleagues[11] have emphasized that, contrary to the rather stereotyped pictures presented in textbooks, delirium tremens presents a rather variable clinical picture in the formation of which personality and cultural factors play a major pathoplastic role. These workers have emphasized that the presence of hallucinations cannot be accounted for entirely on the basis of clouding of consciousness. Hallucinations occur only in approximately 50% of schizophrenics, and their presence must be explained on the basis of additional factors, for example, an inherent propensity to strong imagery.[12] On the other hand, hallucinations are very common in alcoholism. Ninety percent of the patients in the Downstate series with combined diagnoses reported them, but then so did 100% of the outpatient alcoholics who reported having at one time experienced a withdrawal syndrome. In our series, schizophrenics suffered mostly from auditory and visual hallucinations. The alcoholics, on the other hand, tended to report hallucinations that involved a combination of auditory, visual, and tactile modes. The "pure" alcoholics tended not to be delusional, however, while patients with both diagnoses tended to be as delusional as did patients with schizophrenia alone.

There are conflicting views as to just how sharply the phenomenology of hallucinations differs in these two groups. Alpert and Silver[13] found a difference in the quality of hallucinations which alcoholics and schizophrenics subjectively reported. For alcoholics, hallucinations could be localized in space, had a greater frequency of occurrence, and were relatively independent of emotional state. Schizophrenics' hallucinations had a more cognitive "taint" (they are sometimes referred to in classic psychopathology as "thoughts made audible"), were poorly localized, and showed a sensitivity to emotional arousal. Other workers[14] failed to find differences in the quality of hallucinations between diagnostic groups. The important heuristic point is that the presence or quality of hallucinations may make some difference but not a sufficient one upon which to base a diagnosis or choice of treatment.

The clinician may find that a more useful source of information is close attention to the timing of the onset of hallucinations in relation to the patient's medical and alcohol history. For example, it is common to find that patients who become paranoid or hallucinated two or three days after hospital admission, particularly after a surgical stress, will bear close scrutiny for the diagnosis of alcohol withdrawal psychosis, even though the other stigmata of delirium not be present.

One is also sometimes troubled by the sort of patient who presents with chronic hallucinations or delusional thinking, apparently precipitated by alcohol, but long outlasting the stimulus. This remains a controversial issue.

We have seen several of these patients presenting a hallucinosis but without clear symptoms of schizophrenia. Victor and Hope[15] have pointed out that the symptoms of alcohol hallucinosis may persist for lengthy periods of time in a small number of patients. One cannot be absolutely certain, however, that all patients with persistent hallucinations fall into this group. Some of them follow a deteriorating course independent of continued alcohol abuse and begin to look more and more like chronic schizophrenics, despite the fact that during their subacute phase a formal throught disorder was not identified. In general, whatever their diagnosis, these patients respond poorly to drug management although it should be attempted, and the support and social interventions they require must be patterned more closely on the model of ambulatory schizophrenia.

Course of Illness

One reason why the notion that a more than chance interaction might exist between alcoholism and schizophrenia is that patients themselves often report that alcohol plays an ameliorating or exacerbating role in their illness. In principle, this is no more cogent than their attributing their drinking to "nervousness" or their "nervousness" to drinking. Nor is it relevant evidence toward the older clinical concept that alcohol abuse is a defense against schizophrenia. The ultimate extrapolation of the former (ameliorating) case would be to encourage schizophrenics toward some sort of controlled drinking or to prescribe and control the use of medication which is cross-tolerant with alcohol in order to treat the schizophrenia. Although there have been a number of clinical impressions put forth,[16] we are unaware of any direct study of the beneficial effect of alcohol on schizophrenic symptomatology. Minor tranquilizers are ineffective antipsychotics, although they are useful for the short-term treatment of anxiety, and alcoholic schizophrenics have even more reason to be anxious than most alcoholics. Similar comments can be made about the use of alcohol to suppress hallucinations in schizophrenics. Nevertheless, it is a commonly reported clinical experience[2] that both alcohol abusers and drug abusers sometimes show psychotic deterioration including hallucinations and delusions when maintenance treatment is tapered off. Kissin[2] has suggested that there is an indication for the combined use of a major and minor tranquilizer in this population, although, like other authors, he has recommended caution and restraint in the light of the abuse potential of the latter agents. In general, the indications for the use of a minor tranquilizer in this population should be those which would influence the clinician if the schizophrenic symptomatology were not present.

It is important to remember that the schizophrenic alcohol abuser is unable to control the dose and timing of his drinking and often of his medication. Both schizophrenics and alcoholics are notoriously noncompliant, and this would undoubtedly compound the problems of prescribing any maintenance medication.

In our population, 75% of the patients who commented on the issue felt that alcohol had worsened their schizophrenic symptoms.

Long-Term Characteristics and Course

Almost no information exists on the long-term prognosis of patients with the combined diagnosis. It may be that they are sufficiently segregated by the treatment system so that attention has been focused entirely on the predominant problem as it is perceived by the treating clinician. In his comprehensive review of the long-term follow-up of a group of schizophrenics, for example, Manfred Bleuler does not report on the issue of alcohol abuse.[4]

Failing this data, it may be useful to look at some of the impressions we have gained concerning the characteristics of the patients in our sample who bore both diagnoses and to differentiate them from the other two groups ("pure" schizophrenics and alcoholics). The patients with the combined diagnoses appeared to follow a course with features which were somewhat more similar to the alcohol group. For example, they tended to report having become sick an average of six years later than the schizophrenic group, and correspondingly they were considerably older at the time of the first hospitalization (30 years old compared to 21 years old). Although the average number of hospital episodes per patient was approximately the same for the two inpatient groups (schizophrenic and combined diagnosis), the total time in hospitals was *ten times* longer for the pure schizophrenic group than for the patients with combined diagnosis.

It is important to emphasize that the presence of psychotic symptoms is common in the presentation of alcoholism whether the psychosis is schizophrenic or not. Schuckit[17] found evidence of psychotic symptomatology in 43% of 220 alcoholic patients presenting for treatment. What seemed to differentiate them from patients without a history of psychotic symptoms was a significantly higher rate of drug use and a greater frequency of antisocial difficulties among the psychotics. They were similar in their alcohol histories. Although Schuckit's psychotic patients were not schizophrenic, they did resemble in these respects our alcoholic schizophrenics. In our sample the alcoholic schizophrenics were likely to abuse drugs other than alcohol with considerably higher frequency (57% of cases compared to 20% of alcoholics and 0% of schizophrenics). It appears that the presence of alcohol and drug abuse is more likely to affect or dominate the clinical picture of schizophrenia than the other way around.

The alcoholic schizophrenic group is a suicidal group. It had about twice the incidence of suicidal attempts as the alcoholic group. One cannot emphasize strongly enough the impulsivity and suicidal potential of this group of patients. The clinician who undertakes to treat them must bear in mind the responsibility for assuring that these patients have around-the-clock accessibility to emergency services.

Since schizophrenia research appears to indicate that long-term prognosis in that disease is more related to premorbid adjustment than to the specific symptomatology of the acute episode, it is likely that the same premorbid factors (rather poor and similar for all groups in our sample) will have an overriding influence in patients with the combined diagnosis.

Modification of Psychopharmacological Treatment with the Combined Diagnoses

Kissin[2] has pointed out that, while major tranquilizers may exacerbate the clinical state of agitated alcoholics, "diagnosed agitated schizophrenics preferred phenothiazines as their maintenance drug although many find chlordiazepoxide to be a valuable anxiolytic adjunct as well."

Although the use of major tranquilizers would appear to be a necessary but insufficient condition of abstinence of patients with the combined diagnoses, controlled clinical evidence is lacking for this rather self-evident notion. Although alcohol potentiates some effects of phenothiazines, this should not present an absolute contraindication to prescribing them in this group, particularly in light of the short-term and long-terms risks of continued drinking. Optimally, administration of medication should be monitored by a responsible "other" and 24-hour medical support should be available and accessible.

The use of disulfiram which is effective in the treatment of many alcoholics, cannot be recommended for this group. Schizophrenia-like psychoses represent only a small percentage of psychoses described among the psychiatric complications of that agent (which tend to be but are not always, associated with delirium). Whether this is a direct drug effect, an uncovering effect, or the chance occurrence of a concomitant psychosis is unclear. Until we know more about these patients and their response to such treatment under investigative conditions, the high proportion of suicide in disulfiram psychoses (17%)[18] would preclude its use in patients with schizophrenia.

Experienced clinicians such as Kissin[2] have come to the conclusion that for a subgroup of these patients the combination of a major and minor tranquilizer, generally frowned upon as polypharmacy, represents optimal management. When the patient is under long-term care and his condition has been sufficiently clarified, it may be possible to distinguish anxiety related to the various interacting crises to which these patients are prone, for instance, alcohol withdrawal, prolonged abstinence syndrome, schizophrenic decompensation, insufficient major tranquilizer dose (secondary to non compliance or to an increase in psychosocial stress). It should be recalled that the alcoholism literature is increasingly supportive of the concept of the prolonged abstinence syndrome—a lengthy period of psychological and physiological instability following withdrawal. During this period the need for psychotropic medication may be different from the need when the patient is stabilized. For some patients it is unlikely that even intensive scrutiny will achieve the goal of maximum specificity for the pharmacological treatment plan.

Nonpsychopharmacological Aspects of Treatment

Any program which attempts to deal with patients who have combined diagnoses must recognize that while they may, if our sample was typical, represent a somewhat less institutionalized and chronic group, they present formidable problems because of their acting-out behaviors. We have been impressed with how little attention is given to the alcohol problems of the schizophrenic group. Even good treatment programs are necessarily staffed and programmed to deal with patients with the uncomplicated diagnosis of schizophrenia, and referrals to outside agencies are often cumbersome and allow too much opportunity for patient noncompliance. In our sample we found no differences in the kinds of treatments, their effectiveness, or the type or dose of drug prescribed for patients with schizophrenia alone or with combined diagnosis. Alterman et al[19] have reported on the incidence of patients with combined diagnoses in a large VA Neuropsychiatric Hospital. These patients comprised about 10% of their population, and approximately 50% of this group of patients exhibited "multiple adverse consequences of this behavior [which] made it difficult for staff to effectively treat and manage these patients." A large proportion (80%) of these problematic patients had not received specialized treatment for their alcohol abuse. Thus, the VA group and our own appear to share similar characteristics.

Since these patients are apt to demonstrate more disruptive behavior in the hospital than as outpatients, they are at risk for premature discharge from programs which fail to take into account both alcohol and schizophrenia-related behaviors. Therapeutic milieu programs which may summarily discharge even quite ill patients who return from a pass drunk or secrete alcohol on the ward are particularly at fault in this respect. On the other hand, it is commonly observed on drug and alcohol units that patients at risk for functional psychosis may decompensate when alcohol or an opiate has been recently withdrawn; pressure to transfer these patients to a psychiatric facility at a key point in their withdrawal may thus be generated. Obviously, due account must be taken of the patients' need for pharmacological and personal support around these issues, which do not present themselves in the uncomplicated schizophrenic patient. The staff will frequently interpret the exacerbation of symptoms as being related to anxiety over the termination of treatment and incipient discharge. It is not uncommon for this dilemma—the difficulty of sorting out just how much of the patient's symptomatology is determined by his response to separation and how much represents a reemergence of his illness—to serve as the focus of staff dissension. Clearly staff education in and supervision through the prolonged and complicated course of these disorders is a necessary, although hardly sufficient, condition for their management.

When the patient has recompensated and has been reintroduced into an outpatient treatment program, the structure of that program must take into account the particular vulnerability of the schizophrenic patient to treatment relationships which are variable, intrusive, or critical in nature.[20] Schizophrenics may find the confrontational quality of some Alcoholics Anonymous (AA) groups or therapeutic groups too aversive. On the other hand, the consistent, structured, and relatively impersonal quality of some pharmacologically oriented alcohol treatment programs may prove more effective in maintaining these patients in treatment.[21] For these patients a major initial goal must be to assure compliance with medication, since this has been well established as a major determinant of prognosis in recently discharged schizophrenic patients. In a metaphorical sense, the reliable relationship appears to substitute for the addicting agent. The time when a remote and interpretive stance has been acceptable for the great majority of schizophrenic or alcoholic patients in psychotherapy would appear to have passed. A helpful and supportive relationship aimed at stabilizing the patient and assisting the family would appear to be the optimal one, at least during the initial phases of treatment.

It is possible that this group of patients would be most effectively treated by a multidisciplinary staff whose efforts were concentrated on the special problems they present. Until such time as mental health workers are routinely trained in treating both substance abuse and psychiatric illness, it is likely that an intensive period of development and education would be necessary to staff such a unit, and it is unlikely to be effective if it is diffused across a large general mental health facility. The effectiveness of this sort of unit is not yet established, however, and may not be recommended except on a pilot basis.[22] It is possible, for example, that despite its apparent theoretical attractiveness, it would do no better than the units currently in use. On the other hand, the data available about patients with combined diagnoses is both scanty and drawn mostly from chronically ill and handicapped populations. Patients who are not so ill from either alcoholism or schizophrenia may do well in other sorts of settings. It is also possible that the prolonged and intense needs of these patients may make the establishment of these units economically unfeasible in many settings. Weighing against the tentative nature of this recommendation, however, would be the pressing need to gather better data and more clinical experience and the well-established need to begin the problem of staff education in this area with at least a core group of mental health professionals.

References

1. Kaplan HI, Freedman AM, Soddock BJ: *Comprehensive Textbook of Psychiatry III.* Baltimore, Williams & Wilkins, 1980.
2. Kissin B, Begleiter H (eds): *The Biology of Alcoholism.* New York, Plenum Press, 1971.
3. Freed E: Alcoholism and schizophrenia: The search for perspectives. *J Stud Alcohol* 36:853–881, 1975.
4. Bleuler M: *The Schizophrenic Disorders.* New Haven, Yale University Press, 1978.
5. Rimmer J, Jacobsen B: Alcoholism in schizophrenics and their relatives. *J Stud Alcohol* 38:1781–1784, 1977.
6. *Diagnostic and Statistical Manual of Mental Disorders,* ed 3 *(DSM-III).* Washington DC, American Psychiatric Association, 1980.
7. Tupin J: Borderline states and psychosis, in *Transient Psychoses: Diagnosis and Management.* Presented at the 133rd Annual Meeting of the American Psychiatric Association, 1980.
8. Reich LH, Davies RK, Himmelhock J: Excessive alcohol use in manic-depressive illness. *Am J Psychiatry* 131:83–86, 1974.
9. Mayfield DG, Coleman LL: Alcohol use and affective disorder. *Dis Nerv System* 29:467–474, 1968.
10. Bleuler E: *Dementia Praecox, or the Group of Schizophrenias.* New York, International University Press, 1952.
11. Gross MM, Rosenblatt SM, Lewis E *et al*: Hallucinations and clouding of sensorium in acute alcohol withdrawal syndromes: Dependent and independent relationships including evidence for cultural hallucinogenic mechanisms, in Keup W (ed): *Origin and Mechanisms of Hallucinations.* New York, Plenum Press, 1970.
12. West LJ (ed): *Hallucinations.* New York, Grune & Stratton, 1962.
13. Alpert M, Silvers N: Perceptual characteristics distinguishing auditory hallucinations in schizophrenia and acute alcoholic psychoses. *Am J Psychiatry* 127:298–302, 1970.
14. Goodwin DW, Alderson P, Rosenthal R: Clinical significance of hallucinations in psychiatric disorders: A study of 116 hallucinatory patients. *Arch gen Psychiatry* 24:76–80, 1971.
15. Victor M, Hope JM: The phenomenon of auditory hallucinations in chronic alcoholism: A critical evaluation of the status of alcoholic hallucinosis. *Nerv Ment Dis* 126:451–481, 1958.
16. Hallay L: Alcoholism and schizophrenia. *J Med Cincinn* 18:23–28, 1937.
17. Schuckit M: The history of psychiatric symptoms in alcoholics. Presented at the Annual Meeting of the American Psychiatric Association, 1980.
18. Liddon SC, Satran R: Disulfiram (Antabuse) psychosis. *Am J Psychiatry* 123:1284–1289, 1967.
19. Alterman AI, Erdlen FR, McLellan AT: Problem drinking in a psychiatric hospital: Alcohol schizophrenics, in Gottheil E, McLellan AT, Druley KA (eds): *Substance Abuse and Psychiatric Illness,* New York, Pergamon Press, 1980.

20. Hirsch SR: Interacting social and biological factors determining prognosis in the rehabilitation and management of persons with schizophrenia, in Cancro R (ed): *Annual Review of the Schizophrenic Syndrome,* vol 4, 1974–1975. New York, Brunner/Mazel, 1976.
21. Panepinto WC *et al*: Underlying psychiatric diagnosis as an indicator of participation in alcoholism therapy. *Q J Stud Alcohol* 31:950–6, 1970.
22. Weinstein SP, Gottheil E: A coordinated program for treating combined mental health and substance abuse problems, in Gottheil E, McLellan AT, Druley KA, *Substance Abuse and Psychiatric Illness.* New York, Pergamon Press, 1980.

Alcoholism and Affective Disorders

Methodological Considerations

JOEL SOLOMON, MD

The association between alcoholism and affective disorders has been written about extensively from many perspectives, yet there remain many questions unanswered. Several reasons have been suggested for this ambiguity. For example, part of the difficulty in establishing a clear-cut relationship can be based upon the lack of uniform and precisely defined terminology.

Schuckit[1] recently outlined several problems which he feels contribute to the confusion and suggested an approach for clarifying some of the issues involved. Such concepts as "mood and affect," "primary and secondary affective disorder," "drinking practices" and "primary and secondary alcoholism" all must be clearly defined before a clinician or researcher can base findings upon them.

Many attempts at clarification do not adequately differentiate, for example, between mood changes which occur during an alcoholic episode and true affective disorder. The pharmacologic affects of alcohol are capable of producing sadness and despondency which must be differentiated from true affective disorder.

Another difficulty in understanding this relationship may arise from the wide range of prevalence of these two combined conditions. Hamm *et al*,[2] for example, administered the Zung Self-Rating Depression Scale and the Hamilton Depression Scale to a group of young, healthy alcohol abusers and found that none of their patients has a clear-cut indication of depression, although some did score in the borderline range. They felt the low incidence of depression in this group of patients might be due to the relatively younger age of their patients, the absence of severe medical and psychosocial problems, or

JOEL SOLOMON • Clinical Associate Professor, Director, Division of Alcoholism and Drug Dependence, Department of Psychiatry, State University of New York, Downstate Medical Center, Brooklyn, New York 11203.

other aspects of patient selection bias. For example, it is not uncommon for persons to seek treatment when two disorders are present: therefore, by choosing those patients who have actively sought treatment we may be seeing an artifically elevated association of the two conditions.[3] Winokur et al[4] reported finding 3% of male alcoholics interviewed also to have a primary affective disorder. In addition to these lower rates, many reports of high levels of depression among alcoholics can be found throughout the literature.

Shaw[5] found that depression, as determined on the Zung, the Beck Depression Inventory, and the Minnesota Multiphasic Personality Inventory (MMPI), was present in 98% of male alcoholics. Weingold et al[6] found that 70% of alcoholic patients evaluated with the Zung scale exhibited mild to severe depression.

Weissman et al[7] found that 59% of the alcoholics they interviewed were also depressed and that the symptom patterns of the depressed alcoholics were similar to those of the primary depressives. They did find, however, that primary depressives showed a significantly greater severity of all symptoms. Gibson and Becker[8] also found that there were major similarities between the affect described by alcoholics and that of primarily depressed patients.

The wide range of prevalence seen in these studies may also reflect differences in diagnostic criteria or instruments used. Keeler et al[9] interviewed alcoholics and gave them a battery of tests for depression. They found that, according to the method used, 8% (clinical interview), 28% (Hamilton Depression Rate Scale), 43% (MMPI), or 66% (Zung Self-Rating Depression Scale) of the patients were "depressed." Methodological problems in evaluating depression in alcoholics was recently reviewed by Freed.[10]

Implicated in the cause of depression have been neurotransmitters, personality factors, physical illness, psychosocial stress, familial and hereditary factors, and psychiatric disorders. Depression can also be caused by prolonged alcohol consumption. This direct depressive effect of alcohol has been examined by several authors. Tamerin and Mendelson[11] found that "prolonged drinking led to progressive depression, guilt and psychic pain." These conclusions were reached in a controlled setting in which chronic intoxication was found to have a depressive effect upon the subjects, with both rapid relief and little recall of symptoms when they became sober.

Mayfield and Montgomery[12] also described a "depressive syndrome of chronic intoxication" where they found a profound depression following moderately extended periods of intoxication to be consistent with a pharmacologic-metabolic process. This would be supported by the conclusions drawn by Keeler et al,[8] who felt that any work which looks at alcohol and affective illness should consider that "a significant factor may be that the sequelae of chronic alcoholism and/or a recent prolonged spell of excessive drinking and/or recent alcohol withdrawal can produce signs and symptoms similar to those of depression and invalidate self-administered tests."

This was also confirmed by Weingold *et al,*[6] who concluded that although the majority of alcoholic patients in his study were indeed depressed when initially evaluated, the depression in most of these patients remitted spontaneously over time without regard to the type of treatment they were given. Thus, when evaluating alcoholic patients for depression one must pay attention both the the acute and chronic consumption of alcohol, that is, how recently and for how long the patients have been drinking, as well as to the method used to evaluate the depression.

In addition to the direct depressive effects, chronic intoxication may lead to severe physical deterioration by the direct toxic effect and the malnutrition which frequently goes with the alcoholic life-style. The loss of family, friends, and employment which often accompanies alcoholism may precipitate depression, which becomes superimposed upon the direct depressive effects of alcohol itself. If these secondary medical and social consequences are absent, it may take longer for depression to develop in alcoholics; this phenomenon might then account for Hamm's report[2] of a low rate of depression in younger alcoholics.

Several authors attempt to classify people who suffer from both alcoholism and affective illness into two groups: one in which the alcoholism predated and possibly gave rise to the depression (ie, primary alcoholism with secondary depression) and another in which the depression appeared before the alcoholism. Unfortunately, the temporal relationship is rarely clear enough to determine which is primary—the alcoholism or affective illness. Frequently, the relationship becomes tainted with elements of both, making the distinct determination of primacy difficult, particularly while both conditions are active.

When an affective disorder of definite onset is evident with disturbed mood and a number of psychological and somatic symptoms, and there has been on preexisting psychiatric disturbance, then a diagnosis of primary affective disorder can be made. If a psychiatric disorder such as alcoholism has preceeded or accompanies the affective illness, it then is classified as secondary.

Weissman *et al*[7] looked at symptom patterns in primary and secondary depressions and concluded that, although the two groups had similar symptom patterns, they do differ in symptom severity, with the secondary depressives reporting less severe symptoms. The major problem they cite in making this evaluation is the careful determination of chronology which is obviously required for the diagnosis of depression secondary to the diagnosis of alcoholism.

Alcoholics as a group appear to be more depressed than one would expect by mere coincidence. The basis for this depression, however, may vary from one individual to another. The depression may be primary and precede excessive alcohol consumption, which is used in an attempt to relieve the depression. If the depression is a psychopharmacological function of chronic intoxication it may lift when the individual becomes sober. Superimposed upon an individual's primary alcoholism may be losses from the interpersonal, medical, occupational, and financial spheres which further contribute to an alcoholic's depression.

Any attempt to evaluate depression in alcoholics should be concerned with each of these issues, for to ignore them is to propagate the methodological problems which have beset many studies in this area.

In summary:

1. Both alcoholism and affective disorders must be clearly defined and diagnosis for each of them based upon accepted criteria. Alcohol use should be differentiated from alcoholism, and sadness from depression.
2. Subjective reports of feeling bad cannot be unequivocally accepted as depression in the alcoholic, since most alcoholics are uncomfortable, particularly during the acute withdrawal phase.
3. Standard tests for depression show a wide range of results in alcoholics and may very well be measuring the effects of alcoholism (particularly withdrawal phenomena) and not necessarily depression.
4. The point in the alcoholic process, for instance, early, late, acute withdrawal, protracted abstinence, should be specified, for as we mentioned above, symptoms of alcoholism, such as sleep disturbance, may mimic those of depression.
5. The temporal relationship between the alcoholism and depression should be delineated as clearly as possible. Did the alcoholism precede the drinking or vice versa? Is there any relationship between episodic mania or depression and drinking binges?
6. Has there been any effect of antidepressant medication on drinking behavior?

References

1. Schuckit MA: Alcoholism and affective disorder: Diagnostic confusion, in Goodwin DW, Erickson CK (eds): *Alcoholism and Affective disorders*. New York, Spectrum Publications, 1979.
2. Hamm JE, Major LF, and Brown GL: The quantitative measurement of depression and anxiety in male alcoholics. *Am J Psychiatry* 136:580–582, 1979.
3. Weissman MM, and Meyers JK: Clinical depression in alcoholism. *Am J Psychiatry* 137:372–373, 1980.
4. Winokur G, Rimmer J, Reich I: Alcoholism IV: Is there more than one type of alcoholism? *Br J Psychiatry* 118:525–531, 1971.
5. Shaw JA, Donley P, Morgan DW, *et al*: Treatment of depression in alcoholics. *Am J Psychiatry* 132:641–644, 1975.

6. Weingold HP, Lachin JM, Bell AH, Coxe RC: Depression as a symptom of alcoholism: Search for a phenomenon. *J Abnorm Psychol* 3:195–197, 1968.
7. Weissman MM, Pottenger M, Kleber H, *et al*: Symptom patterns in primary and secondary depression. *Arch Gen Psychiatry* 34:854–862, 1977.
8. Gibson S, Becker J: Alcoholism and depression: The factor structure of alcoholics' responses to depressive inventories, *Q J Stud Alcohol* 34:400–408, 1973.
9. Keeler MH, Taylor CI, Miller WC: Are all recently detoxified alcoholics depressed? *Am J Psychiatry* 136:586–588, 1979.
10. Freed EX: Alcoholism and manic-depressive disorders. *Q J Stud Alcohol* 31:62–69, 1970.
11. Tamerin JS Mendelson JH: The psychodynamics of chronic inebriation: Observations of alcoholics during the process of drinking in an experimental group setting. *Am J Psychiatry* 125:886–899, 1969.
12. Mayfield DG, Montgomery D: Alcoholism, alcohol intoxication and suicide attempts. *Arch Gen Psychiatry* 27(3):349–353, 1972.

Alcoholism and Affective Disorders

The Basic Questions

DONALD W. GOODWIN, MD

> Melancholy is at the bottom of everything, just as at the end of all rivers is the sea. . . . Can it be otherwise in a world where nothing lasts, where all we have loved or shall love must die? Is death, then, the secret of life? The gloom of an eternal mourning enwraps every serious and thoughtful soul, as night enwraps the universe.
>
> —Henri-Frederic Amiel (1893).

> And Malt does more than Milton can
> To Justify God's ways to man.
>
> —A. E. Housman (1894).

God's ways have struck many people, including Amiel, as pretty depressing. What is a good cure for depression? Alcohol, Housman says, and through the ages people have agreed with him.

But is it so? Does alcohol relieve depression? Will it relieve *serious* depression, the kind seen by psychiatrists?

More importantly, does depression *cause* alcoholism? Are alcoholics really just depressed people who drink to feel better (and better, and better) until drinking becomes uncontrolled, a habit with its own propulsion, progressing independently of the depressed feelings that caused it?

Some believe it. What is the evidence? Here are the questions that need to be asked:

DONALD W. GOODWIN • Chairman, Department of Psychiatry, University of Kansas Medical Center, Kansas City, Kansas 66103.

How Many Alcoholics Have an Affective Disorder?*

Many alcoholics become depressed. Their depressions resemble the depressions seen in nonalcoholic ("primary") affective disorders.[1-3] The alcoholics become irritable and can't sleep. They feel blue and sad. They experience feelings of guilt and remorse. They lose interest in life and contemplate suicide. Depressed alcoholics, on the other hand, rarely show psychomotor retardation.[1]

Suicide, indeed, is a common outcome of alcoholism.[4] Except for manic-depressives, alcoholics commit suicide more often than any other group. One reason to believe that alcoholism and manic-depressive disease are related is that in Western countries most people who commit suicide have one or the other illness.

Many psychoanalysts believe that alcoholism and manic-depressive disease have the same origin: victims of both illnesses are orally fixated and, instead of feeling angry toward others, feel angry toward themselves.[5] Aggression directed toward one's self is experienced as a feeling of depression. The ultimate act of self-aggression is suicide. Alcoholism has been called "slow suicide."[6]

This is an interesting theory, but difficult to prove scientifically. Although the depression experienced by alcoholics resembles manic-depressive depression, there is a difference: when the alcoholic stops drinking, the depression often goes away.[1] Alcohol is a toxin and in large amounts produces depression, anxiety, irritability. The alcoholic feels guilty and for good reason: he *has* botched up his life and knows it.

From most studies it appears that *in men* alcoholism causes depression more often than depression causes alcoholism.[7,8] The cure for alcohol-induced depression is not antidepressant medication nor electroconvulsive therapy but abstinence.[9] (The toxic effects, incidentally, may last for weeks or months after a person stops drinking. Sleep, in particular, may take several months to become normal again.)

Most studies indicate that women alcoholics are different from men alcoholics: they more often have depressions *preceding* the onset of heavy drinking. In women more than in men a case can be made that alcoholism is sometimes a manifestation of a depression.[10] Women, as a group, start drinking heavily at an older age than do men, and in people who are drinking heavily it is often difficult to tell whether the depression or alcoholism came

---

*As used in this paper, "affective disorder" refers to *all* of the affective disorders described in DSM–III (major depressive episodes, manic episodes, bipolar disorder, cyclothymic disorder, dysthymic disorder, atypical bipolar disorder, and atypical depression). The older term "manic-depressive disorder" is used in this paper as a synonym for all of these entities; their cross-sectioned clinical pictures overlap, and none of the studies cited used DSM–III criteria.

first. Since women become alcoholic at an older age than men, there is more time for depression to occur before heavy drinking. Depression may promote heavy drinking in men as often as it appears to in women, but, because men start drinking heavily at an earlier age, it is impossible to determine whether the depressions are a cause or consequence of the drinking.

The above observations were based on samples of *patients*. It is well known how skewed patient samples can be. Depression, for example, may be seen more often in treated alcoholics than in untreated alcoholics simply because depression is often the proximate cause for seeking treatment.

There has been only one study in the United States of a sample of individuals selected randomly from the general population for the specific purpose of diagnosing psychiatric disorders, including alcoholism, by *contemporary* research criteria. The study was conducted by Weissman and associates in New Haven, Connecticut.[11,12] A probability sample of 1,095 households was selected, and one adult (18 years of age or older) was chosen at random from each household for inclusion in the sample. Of this group, 86% were interviewed in person, with two subsequent follow-up interviews of somewhat smaller numbers over a nine-year period.

Weissman *et al* found that 2.6% of the interviewed individuals were currently alcoholic. More men than women were alcoholic by about a three-to-one ratio. More nonwhites, Protestants, middle-aged, divorced people, and members of the lower social class were alcoholic. (Interestingly, no alcoholics were found among Jews, supporting the widespread impression that alcoholism among Jews is uncommon and perhaps has not even increased with trends toward greater assimilation. The higher rates in Protestants reflected the higher rates in nonwhites, most of whom were Protestant.)

The "lifetime" prevalence rates for alcoholism in the sample were 10.1% for men and 4.1% for women. "Lifetime" referred to the period preceeding the final interview in the three-phase longitudinal study. The presumed age of risk for alcoholism (perhaps 15 to 45 in men and older in women) had not been transversed by some members of the sample (M. Weissman, personal communication, 1981). However, both the point prevalence and lifetime prevalence rates reported by Weissman *et al* are roughly comparable to findings of other population surveys. Mulford found that 10% of 1,509 persons he sampled had been in trouble because of heavy drinking at some time during their lifetime.[13] In a household survey in Sweden, Hagnell and Tunving found a lifetime rate of 10.3% for men.[14] Helgason, using the World Health Organization's definition of alcoholism and the Stromgren method to adjust for the age of risk and the age of the sample, found a lifetime expectancy of about 9% in Iceland.[15] From these studies it appears that about 10% of men can be considered alcoholic at some point in their lifetime.

The study by Weissman *et al* used a structured interview (SADS).[16] The Reasearch Diagnostic Criteria (RDC), which are similar to diagnostic criteria used in clinical settings, were applied to the data obtained from this interview.[17] Each subject was evaluated for a broad range of psychiatric disorders. Weissman *et al* found that, among those ever diagnosed as alcoholic, 70% had been diagnosed at some point in their lives as having at least one other psychiatric disorder.[16] These rates did not differ by sex (an exception to the often reported overrepresentation of depression in alcoholic women). The most frequent of the other diagnoses were major depression (44%), depressive personality (17%), minor depression (15%), and drug misuse (12%). The broad range of other diagnoses included "generalized anxiety" (9%), bipolar disorder (6%), and phobia (3%). These diagnoses were not mutually exclusive. About half of the alcoholics received a diagnosis consistent with affective disorder, compared to about a quarter of non-alcoholics in the sample (M. Weissman, personal communication, 1981). Of the 44% of the alcoholics diagnosed as having a major depression, depression was reported to be the "primary" diagnosis in 60%. However, Weissman conceded that separating "primary" from "secondary" was exceedingly difficult and that the 60% figure could only be based on a rough estimate (personal communication).

To summarize these findings, it would appear that alcoholism in the general population (or at least in New Haven in the 1960s and 1970s) is often associated with depression, with continued uncertainty about whether depression preceeds the alcoholism and may even act as an etiological factor in the alcoholism, or occurs after the onset of heavy drinking with all the confusion this causes in separating cause from effect. The prevalence rates found by Weissman *et al* were gratifyingly similar to those reported in other studies using a variety of interview schedules and diagnostic criteria (or, in some cases, no diagnostic criteria).

How Many Manic-Depressives Are Alcoholic?

This sounds like the same question as the one above, but isn't. If you study a group of manic-depressive patients, how many are alcoholic? Such studies have been conducted, with conflicting results. In one study, one third of manic-depressives were alcoholic.[18] In another study, 8% were alcoholic.[19] Eight percent is not much higher than the overall prevalence of affective disorder (as broadly defined in this paper). A third is much higher. Which is correct? Nobody knows.

Do Manic-Depressives Drink More When They Are Manic or When They Are Depressed?

If one leaves aside alcoholic manic-depressives, some drink more and some drink less. Probably more manic-depressives cut down on their drinking when depressed than increase their drinking.[7,20,21]

One investigator gave alcohol to hospitalized manic-depressives.[22] A small amount of alcohol improved their mood. A large amount made them more depressed. The same is true of alcoholics. Bring alcoholics into an experimental ward, give them alcohol for a long period, and, instead of feeling happy, they feel miserable.[3] Alcohol, it turns out, is a rather weak euphoriant compared, for example, to stimulants such as cocaine and the amphetamines. The hedonistic explanation for alcoholism, contrary to popular opinion, has little support in science.

After giving alcohol to many psychiatric patients, including manic-depressives and alcoholics, Mayfield[22] reached the following conclusions:

> If you feel bad, drinking will make you feel a lot better. If you drink a lot, it will make you feel bad. Feeling bad from drinking a lot does not seem to make people choose to stop. Feeling a lot better from drinking does not seem to encourage people to continue drinking.

Do Manic-Depressives Drink More When They Are Manic?

Definitely. Many manics who ordinarily drink little or nothing start drinking heavily when manic.[20,23,24] The explanation is not clear, but it appears that alcohol has almost a specific ameliorative effect on the manic mood. Manics often feel *too* high, uncomfortably high, and alcohol seems to reduce the unpleasant effects of the mania while amplifying the pleasant ones. In two controlled studies,[25,26] lithium, an effective drug for mania,[27] was given to alcoholics and appeared to reduce the frequency of relapse, particularly if the alcoholics were depressed. More studies are required before it can be known definitely whether lithium is helpful for alcoholism.

A recent study of 32 college freshmen males later hospitalized for alcoholism provides some support for the hypothesis that affective disorders, particularly mania, are related to alcoholism.[28] The Minnesota Inventory (MMPI) scores of the prealcoholics were compared with scores of 148 male classmates. The prealcoholics were significantly higher on Scales F,4 (psychopathic deviate), and 9 (hypomania).

Nevertheless, the mania-alcoholism association perhaps is still best supported by clinical observations reported for a century or more. Isaac Ray, in his 1838 classic textbook on psychiatry, *A Treatise on the Medical Jurisprudence of Insanity*, said that alcoholism strongly reminded him of mania and expressed the conviction that the two conditions had a common etiology:[29]

> "It is now well understood that this vice (alcoholism) sometimes assumes a *periodical* character, persons indulging in the greatest excesses periodically, who are perfectly sober during the intervals, which may be from a space of a month to that of a year. From a state of complete sobriety, they suddenly lapse into the most unbounded indulgence in stimulating drinks, and nothing by absolute confinement can restrain them.

Alcoholics, he also observed, "seem quite aware of the uncontrollable nature of their passion."

Esquirol, the famous eighteenth-century French psychiatrist, often called the father of psychiatry, also noted a similarity between mania and alcoholism. Alcoholics, he wrote, were "true monomaniacs" with "all the characteristic features of partial madness."[29(p423)]

What these astute physicians observed so long ago is still being talked and written about today—with almost as little systematic data to support the connection as existed 200 years ago.

What Is the Possibility That an Alcoholic May Have an Independent Concomitant Affective Disorder, or Vice Versa?

About 4% of the population has "major" unipolar depressions.[30] If perhaps 5% of men are alcoholic, then the expected concomitance of alcoholism and unipolar affective disorder would be about 0.2%. For bipolar illness, which is estimated to effect 1% to 2% of the population,[31] the rate of concordance would be about 0.04%.

Do Alcoholism and Manic-Depressive Disease Run in the Same Families?

If they *did* run in the same families, this would suggest a common genetic predisposition. There is evidence that both alcoholism and manic-depressive disease are influenced by genetic factors, but are they the *same* genetic factors?

The evidence is mixed. Some studies demonstrate an increase of depression in the families of alcoholics and of alcoholism in the families of manic-depressives.[32,33] Other studies fail to show this.[34] Those that show an overlap have resulted in a concept called "depressive spectrum disorder."[35] In this still hypothetical condition, alcoholism occurs on the male side of families and depression on the female side. There is also some evidence, based on adoption studies,[36] that daughters of alcoholics suffer depressions when they are raised by their alcoholic parents by not when they are separated from their alcoholic parents and raised by nonalcoholic adoptive parents. This suggests that the depression seen in female relatives of alcoholics may be influenced less by heredity than by the environmental circumstance of being raised by an alcoholic parent.

A recent study by Taylor and Abrams[37] confirms an original observation that manic-depressives who become ill at a young age are more likely to have first-degree relatives with *both* affective disorder and alcoholism than are manic-depressives who become ill for the first time after age 30. Information for the study was obtained from a sample of 134 bipolar probands interviewed with a semistructured form permitting application of diagnostic criteria. The findings no doubt will encourage future investigators of a possible relationship between affective disorder and alcoholism to divide their subjects into early- and late-onset groups.

Does Antidepressant Medication Relieve Alcoholism?

If it did, this would somewhat support the idea that alcoholism was caused by depression. The best carried-out studies, however, do *not* indicate that antidepressant medication is useful for alcoholism. Of nine *uncontrolled* studies of the use of antidepressants for alcoholism, seven showed benefit; of seven *controlled* studies, none showed benefit.[38,39]

Summary

The literature on alcoholism and affective disorders has a long and confusing history. Alcohol may make depressed people feel a little better, but not for long. It may, indeed, make them *more* depressed. The evidence that depression causes alcoholism is weak. Women, more often than men, become alcoholic following or during a depression, but the causal connection is still not established. Even if depression does not cause alcoholism, alcoholism certainly is depressing, and most drinking alcoholics are depressed a good deal of the time.

References

1. Gibson S, Becker J: Alcoholism and depression. *Q J Stud Alcohol* 34:400–408, 1973.
2. Nathan PE, Lisman SA: Behavioral and motivational patterns of chronic alcoholics, in Tarter RE, Sugarman AA, eds: *Alcoholism: Interdisciplinary Approaches to an Enduring Problem.* Reading, Mass., Addison-Wesley, 1976, pp 479–522.
3. Tamerin JS, Weiner S, Mendelson JH: Alcoholics' expectancies and recall of experiences during intoxication. *Am J Psychiatry* 126:1697–1704, 1970.
4. Goodwin DW: Alcohol in suicide and homicide. *Q J Stud Alcohol* 34:144–150, 1973.
5. Ullman AD: Alcoholism and depression. *Q J Stud Alcohol* 13:602–608, 1952.
6. Rado S: *Psychoanalysis of Behavior.* New York, Grune & Stratton, 1956.
7. Campanella G, Fossi G: Alcoholism and depression. *Rass Stud Psichiatr* 52:617–632, 1963.
8. Pauleikhoff B: Ueber die seltenheit von Alkoholabusus bei syklothym Depressiven. *Nervenarzt* 24:445–448, 1953.
9. Ends E, Page C: Group psychotherapy and concomitant psychological change. *Psychol Monogr* 73:1–31, 1959.

10. Schuckit MA, Winokur G: A short term follow up of women alcoholics. *Dis Nerv Syst* 33:672–678, 1972.

11. Weissman MM, Pottenger M, Klever H, *et al*: Symptom patterns in primary and secondary depression. *Arch Gen Psychiatry* 34:854–862, 1977.

12. Weissman MM, Meyers JK, Harding PS: The prevalence rates and psychiatric heterogeneity of alcoholism in a United States Urban community. *J Stud Alcohol* 41:672–681, 1980.

13. Mulford HA: Drinking and deviant drinking, U.S.A., 1963. *J Stud Alcohol* 25:634–650, 1964.

14. Hagnell O, Tunving K: Prevalence and nature of alcoholism in a total population. *Soc Psychiatry* 7: 190–201, 1972.

15. Helgason T: *Epidemiology of Mental Disorders in Iceland*. Copenhagen, Munksgaard, 1964.

16. Weissman MM, Myers JK, Harding PS Psychiatric disorders in a U.S. urban community, 1975–76. *Am J Psychiatry* 135:459–462, 1978.

17. Spitzer RL, Endicott J, Robins E: Research diagnostic criteria rationale and reliability. *Arch Gen Psychiatry* 35:773–782, 1978.

18. Parker J, Spielberger CD, Wallace DK, *et al*: Factors in manic-depressive reactions. *Dis Nerv Syst* 20:506–511, 1959.

19. *Sixty-fourth Annual Report*, Department of Mental Hygiene., State of New York, 1952.

20. Mayfield DG: Psychopharmacology of alcohol. II. Affective tolerance in alcohol intoxication. *J Nerv Ment Dis* 146:322–327, 1968.

21. Cassidy WL, Flannagan NG, Spellman M, Cohen ME: Clinical observations in manic-depressive disease. A quantitative study of one hundred manic-depressive patients and fifty medically sick controls. *JAMA* 164:1535–1546, 1957.

22. Mayfield DG, Coleman CC: Alcohol use and affective disorder. *Dis Nerv Syst* 29:467–474, 1968.

23. Pitts FN, Winokur G: Affective disorder, VII: Alcoholism and affective disorder. *J Psychiat Res* 4:37–50, 1966.

24. Reich LH, Davies RK, Himmelhoch JM: Excessive alcohol use in manic-depressive illness. *Am J Psychiatry* 131:83–86, 1974.

25. Merry J, Reynolds CM, Bailey J, Coppen A: Prophylactic treatment of alcoholism by lithium carbonate: A controlled study. *Lancet* 2:481–482, 1976.

26. Kline NS, Wren JC, Cooper TB, Varga E, Canal O: Evaluation of lithium therapy in chronic and periodic alcoholism. *Amer J Med Sci* 268:15–22, 1974.

27. Davis JM: Overview: Maintenance therapy in psychiatry: II. Affective disorders. *Am J Psychiatry* 133:1–14, 1976.

28. Loper RG, Kammeier ML: *J Abnorm Psychol* 82 (1), 159–162, 1973.

29. Ray I: *Medical Jurisprudence of Insanity*. Charles C. Little and James Brown, Boston, 1838.

30. Winokur G: Genetic findings and methodological considerations in manic-depressive disease. *Br J Psychiatry* 117:267–274, 1970.

31. Freed EX: Alcoholism and manic-depressive disorders. *Q J Stud Alcohol* 31:62–89, 1970.

32. Winokur G, Clayton PJ, Reich T: *Manic-depressive Illness*. St. Louis, Missouri, C.V. Mosby, 1969.

33. Winokur G, Reich T, Rimmer J, Pitts FN, Jr: Alcoholism. *Arch Gen Psychiatry* 23:101–111, 1970.

34. Morrison JR: Bipolar affective disorder and alcoholism. *Am J Psychiatry* 131:1130–1134, 1974.

35. Winokur G, Rimmer J, Reich T: Alcoholism. IV. Is there more than one type of alcoholism? *Br J Psychiatry* 118:525–531, 1971.

36. Goodwin DW, Schulsinger F, Knop J, Mednick S, Guze SB: Alcoholism and depression in adopted-out daughters of alcoholics. *Arch Gen Psychiatry* 34:751–755, 1977.

37. Taylor MA, Abrams R: Early- and Late-Onset Bipolar Illness. *Arch Gen Psychiatry* 38:58–61, 1981.
38. Ditman KS: Review and evaluation of current drug therapies in alcoholism. *Int J Psychiatry* 3:248–258, 1967.
39. Viamontes JA: Review of drug effectiveness in the treatment of alcoholism. *Am J Psychiatry* 128:120–121, 1972.

CHAPTER 8

Alcoholism and Suicide

JOEL SOLOMON, MD

The literature relating morbidity and mortality to the abuse of alcohol is rather extensive. This literature has consistently revealed a higher incidence of illness and death among the substance-abusing group than is found among comparable populations.[1-3] Additionally, these studies as well as a number of others have demonstrated suicide to be a cause of death which occurs at a far higher rate among alcoholics than is found among the general population.[4,5] These studies focus primarily on the overt suicide, that is, those persons who have consciously and intentionally taken or attempted to take their lives by one means or another.

There is also an increasing body of work which addresses yet another aspect of self-destructive behaviors common to alcoholics but is more covert in nature. This would include the chronic ingestion of a toxic substance, alcohol, fatal accidents, overdoses, homicides, severe medical problems, and other forms of "chronic suicide" as described by Menninger.[6] Although these may not be as obvious, they are nevertheless equally destructive. Although the relationship between these deaths and overt suicide may not be readily apparent, there do appear to be elements which are common to both.

Research which attempts to correlate alcoholism and suicide are of two general types; first, there are the studies which retrospectively review the alcohol consumption patterns of attempted and successful suicides and secondly, the studies which attempt to determine the incidence of suicide among alcoholics.

Estimates of alcoholism among the general adult population run between 4% and 7%.[7] In studying the alcohol consumption patterns among attempted and successful suicides, numerous authors have found this rate to run consistently higher than that found in the general population.

JOEL SOLOMON • Clinical Associate Professor, Director, Division of Alcoholism and Drug Dependence, Department of Psychiatry, State University of New York, Downstate Medical Center, Brooklyn, New York 11203.

East[8] reviewed 1,000 consecutive cases of attempted suicide and found alcoholism to be present in 39%. Among these cases he also found "33 cases of alcoholic insanity, 16 with weak-mindedness, 141 unconscious impulse, 171 impulsive with memory-retained, 31 post-alcohol depression, and one an alcoholic accident." These diagnostic categories, although no longer in use, do indeed have their present-day equivalents, as will be seen. Batchelor[9] observed 200 consecutive cases of attempted suicide admitted to a general hospital and found that 21.5% of them gave a history of excessive drinking. Of interest is that 46.5% of this group were not under the influence of alcohol at the time of their attempt. He also found a history of alcoholism in first-degree relatives in 28.5% of his cases. There are, in addition, several other studies which consistently support the finding of an increased incidence of alcoholism among both attempted as well as successful suicides. These studies found alcoholism present in the general area of 30%.[10-17]

From the other perspective, authors have also studied the rates of suicide among groups of alcoholics. Kessel and Grossman[4] reported that in two series of 131 and 87 chronic alcoholics, 8% and 7% respectively of the men in these series committed suicide. This, they conclude, is 75 to 85 times greater than the expected figures for males of comparable age groups. There was no report, however, of the rate of attempted suicide by this population. Similarly, Nørvig and Nielsen[18] report a 7% rate of completed suicide on follow-up of 221 male alcoholics who had been treated for their alcoholism and on whom follow-up could be established. Other authors have also reported similar high rates of suicide among populations of alcoholics.[10, 19-21] It is also of interest to note the significantly high number of repeated suicide attempts among alcoholics.

Several authors have described the association between suicidal ideation, attempted suicide, and alcoholism. Palola et al[12] in a retrospective review examined, by means of a questionnaire, the incidence of suicidal thoughts and attempts in a sample of active skid row alcoholics and in a sample of members of Alcoholics Anonymous (AA) who were no longer drinking. They found that 17.1% of the combined sample had attempted suicide, while an additional 29.3% had seriously contemplated such attempts. They report, however, a higher incidence of suicidal ideation among the AA members as compared to active skid row alcoholics. They attribute this difference to the supportive nature of the skid row subculture which, though perceived as deviant by society, nonetheless provides a setting of nonjudgmental acceptance to the active drinker. It was felt that the members of AA, on the other hand, because of their predominantly middle-class origins, could not avail themselves of the skid row subculture when they were actively drinking and consequently closed off this type of social support.

The authors of this report also addressed themselves to the issue of whether suicidal preoccupation preceded alcoholism, or vice versa. They found the predominating pattern in this combined sample of alcholics to be one in which suicidal preoccupations, either in the form of thoughts or attempts, preceded the loss of control over drinking behavior, a cardinal sign of alcoholism. They found evidence suggesting that suicide attempts which occurred in this sample had frequently been preceded by bouts of drinking which had themselves been precipitated by spontaneously occurring suicidal thoughts.

Attempts have been made to delineate variables that might distinguish those alcoholics who have attempted suicide and those without a history of such attempts. Koller and Castanos[22] found:

> Suicidal patients tend to be male, to have a higher incidence or parental loss, and to have been reared by relatives rather than the remaining parent after such a loss. Further, they come from smaller families, display more 'neuroticism' (on the Eysenck Personality Inventory) and begin addictive drinking earlier.

Rushing[23,24] and James[25] also described the association between alcoholism and suicide to be stronger in males.

Attkisson,[26] in his study of skid row alcoholics, found a higher incidence of suicide among younger alcoholics, a finding in agreement with Sundby's report[3] that suicide appears to be more frequent among early-stage alcoholics than among those in the later stages of the disease. Goodwin[27] hypothesizes that late-stage alcoholism may actually be protective against suicide because (a) the alcoholic has less to lose in the way of wealth, status, and interpersonal relationships and (b) brain damage associated with alcoholism makes suicide less probable. Rushing[23,24] also reports the alcohol–suicide association to be stronger in whites than in blacks.

Although one might expect depression to be present in all alcoholics who committed suicide, this is not necessarily the case. Murphy *et al*[28] in a recent study of predictors of suicide in alcoholics found evidence of a definite affective disorder in 56% and probable affective disorder in 8% of his patients. Twenty-two percent were found to have uncomplicated alcoholism. Also noticeably absent in this study of suicides were patients diagnosed as antisocial personalities.

Among their most important findings was a significantly high frequency of loss of a close personal relationship in the six weeks immediately preceding the suicide. This was not the case with the nonalcoholic controls who committed suicide.

Thus, there appears to be little question about the strong association between suicide and the abuse of alcohol. This association is most clear for the overt suicide and becomes somewhat speculative in the area of covert suicide, but the association still remains too strong not to consider many of the accidental overdoses, other types of accidents, medical illness and homicide, also as cases of suicide.

Alcoholism is presently considered to result from the complex interaction of physiological, psychological, and social factors. Each of these three factors may play a role in the genesis, development, perpetuation, and termination of an individual's alcoholism. One way in which this process may be terminated is by suicide. In order to understand the various roles these factors may play, three theoretical frameworks will be described in which to view the possible relationships between alcoholism and suicide.

Alcoholism as a Cause of Suicide

If suicide is viewed as the result of the chronic compulsive use of alcohol, contributions to this suicidal outcome may be from the medical, psychological, and social spheres of an individual's functioning.

The toxic effects of alcohol on every organ system of the body are well known and documented throughout the scientific literature. What is less evident, but appears to be equally as important, is the direct psychotoxic effect which alcohol may have on an individual, irrespective of the social context. Tamerin and Mendelson[29] found that "prolonged drinking was characterized by progressive depression, guilt, and psychic pain," which in themselves are known to be frequent antecedents of suicide. The importance of this study should be underscored, for in a controlled setting chronic intoxication was shown to have a direct depressive effect upon an individual with rapid relief of symptoms and little recall for them when experimental alcoholization was stopped.

Mayfield and Montgomery[30] have described a "depressive syndrome of chronic intoxication." They feel that this type of profound depression following fairly long periods of intoxication is "consistent with a pharmacologic-metabolic process." They also stress that suicide attempts made by alcoholics while in this type of depression are particularly serious.

This direct depressive effect of alcohol, which disappears with the cessation of drinking, obviously has important implications for treatment.

Chronic intoxication may additionally lead to severe physical deterioration by both the direct toxic effect of alcohol and the poor nutrition which frequently accompanies some alcoholics' lifestyles. Physical deterioration is also a well-known antecedent to depression, which then becomes superimposed upon the direct depressive effects of the alcohol.

In addition to these medical and psychological consequences of alcoholism, the social disruption which it often causes can have a profound effect upon the individual. Loss of family, friends, and employment are common results of chronic alcoholism. These losses frequently precipitate a concomitant depression which the alcoholic often attempts to combat through the increased use of alcohol. This pattern often develops into a downward spiral which continues to alienate family and friends and, when there appears to be little or no hope for recovery, may ultimately end in a suicide attempt. Rushing,[23,24] in particular, explored the possibility that alcoholism was among the deviant forms of behavior that frequently culminated in suicide. He also found that suicide as a consequence of alcoholism was more frequent when accompanied by unemployment and marital isolation. This model of interpersonal disruption as an antecedent to suicide, although not unique to it, was particularly pronounced in alcoholics.[28]

Thus, whether it be through the deterioration of interpersonal relationships, or the direct effects of alcohol on physical and emotional well-being, or most likely some combination of all of them, there is little doubt that alcoholism may indeed be an important cause of suicide.

Alcoholism as a Form of Suicide

Self-destruction in some individuals is manifest by the intentional attempt openly to take their lives. There are, however, some people in whom this drive may be active and strong, and yet for some reason, they are unable to commit this final act of self-destruction. The drive does not disappear but may emerge in some other form. This may be in a symptomatic way, such as frequent accidents, or an occupation which appears adaptive but nevertheless would be considered "high risk." Or the drive may be more directly expressed through the chronic ingestion of a toxic substance and a lifestyle which in great measure is determined by the abuse of this substance.

Menninger[6] described alcoholism as a form of "chronic suicide," and studies have been carried out which both support[12] and refute[13] this thesis. These two studies were based on the temporal relationship of suicidal thoughts to alcohol abuse. In spite of these contradictory findings, there can be little question that, at least in some alcoholics, both the chronic ingestion of alcohol as well as their general lifestyle is in some degree directed towards self-destruction, irrespective of conscious intent. Meerlo[31] has also written about this form of "hidden suicide." As a form of suicide, there appear to be two distinct methods by which alcohol may be used: by its direct toxic effect and by its effect upon the lifestyle in which the alcoholic becomes involved. In both cases, the chronic alcoholism becomes the form in which the suicide is carried out.

As we stated in the previous section, the toxic effects are probably most important among alcoholics. The direct toxic effect of alcohol on the human body is well known and includes most organ systems. In addition, the indirect effects of alcohol predispose the alcoholic to a wide range of illnesses. A review of these medical complications is well covered by Seixas et al[32] Palola et al[12] described alcoholism as an "ambivalent suicide" which may serve as a substitute or defense against total self-destruction, and Goodwin[27] found an association between drinking and homicide in 15 studies over the past 30 years.

In addition to the direct toxicity of the drug, there are other less apparent ways by which alcohol may become the suicidal method. The question of accidental overdose presents a particularly important aspect of drug abuse as the form of suicide, for superimposed upon chronic use is the acute self-destructive act. Proudfoot and Park,[33] for example, found that 64% of male admissions had consumed alcohol before taking some other poison in a suicide attempt. Whether the initial dose of alcohol disinhibited them enough to attempt suicide by poisoning is obviously speculative, but nevertheless worthy of attention.

This association between alcohol and violent death is probably nowhere more apparent then in deaths due to automobile accidents. Pearson[34] found elevated blood alcohol levels in 39.4% of 121 victims of fatal traffic accidents. Others have found this rate to be as high and higher. The issue is obviously speculative as to how "accidental" these accidents actually were but, again, as with other forms of violent death, the association occurs far too often to be merely coincidental. In studying 246 consecutive violent dealths, Spain et al[35] found that alcohol was a contributing or responsible factor in 27% of their cases.

The role of acute intoxication in the actual attempt appears to be that of a disinhibitor in that the social and personal restraints which prevent an individual from attempting suicide are often lifted during an episode of intoxication. During these intoxicated states, there often appears to be amnesia for the suicidal attempt.[15] Alcoholic "blackouts" which occur at some time in nearly two thirds of alcoholics[36] may play an important part in suicidal attempts, although when they are successful they obviously cannot be studied. However, Morrison and Pendery[37] felt that a "great many people may be at risk for suicidal behavior which they cannot remember," and Ryback[38] suggests that many suicides are attempted while under the influence of alcohol because the amnesia and dissociative states which represent a loss of higher (cortical) control would put the potential suicide in a particularly high-risk situation while intoxicated. In carrying this thinking one step further, Moore[11] felt that the alcohol itself was a major factor which "appeared to derange, inhibit, or render generally less efficient the technique and planning used in carrying out the suicidal attempts." He found that 5% of alcoholic suicidal patients actually died as a result of their attempts, as opposed to 11% of the total number of suicidal patients in his sample. It would seem, therefore, that, although alcohol might stimulate suicidal ideation and lift prohibitions, thereby accounting for the high rate of suicidal attempts, it nevertheless may also act as a deterrent to the successful completion of the suicidal act. Mayfield and Montgomery[30] also comment on this phenomenon, distin-guishing between suicide attempts made following an extended period of heavy drinking and those made after an episode of acute intoxication. The latter occur, according to the authors, "in a context of interpersonal interaction and are accompanied by anger, aggression, and hyperactivity." These attempts rarely result in serious injury. The series of events following an episode of acute intoxication has been termed by the authors an "abreactive syndrome." On the other hand, suicide attempts which occurred following extended periods of heavy drinking were characterized by their lethality.

Other reports, however, indicate that acute intoxication may be implicated in both attempted and completed suicide to a far larger degree than is generally appreciated. James et al[39] report on the blood alcohol levels of a series of 50 attempted suicides, many of which were very severe in nature. They note that 31 of the 50 had blood alcohol levels over 0.05 mg%. Fourteen of these had levels over 0.15 mg%, levels compatible with acute intoxication. In a study of successful suicides, James[25] reports that more than a third of the sample had elevated blood alcohol levels.

There is clearly much work which must be done in this somewhat speculative area, for, if this association between "chronic," "hidden," or "covert" suicide and overt suicide were to be made more apparent, there would obviously be many important implications, particularly in the area of prevention. It is impossible to estimate how many homicides, fatal car and other accidents, and deaths from potentially reversible or preventable conditions could be stopped if they were to be viewed in a theoretical framework in which they were acknowledged as suicidal equivalents. This is particularly pertinent concerning alcoholic populations, where both the direct toxic effects of the abused substance as well as the general lifestyle of the abuser contribute so strongly to so many of their deaths and may very well be the form in which many of them carry it out.

Alcoholism and Suicide as Manifestations of a Common Etiology

Depression and alcoholism are intimately linked. This has been noted by many authors (see Chapters 7A and 7B). This association strongly suggests the possibility that at least some are, in effect, self-medicators and that the impetus toward both alcohol abuse and suicidal behavior lies in the underlying painful tensions and emotions which they experience. Rado,[40] in a psychoanalytic study of this phenomenon, coined the term "pharmacothymia" to describe a disorder in which drugs are taken by certain people to find surcease from intolerable psychic pain. He stresses the magical qualities that alcohol comes to possess in bringing about a sense of heightened self-esteem and a brighter mood.

Much of the psychoanalytic literature describing the premorbid personalities of alcoholics describes a constellation of characteristics centering about intense conflict concerning powerful and unresolved oral dependency needs. These needs stem, according to the literature, from severe parental deprivation at very early stages of development, leaving the developing individual with a residue of inferiority, frustration, and rage, and as adults they experience great difficulties in establishing satisfying interpersonal and other social relationships. Their extreme sensitivity to rejection, combined with the insatiable neediness which characterizes their relationships with others, leads them to experience social situations as events which produce anxiety and depression. When significant relationships are destroyed, as they so frequently are, because of the intolerable nature of the substance-abusers' mode of behavior, these people experience intense frustration, rage, and significant depression as the injuries of childhood are reawakened and reexperienced.[41,42] Chafetz[43] notes that, as a result of this kind of development disturbance, the premorbid personality of the alcoholic is characterized by gross disturbances in interpersonal relationships, with poor adjustment in school, occupational instability, and a high rate of marital disintegration. He states, "Most striking in the total pattern of responses is the self-destructive component."

The proclivity of alcoholics to social disruption and their sensitivity to such disruption has also been noted by authors employing more rigorous research methodology. Murphy and Robins[44] compared the relative importance of social factors as precipitants of completed suicides in a group of nonalcoholic depressed subjects and a group of alcoholics. They did not, unfortunately, comment on the degree of depression among the alcoholics. Nonetheless, important differences were discerned between the two groups. A significantly lower percentage of the alcoholics were married at the time of suicide as compared to the nonalcoholic depressed group, while a significantly higher percentage of alcoholics were divorced. Half of the married alcoholics were separated at the time they committed suicide, again a significantly higher rate than that of the nonalcoholic group. Over half of the alcoholic sample, moreover, were living alone when they committed suicide, a markedly higher rate than that of the nonalcoholic group. The importance of these findings becomes even more striking in view of the authors' findings that 48% of the alcoholic subjects had experienced the loss of a major social relationship within one year of suicide as compared to 15% of the depressed nonalcoholics. Fully two thirds of these events among the alcoholics, moreover, had taken place in the six weeks preceding the suicidal act. These findings of Murphy's group were confirmed and updated in a subsequent report.[28] Palola et al[12] also note the sensitivity of alcoholics to social loss, the most common losses reported being marital separation and divorce. They also mention, however, the importance of loss of job as being one of the precipitating causes of suicide, especially job loss as a result of drunkenness.

Further confirmation of the sensitivity of the alcoholic to his environment is provided by the work of Witkin et al,[45] who have applied the easily quantifiable function of field dependence to investigations of personality in alcoholics. According to Witkin, both field-dependent and field-independent cognitive styles are associated with separate clusters of personality characteristics, which are developed in childhood and are fairly stable over time. Field-dependent individuals depend on their surrounding environment for structure and support. They have difficulty in dealing analytically with the world around them and characteristically react to it in a passive manner. They tend to have, among other traits, a poor sense of separate identity, poor impulse control, and low self-esteem. Field-independence, on the other hand, is associated with the ability to separate oneself from one's environment and to deal with it in a more critical and analytic way. Field-independent people are characterized by activity and independence in relation to the world around them, better impulse control, higher self-esteem, and a more mature body image. Field dependence-independence can be easily measured by instruments such as the Rod and Frame Test, which has established reliability and validity.[46]

Studies of field dependency in alcoholics by Witkin *et al*[45] and Karp *et al*[47] have repeatedly demonstrated that alcoholics are in general significantly more field-dependent than normal controls. Karp *et al*[48] report that the mean performance of alcoholic groups tends to be one to two standard deviations above that of control groups in the direction of field-dependence. They also note that, in addition to the extreme field-dependence of alcoholics as a group, female alcoholics are significantly more field-dependent than males.[49]

The research described above supports that concept that many alcohlics suffer from a distortion of personality development preexisting alcohol abuse. This kind of personality development leaves them particularly dependent on environmental support and sensitive to rejection. When this support is lacking, is present in insufficient quantity, or is removed, the alcoholic may experience anxiety and depression, leading to severe personality disorganization for which an immediate and readily available solution is alcohol use. Unfortunately, this kind of solution frequently increases the alcoholic's alienation from supportive elements in his environment such as family or employment, thereby creating a vicious cycle that in turn leads to further alcohol abuse and in some individuals culminates in suicide.

It should be noted that the three frameworks described are by no means mutually exclusive. For example, in some individuals the preexisting personality structure may lend itself to the relief of anxiety and depression through the use of alcohol. Its increased use may then interfer with whatever relationships may have developed, deepening the depression and leading to a suicide attempt which may involve the use of alcohol as the method employed. Clearly, each case must be evaluated on its own merits and not be forced into one particular framework. This will be particularly apparent concerning treatment when it is essential to evaluate the individual and then develop a treatment plan based on that evaluation.

Alcoholics who are overtly suicidal present a particular treatment problem, for, in addition to the suicidal behavior, they may be depressed, often socially disrupted, and frequently physically dependent on alcohol and possibly other drugs. When one is attempting to develop an orderly and workable treatment plan, these factors must all be kept in mind, for, as we mentioned earlier, alcohol may play a variety of roles in the physical, psychological, and social events leading to suicide attempts.

Modes of Treatment

The initial step in treatment should be directed toward the elmination of alcohol and other drugs from this complex system of interactions. To this end, the first element to be considered is whether or not the patient is physically dependent. Those drugs with a potential for physical dependence include alcohol, narcotics, and the sedative-hypnotics such as barbiturates, other sleeping medications, and minor tranquilizers such as benzodiazepines. If the patient is physically dependent, as manifest by an abstinence syndrome upon discontinuation of drinking, then a detoxification regime should be instituted.

This aspect of treatment should take place in a hospital under careful medical and psychiatric supervision. Suicide may now become an even greater danger, for it is often during this period, when symptoms which have been masked by alcohol or other drugs, become more overt. In addition, withdrawal symptoms from depressant drugs such as alcohol and the sedative-hypnotics may constitute a medical emergency and require vigorous treatment. The importance of this initial phase of treatment cannot be overstated, for until the patient is free of alcohol or other drugs, treatment cannot proceed successfully; craving will continue to superimpose itself on treatment and thereby block its effectiveness. Additionally, the drug will continue to exert its physical and psychological toxicity upon the individual.

Once detoxification is completed and the patient is drug-free, the causes and effects of the patient's drug-taking behavior can be evaluated. This evaluation must take into account the pharmacological action of the drug, the psychological structure of the individual, and the social context in which the drug is taken. The importance of viewing alcoholism or drug abuse within this multidimensional framework is essential if one hopes to understand the pathogenesis of alcoholism as it applies to any individual patient. It is particularly inappropriate and counterproductive to categorize all alcoholics as a single personality type or psychiatric disorder and then attempt to treat that entity. The social context in which the alcohol abuse took place is one of the factors which only recently have begun to receive the attention they deserve. Kissin[50] gives a particularly rich presentation of how these patients variables may be evaluated and then translated into a treatment approach.

Following alcohol detoxification, treatment may then take a number of directions, depending on the results of the initial evaluation as well as the availability of treatment modalities. The first consideration at this point is the continued suicidal risk that the patient presents and whether or not he requires hospitalization. Once this is assessed, treatment may proceed in either an inpatient or outpatient setting. In either case, a chemotherapeutic approach may be taken and various psychotherapeutic modalities may be employed.

Disulfiram (Antabuse) is a form of therapy commonly used in many alcoholism treatment programs, and, although it can be an important form of treatment for alcoholism, it should be used with caution in depressed patients. Nørvig and Nielson[18] found that of the 15 suicides in their study 10 had received disulfiram at some point in their treatment. They conclude that "no longer able to escape by means of alcohol, for some of our patients the only way out became suicide."

In addition to the chemotherapies specifically directed to alcoholism, many programs will use other psychoactive agents where indicated for the treatment of underlying psychiatric disorders.[52] It should be recognized, however, that chemotherapeutic agents are only one aspect of treatment. The psychological and social factors underlying and contributing to the alcoholism or drug abuse must also be addressed.

Since social disruption plays such a significant role both as a cause and consequence of alcoholism, unique psychotherapeutic modalities employing peer group support have been developed for the psychological treatment of these disorders, such as Alcoholics Anonymous, in which the only requirement for membership is that the individual have a genuine desire to stop drinking. It offers the often guilt-ridden alcoholic the opportunity to ventilate his feelings in an accepting, nonjudgmental atmosphere, where he may feel a sense of support and belonging which has often been lost to him. It should strongly be considered a part of any treatment plan for the chronic alcoholic. Al-Anon is similar in concept to Alcoholics Anonymous but is for the close family members of the alcoholic.

Family therapy has recently become a major modality of treatment for the alcoholic and those around him. The familial disruption caused by alcohol and drugs can be devastating and often the last step before a suicide attempt. Previously cited studies report marital breakup as an important antecedent to suicide, and it is not uncommon for drug or alcohol abuse to play many roles within a family structure, some of which may even be adaptive.[53] However, when abuse goes beyond the bounds that are tolerable, severe disruption of family organization takes place, often with profound effects upon all family members.

There is some controversy as to the effectiveness of individual psycho-analytic psychotherapy in the treatment of alcoholism. This method of treatment has been considered inappropriate for these disorders, patients often being labeled impulsive, uncooperative, prone to "acting-out," narcissistic, and thereby unamenable to sustained therapy. To the contrary, several of the authors of this book have met with success in treating large numbers of these patients in individual psychotherapy. The difficulties encountered in treatment are often a function of the feelings of the therapist toward these patients or the labels which have been imposed upon them. It should not, therefore, be excluded *a priori* from one's treatment alternatives. (See chapters 14 and 15).

Conclusion

The problems of alcoholism and suicide are, in many cases, intimately linked. Alcoholism may be a cause of suicide, may be the form of suicide, or may share a common etiology with suicidal behavior. Treatment of the suicidal alcoholic must be vigorous, for to ignore either aspect can lead to continued social and psychological loss culminating in further suicidal behavior.

References

1. Pearl R: *Alcohol and Longevity*. New York, Kripf, 1926.
2. Schmidt W, deLint J: Causes of death in alcoholics. *Q J Stud Alcohol* 33:171–185, 1972.
3. Sundby P: *Alcoholism and Mortality*. Oslo: Universitetsforcaget, 1967.
4. Kessel N, Grossman G: Suicide in alcoholics. *B J Med* 2:1671–1672, 1961.
5. Hendin H: Attempted suicides: A psychiatric and statistical study. *Psychiatr Q* 24:39–46, 1950.
6. Menninger KA: *Man Against Himself*. New York, Harcourt, Brace, 1938.
7. Cahalan D, Cisin IH: Drinking behavior and drinking problems in the United States, in Kissin B, Begleiter H (eds): *The Biology of Alcoholism*, vol 4. New York, Plenum Press, 1976.
8. East WN: On attempted suicide, with an analysis of 1,000 consecutive cases. *J Ment Sci* 59:428–478, 1913.
9. Batchelor IRC: Alcoholism and attempted suicide. *J Ment Sci* 100:451–461, 1954.
10. Dahlgren KG: On death-rates and causes of death in alcohol addicts. *Acta Psychiatr Neurol* 26:297, 1951.
11. Moore M: Alcoholism and attempted suicide. *N Engl J Med* 221:691–693, 1939.
12. Palola EG, Dorpat TL, Larson WR: Alcoholism and suicidal behavior, in Pittman DJ, Snyder CR (eds): *Society, Culture and Drinking Patterns*. New York, John Wiley & Sons, 1962.
13. Ross M: Suicide among physicians. *Dis Nerv Syst* 34:145–150, 1973.
14. Stenback A, Achté KA, Rimón RH: Physical disease, hypochondria, and alcohol addiction in suicides committed by mental hospital patients. *Br J Psychiatry* 111:933–937, 1965.
15. Sullivan WC: The relation of alcoholism to suicide in England with special reference to recent statistics. *J Ment Sci* 46:260–281, 1900.

16. Sullivan WC, Scholar S: Alcoholism and suicidal impulses. *J Ment Sci* 44:259–269, 1898.
17. Yessler PG, Gibbs JJ, Becher HA: On the communication of suicidal ideas. II: Some medical considerations. *Arch Gen Psychiatry* 5:12–29, 1961.
18. Nørvig J, Nielsen B: A follow-up study of 221 alcohol addicts in Denmark. *Q J Stud Alcohol* 17:633–642, 1956.
19. Ciompi L, Eisert M: Mortalite et causes de décès chez les alcooliques. *Soc Psychiatry* 4:159–168, 1969.
20. Lemere F: What happens to alcoholics? *Am J Psychiatry* 109:674–676, 1953.
21. Ritson EB: Suicide among alcoholics. *Br J Med Psychol* 41:235–242, 1968.
22. Koller KM, Castanos JN: Attempted suicide and alcoholism. *Med J Aust* 13:835–837, 1968.
23. Rushing WA: Suicide as possible consequence of alcoholism, in Rushing WA (ed): *Deviant Behavior and Social Process.* Chicago, Rand-McNally, 1969.
24. Rushing WA: Deviance, interpersonal relations and suicide. *Human Relations* 22:61–76, 1969.
25. James JP: Blood alcohol levels following successful suicide. *Q J Stud Alcohol* 27:23–29, 1966.
26. Attkisson CC: Suicide in San Francisco's skid-row. *Arch Gen Psychiatry* 23:149–157, 1970.
27. Goodwin DW: Alcohol in suicide and homicide. *Q J Stud Alcohol* 34:144–156, 1973.
28. Murphy GE, Armstrong JW, Hermele SL, *et al*: Suicide and alcoholism: Interpersonal loss confirmed as predictor. *Arch Gen Psychiatry* 36:65–69, 1979.
29. Tamerin JS, Mendelson JH: The psychodynamics of chronic inebriation: Observations of alcoholics during the process of drinking in an experimental group setting. *Am J Psychiatry* 125:886–899, 1969.
30. Mayfield DG, Montgomery D: Alcoholism, alcohol intoxication, and suicide attempts. Arch Gen Psychiatry 27:349–353, 1972.
31. Meerlo JAM: Hidden suicide, in Resnick HLP (ed): *Suicidal Behaviors.* Boston, Little, Brown & Co, 1968.
32. Seixas F, Williams K, Eggleston S (eds): *Medical Consequences of Alcoholism.* New York, Annuals of the New York Academy of Sciences, vol 252, 1975.
33. Proudfoot AT, Park J: Alcohol and self-poisoning, in Edwards G, Grand M (eds): *Alcoholism: New Knowledge and New Responses.* Baltimore, University Park Press, 1976.
34. Pearson J: Alcohol and fatal traffic accidents. *Med J Aust* 2:166–167, 1957.
35. Spain DM, Bradness VA, Eggston AA: Alcohol and violent death. *JAMA* 146:334–335.
36. Goodwin DW, Crane JB, Guze SB: Alcoholic "blackouts": A review and clinical study of 100 alcoholics. *Am J Psychiatry* 126:191–198, 1969.
37. Morrison JR, Pendery M: Suicidal behavior during alcoholic blackouts. *Q J Stud Alcohol* 35:657–659, 1974.
38. Ryback RS: Self-mutilation during alcohol amnesia. *Br J Psychiatry* 118:533–534, 1971.
39. James JP, Scott-Orr DN, Crenow DH: Blood alcohol levels following attempted suicide. *Q J Stud Alcohol* 24:14–22, 1963.
40. Rado S: Psychoanalysis of pharmacothymia. *Psychoanal Q* 2:1–23, 1933.
41. Knight RP: Psychodynamics of chronic alcoholism. *J Nerv Ment Dis* 86:538–548, 1937.
42. Shilder PF: Psychogenesis of alcoholism. *Q J Stud Alcohol* 2:12, 1941.
43. Chafetz ME: Addiction III: Alcoholism, in *Comprehensive Text Book of Psychiatry.* Baltimore, Williams & Wilkins Company, 1967.
44. Murphy GE, Robins E: Social factors in suicide. *JAMA,* 199:303–308 1967.
45. Witkin HA, Karp SA, Goodenough DR: Dependence in alcoholics. *Q J Stud Alcohol* 20:493–504, 1959.
46. Witkin HA, Dyk RR, Faterson HF, Goodenough DR: *A Psychological Differentiation.* New York John Wiley & Sons, 1962.
47. Karp SA, Witkin HA, Goodenough DR: Alcoholism and psychological differentiation: Effect of alcohol on field dependence. *J Abnorm Psychol* 70:262–265, 1965.

48. Karp SA, Kissin B, Hustmyer FE, Jr: Field dependence as a predictor of alcoholic therapy dropouts. *J Nerv Ment Dis* 150:77–83, 1970.
49. Karp SA, Poster DC, Goodman A: Differentiation in alcoholic women. *J Pers* 31:386–393, 1963.
50. Kissin B: Theory and practice in the treatment of alcoholism, in Kissin B, Begleiter H (eds): *The Biology of Alcoholism,* vol 5. New York, Plenum Press, 1977.
51. Kissin B: The use of psychoactive drugs in the long-term treatment of chronic alcoholics. *Ann Acad Sci* 252:385–395, 1975.
52. Davis D, Berenson D, Steinglass P, Davis S: The adaptive consequences of drinking. *Psychiatry* 37:209–215, 1974.

CHAPTER 9

Alcoholism and Sociopathy

JOEL SOLOMON, MD, and MEREDITH HANSON, MSW

The relationship between alcoholism or alcohol abuse and sociopathy is more difficult to unravel than most other psychiatric diagnoses. The degree of overlap between the two conditions is remarkable, for many persons diagnosed as sociopaths engage in excessive drinking and many alcohol abusers also exhibit antisocial behavior patterns. The associations between alcohol consumption and aggressive behavior, [1-5] criminal activity, [6-9] violent death, [10,11] and the family incidence of sociopathy [12-14] have been studied widely. Yet, conceptual and diagnostic confusion about the conditions persists.

Antisocial personality disorders (sociopathy) are described in the third edition of the *Diagnostic and Statistical Manual of Mental Disorders* as those in which "there are a history of continuous and chronic antisocial behaviors in which the rights of others are violated, persistence into adult life of a pattern of antisocial behavior that began before the age of 15, and failure to sustain good job performance over a period of several years." Childhood and adolescent signs include lying, stealing, fighting, truancy, resisting authority, unusually early or aggressive sexual behavior, and excessive drug use.

> In adulthood, these kinds of behavior continue, with the addition of inability to sustain consistent work performance or to function as a responsible parent and failure to accept social norms with respect to lawful behavior. [15]

Obviously, many of the behaviors and patterns characteristic of the antisocial personality disorders also apply to the alcohol abuser. This point is illustrated clearly by Robins' longitudinal study of children who were treated at a St. Louis child guidance clinic. In her study, in order to be categorized as a

JOEL SOLOMON • Clinical Associate Professor, Director, Division of Alcoholism and Drug Dependence, Department of Psychiatry, State University of New York, Downstate Medical Center, Brooklyn, New York 11203.   **MEREDITH HANSON** • Clinical Instructor, Division of Alcoholism, State University of New York, Downstate Medical Center, Brooklyn, New York 11203.

"sociopathic personality" the subjects had to possess 5 to 9 criteria for this diagnosis. Although a number of other diagnostic groups shared symptoms with the sociopath category, "the diagnostic group (excluding sociopathic personality) with the highest proportion of cases meeting the minimum criteria of five sociopathic symptoms was alcoholics, 70% of whom had five or more symptoms."[16]

This situation is further exacerbated by the fact that typically all alcoholics and all sociopaths do not share the same (or even a majority) of symptoms and characteristics, and standardized tests often inadequately discriminate facets of psychopathology. Thus, as Hoffmann, Jackson, and Skinner, in discussing the MMPI scores of alcoholic patients, observed,

> A diagnosis of "sociopathic personality disorder" might result from observations of marked interpersonal conflict or antisocial behavior, or from a lack of impulse control. An elevated Pd scale by itself would not provide an indication of which kind of behavior was more likely.[17]

In short, as with attempts to define the "alcoholic personality" (see, for example, Barnes's reviews[18,19]), the attempt to define a simple "sociopathic and alcoholic personality" appears to have defied possibility.

To resolve some of the confusion surrounding the two diagnostic categories, Schuckit[20] thought that is was particularly important to distinguish between the alcoholic, who due to alcohol abuse becomes involved in actions such as criminal activities, frequent fights, and impulsivity which could be labelled sociopathic, and the sociopath, who is diagnosed by a wide range of behavior among which is excessive alcohol use. According to Schuckit, "primary alcoholism" is a condition exhibited by persons who have no history of psychiatric disorder antedating their alcohol abuse; "sociopathy" is a chronic disorder, with onset prior to age 15 and manifesting at least four of eight symptoms (which are similar to those listed in the *DSM–III*). He stresses that "manifestation of some antisocial behavior is not synonomous with a diagnosis of antisocial personality." He reserves the diagnosis of "sociopathic alcoholism" for situations in which there is an onset of alcohol abuse "in a person with ongoing *antisocial personality or sociopathy*. . . . The sociopathic alcoholic usually has 7 to 10 years of prior severe antisocial behavior" before he develops alcoholism.

Podolsky,[21] in a descriptive paper on the sociopathic alcoholic, felt that, when sober, the alcoholic sociopath was blander, more passive, and more inadequate than the nonalcoholic sociopath. He also thought:

> Most alcoholic sociopaths are hedonists, compulsively seeking immediate impulse gratification of the total disregard of the reality principle and of long-term goals. They need a moderate degree of intoxication to inhibit anxiety and guilt, but after enough successful deceits such fears are allayed and dishonesty becomes habitual and callous.

Podolsky, while describing the alcoholic sociopath and how alcohol can catalyze the sociopathic behavior, did not look at the alcoholic who may engage in what appears to be sociopathic behavior but may not fulfill the criteria for a diagnosis of sociopathy.

In his review of sociopathy and alcohol abuse, Rada[22] asserted that "although it would appear that sociopaths and alcoholics do share a number of similar personality characteristics, as well as a tendency to abuse alcohol, they do not share the same basic personality structure." He proceeds to differentiate the two conditions by observing that "unlike the alcoholic who expresses remorse when he has fallen off the wagon, the sociopath often shows no concern" about his excessive drinking. "The point to be emphasized is that the sociopath's drinking. . . [is] not inconsistent with other aspects of his personality and behavior." Rada also makes a distinction between the "alcoholic sociopath," who is characterized by the onset of sociopathic behavioral symptoms before the abuse of alcohol, and the "sociopathic alcoholic," who does not have a history of sociopathy prior to the age of 15 but possesses personality features of the sociopath such as lack of insight and impulsivity.

The preceding three papers on sociopathy and alcoholism, while shedding some light on the points of convergence and divergence between the two conditions, highlight the presence of a conceptual morass. A major problem, of course, in looking at the relationship between these two conditions, is that alcoholics and sociopaths share so many behavioral characteristics (for example, one criterion by which to define an antisocial personality disorder is the abuse of alcohol at an early age). In fact, a primary means by which to differentiate the two conditions appears *not* to be the presence or absence of various symptoms, but rather the temporal sequencing of the symptoms. That is, if sociopathic patterns occurred first and prior to the age of 15, the person is considered primarily a sociopath or antisocial personality. If the person began to abuse alcohol first, he is considered primarily an alcoholic. Unfortunately, many of the studies attempting to clarify the relationship between the two conditions are retrospective in nature and do not adequately determine the time sequence involved in the emergence of the conditions.

In order better to understand the relationship between the two conditions, it is useful to examine some of the studies that draw correlations between alcoholism, antisocial behavior, criminal activity, violence, and aggression. The use of alcohol is related to crime in at least two ways: (1) The use of alcohol by certain age groups, drinking alcohol at different times in different places, and public intoxication have been defined as crimes at various times, by different localities. Thus, the use of alcohol in violation of public sanctions and normative standards might be considered antisocial behavior. (2) The use of alcohol is related to the commission of other crimes. Alcohol intake by either the offender or the victim, or both, has been demonstrated shortly before the occurrence of various crimes. In a 1960 survey of 2,325 male felons incarcerated by the California Department of Corrections, it was determined that 98% had used alcoholic beverages at some time in their life (compared to 70% for a United States sample of adult males). In addition, 29% claimed that they were intoxicated at the time they committed the crime for which they were currently imprisoned. This proportion varied from 50% for those imprisoned for automobile theft to 10% for those imprisoned for narcotics offenses.[23]

Similarly, Shupe[6] reported that over 72% of the persons in his study who were arrested following the commission of a felony were under the influence of alcohol at the time of their crime; a higher proportion of persons convicted of assault than of those convicted of other crimes, for instance, robbery, had blood alcohol concentrations greater than 0.10% at the time of their arrest. Studies of prison populations in different countries consistently report that a high percentage of prisoners are excessive drinkers. For example, Batholomew's 1968 study, in which Australian prisoners and their family members were interviewed, concluded that 43% of Austrialian recidivists were alcoholic[24]; Gibbens and Silberman's 1970 study of British prisoners found that, after excluding "drunks," of those persons serving sentences under 28 days, 40% were excessive drinkers.[25]

In a comprehensive study of 935 hospitalized British alcoholics, Edwards *et al*[9] found that 32% of the men and 17% of the women had a criminal record. For both sexes, "theft constituted by far the commonest first offense, fraud being second." Further, the alcoholic first offender was on average an offender of late onset. The authors felt that their data suggested that this relationship indicated that "the man who up to a certain age has led a law-abiding life will, under the influence of developing alcoholism . . . engage in behavior which would previously have been foreign to his nature." Finally, they note that a history of excessive drinking carries with it a prognosis for recidivism. Although they acknowledge that the findings on recidivism and on age of onset do not "prove causality," they assert:

> The conjoint facts that alcoholics are both offenders of late onset and then of high recidivism are congruent with what would be expected if alcoholism is indeed contributing to the genesis of crime.

In other words, the authors are suggesting that among their population the alcoholism antedated the criminality. Therefore, the antisocial patterns would be secondary to alcoholism, and the majority of their sample members would fall within Rada's sociopathic alcoholic classification.[22]

In 1962, Guze and his colleagues[26] attempted to determine whether or not psychiatric disorders occurred more frequently among criminals than among the general population. To answer this question, they carried out a systematic, structured psychiatric interview with 223 consecutive male criminals, including probationers, parolees, and "flat-timers" who were under the jurisdiction of the Missouri Board of Probation and Parole. Forty-eight percent of their subjects received no psychiatric diagnosis other than sociopathic personality. Fifty-two percent were found to have some other psychiatric disorder, as well—with alcoholism, the most frequent diagnosis, found in 43% of those cases. Alcoholism was shown to be associated with an increase in family history of alcoholism and suicide, an increased personal history of suicide attempts, and a variety of other sociopathic behaviors. Comparisons between alcoholics and nonalcoholics indicated that there were no differences in the prevalence rates of delinquency, antisocial behavior, and criminal activity before the age of 15.

> Furthermore, it should be noted that of the 51 alcoholics who reported antisocial behavior before age 15, 66 percent claimed that this behavior preceded the onset of heavy drinking; and of the 23 alcoholics reporting criminal behavior before age 15, 87 percent claimed that the crimes preceded the heavy drinking.[26]

The authors interpreted these figures to indicate that the onset of antisocial behavior preceded heavy drinking for most of the alcoholics and that "there were no differences, other than in family history of alcoholism and suicide, between the alcoholics and nonalcoholics prior to the heavy drinking itself." Thus, while some of this study's findings resembled those later discovered by the Edwards group[9] (for example, in both studies alcoholism was associated with recidivism or with continuance in the criminal career), it appears that the Guze sample of criminals was composed of primarily alcoholic sociopaths, while the Edwards sample of hospitalized alcoholics was composed primarily of sociopathic alcoholics (using Rada's classification scheme).

Eight years after the original Guze study, Goodwin *et al* attempted to follow up on the cases.[27] Of the original sample, 94% were located, of whom 5 had died, 2 were abroad, and 26 refused to be interviewed. Table I compares the alcoholics to the nonalcoholics according to the variables found significant at follow-up. Particularly impressive is the diagnosis of sociopathy and the other antisocial behaviors in the alcoholic group.

Other relevant studies include Rosenberg's study of young (under the age of 30) Australian alcoholics, 28% of whom engaged in serious antisocial behavior.[28] It is important to note that Rosenberg found an increased level of antisocial behavior in men who began alcohol use at an earlier age, a finding confirmed by other investigators.[13,29,30] It should be recognized, however, that in commenting on one of the studies[29] Schuckit observes

> that even though more antisocial behavior was present [in the younger onset alcoholics], it was mild or moderate in extent and did not meet the criteria for a

TABLE 1. Comparison of Alcoholic and Nonalcoholic Felons, in Percent[a]

	Alcoholics (N = 118)	Nonalcoholics (N = 58)
White	78	57
Sociopathy	70	39
Repeated year of school	33	0
Dishonorable discharge from military service	10	2
History of wanderlust	48	23
Rage reactions	50	19
More than 20 sex partners	55	17
Arrests for fights	42	10
Arrests for vagrancy	26	2
Arrests for peace disturbance	66	17
Fights before age 18	64	43
Fights after age 18	69	34
More than 6 arrests	68	42
Often irritable	46	11
Depressive symptoms	31	9
Reared in orphanage	10	0

[a] Differences between groups significant at the 0.05 or 0.01 level (chi-square with Yates's Correction) from Goodwin[27].

diagnosis of sociopathy or antisocial personality; among other things the onset of antisocial problems in this group was not evident by age 15.[20]

Based on the several studies reviewed which investigated the correlation between alcoholism and criminal and other antisocial behavior, it would appear that there are heterogeneous groups of persons who exhibit both alcoholic and sociopathic behavior. At the very least, there are two groups, one of which is characterized by an early onset of antisocial behavior and alcohol abuse, the other of which is characterized by a later onset of the conditions. As we will discuss later, the age of onset is important in the prognosis for members of these two groups. Before a discussion of prognostic factors and treatment implications, however, it will be useful to comment on the studies themselves and to review information from another source—familial incidence of the two conditions.

A major problem with studies that attempt to draw conclusions about the relationship between alcoholism and sociopathy by investigating crime statistics and surveying prison populations is one of sampling. By using criminal statistics, a bias is introduced due to unequal enforcement of laws by different communities or by the same police departments in different neighborhoods of the city.[31] Further, one cannot assume that a sample of prisoners is representative of persons who break laws. This group represents only a subgroup of lawbreakers who have been caught, tried, and imprisoned. Related to this sampling bias is another sampling bias that is highlighted by the Guze study.[26] Guze and his colleagues observed that their sample was drawn "almost entirely from lower socioeconomic levels of the community."

There is a large sociological literature that discusses the potential problems involved in generalizing from such skewed samples to the population in general. Chief among the problems is the fact that secondary status characteristics (that is, those which are not directly related to the person's alcoholism and/or his criminal behavior) rather than the crime (or alcohol abuse) itself may be influencing the community's reaction to the person and consequently his inclusion in a criminal and alcoholic population.[32,33] This point is illustrated clearly by studies which investigate the involvement of female alcoholics with the police. Orfore et al,[34] for example, reported that in England there is a male–female sex ratio of 5:1 for university students who have ever has any alcohol-related police contacts. At the same time, the sex ratio is only 2:1 for the incidence of self-reported alcohol-related law breakings in which the police were not involved. Further evidence for the impact of secondary status characteristics on the diagnostic process is provided by two papers that examine social factors that affect the diagnosis of alcoholism.[35,36] In a study of emergency room physicians employed in a large metropolitan hospital, an analysis of interview protocols demonstrated:

> Diagnostically, physicians behave as though alcoholism were primarily a disorder of derelicts. . . , they tend not to recognize alcoholics who are other than derelict, and when they do, are hesistant to make the diagnosis of alcoholism.[36]

Such discrepancies in diagnosis and police contacts lead one to question the representativeness of many study samples. The persons included in the samples may be as much a function of the community's social structure[37-] as it is a function of individual characteristics. As Edwards et al[9] correctly observe, this style of research has "very real limitations," because rather than exploring the relationships between two real conditions the insensitive researcher actually may be exploring "statistical relationships between labels ('alcoholic,' 'criminal')."

Even if one were to assume that samples of prisoners and criminals were representative of the population of lawbreakers, a problem arises when one attempts to compare these groups to the population at large. Often in studies of crime and alcohol, matched groups of representatives from noncriminal populations are not compared to the criminal group. As Wolfgang observes:

> The presence of alcohol in two-thirds of the homicide situations, where alcohol had been ingested just prior to the homicide by the offender, the victim, or both, is a statistic that has not been (and perhaps cannot be) stated in relation to the abundance of other occasions of social intercourse in which alcohol was an ingredient.[38]

A final criticism of studies which attempt to establish a linkage between alcoholism and sociopathy by referring to the association between alcohol/alcoholism and crime and antisocial behavior as pointed out by Rada:

Although many criminals are sociopaths, not all crimes associated with alcoholism
are committed by sociopathic personality types. For example, homicide, except for
gangland slayings, is not clearly associated with sociopathy.[22]

In addition, according to Goodwin, although homicide is associated with
drinking, it may not be associated with alcoholism.[8] Similarly, although rape
is correlated highly with alcohol consumption, and possibly with alcoholism,
it has not been established that convicted rapists have predominantly
antisocial personality disorders.[39] Therefore, solely on the basis of the
association between alcohol consumption and criminal activity, it is not safe
to conclude that alcoholism is correlated with sociopathy/antisocial personality disorder.

The familial and genetic association between alcoholism and sociopathy
is higher than would be expected by coincidence. In fact, Rada[22] asserts that
the strongest evidence supporting the association between sociopathy and
alcoholism is to be found in studies of familial and genetic associations of the
two. In Robins' longitudinal study of children treated at a child guidance
clinic,[16] children who were referred for antisocial behavior had a much higher
rate of medical and social problems as adults, suggesting "that children
referred for antisocial behavior have a special predisposition to develop
alcoholism which goes beyond the fact that they may more often than other
patients live in a culture which is acceptant of heavy drinking." In addition,
the adult alcoholics resembled adult sociopaths not only in the childhood
behavior problems "but also in their family backgrounds"—both groups
coming from families with a high rate of divorce and separation, living in
broken homes, and having siblings who were frequently antisocial. The
alcoholics, however, had the highest rate of parental loss due to death and
more often were raised in self-supporting families. In a related study, Robins
et al[40] reported that a significantly higher proportion of the child guidance
patients developed alcoholism as adults than did a matched group of controls.

Other studies have reached similar conclusions: Glueck and Glueck[41]
found drunkenness, crime, and/or immorality in the homes of 90.4% of 500
delinquent boys they studied, while observing the same patterns in 54% of a
matched control group; in 1951, Amark[42] uncovered a statistically significant
increase in the diagnosis of sociopathy in both the siblings and parents of his
alcoholic subjects; Winokur et al[13] found a higher incidence of sociopathy in
close male, but not female, relatives of sociopathic alcoholics; and, more
recently, Frances et al[43] found that alcoholics who reported at least one family
member with a possible drinking problem demonstrated not only more
symptoms of alcoholism, but also more antisocial behavior. Commenting on
the association between alcoholism and psychiatric illnesses, Goodwin[14]
observed that several studies [12,13,42,44,45] have indicated:

There is an excess of depression, criminality, sociopathy, and "abnormal
personality" in the families of alcoholics. Typically, depression occurs most often

in female relatives and alcoholism or sociopathy in male relatives. Relatives of alcoholics apparently are no more often schizophrenic, mentally defective, manic, or epileptic than are relatives of nonalcoholics.

The preceding studies are very persuasive in their documentation of the familial association between antisocial personality disorders and alcoholism. It is not clear, however, whether these familial associations indicate that a specific genetic/hereditary factor is present. Cloninger,[46] however, asserts that studies of hormonal factors, as well as adoption and twin studies, suggest the presence of congenital factors—probably genetic—in antisocial personality disorders. He suggest that the genetic factor may not be as strong as in the case of alcoholism. Of particular importance are the studies of monozygotic and dizygotic twins in which the monozygotic twins show a higher concordance rate for criminality than do the dizygotic twins. Equally interesting is the finding of Danish adoption studies in which it was demonstrated that the likelihood of male adoptees' becoming criminal ranged from 10%, if neither adoptive nor biological parents were criminal, to 36% if both sets of parents were criminal. Unlike adoption studies in alcoholism,[14] in which the alcoholism of the adoptive parents did not increase the probability that the children would become alcoholic, in the studies of criminality the criminal behavior of the adoptive parents did increase the risk of the adoptee's becoming a criminal. This finding, along with findings on the effect of socioeconomic status (lower status groups have a higher rate of sociopathy) and parental discipline (children whose parents supplied "firm and consistent" discipline had a lower risk of becoming sociopaths), led Cloninger[46] to conclude that, although sociopathy (like alcoholism and schizophrenia) has a significant genetic component, it is associated with major environmental variable.

Currently, the evidence for the role of genetic, hereditary, and environmental (eg, familial) factors in the etiology of sociopathy and alcoholism remains inconclusive. It is possible that when there is increased study of conditions such as the hyperactive child syndrome, especially to clarify its relationship (if any) to the fetal alcohol syndrome and adult alcoholism, the role of genetics and heredity in the development of alcoholism and antisocial personality disorders will be clarified. Current knowledge permits us only to make the connection between family history, sociopathy, and alcoholism. As Robins et al[40] observe, this relationship is most likely one in which not only a pathological individual but exposure to a facilitating social setting is necessary for a person to become alcoholic. At present, it is probably most appropriate for professionals to avoid premature closure around any single factor—be it genetic, environmental, or hereditary—and examine the full range of interacting variables that lead to a fuller understanding of the two conditions.

Standardized self-report inventories often have been used to investigate the personality traits of alcoholics and sociopaths. The most commonly used of these tests in the Minnesota Multiphasic Personality Inventory (MMPI).[47] According to Hare and Cox, persons are classified as psychopathic (ie, sociopathic) on the MMPI on the basis of elevated scores on the Psychopathic Deviate (Pd) and Hypomania (Ma) scales.[48] Interestingly, a frequent finding in studies that use the MMPI with a known alcoholic population is an elevated Pd scale among alcoholics.[18,49] In fact, according to Barnes,[18] "the Pd scale [is] the one that has most frequently been reported as higher in alcoholics than in either controls or MMPI norms."

The search for common personality traits among sociopaths and alcoholics reflects similar searches for the "alcoholic personality," "pre-alcoholic personality," and the "criminal mind." Just as with these other searches, the discovery of an alcoholic-sociopathic character trait may prove impossible. The use of the MMPI as a standardized means to conduct this search is interesting in its own right, however. As we mentioned above, the search for commonalities seems to center around an elevated Pd scale. Yet, when the MMPI was orginally devised, the Pd scale was considered to apply specifically to the asocial psychopathic personality type.[50] From the very start the scale has not been used by researchers with this original meaning in mind. More often that not, an elevated Pd scale has been interpreted as indicating more of an antisocial tendency than an asocial tendency.

> On this basis alone, then, it is inappropriate to interpret a Scale—4 [Psychopathic deviate] elevation in the composite MMPI profile of alcoholics as prima facie grounds for asserting that the typical alcoholic is a "psychopathic deviate."[50]

In examining the MMPI in general and the Pd scale in particular it becomes clear that (1) MMPI scores may be too global and broad to discriminate adequately between subleties of pathology[17]; and (2) Pd scale elevations alone may lead to invalid conclusions about alcoholism and sociopathy.[18,49,50] For example, although MacAndrew and Geertsma[50] found that statistically the Pd scale significantly differentiated alcoholic outpatients from psychiatric outpatients, by deleting three items—"I have used alcohol excessively" (true), "I have never been in trouble with the law" (false), "I have not lived the right kind of life" (true)—from the scale they were able to eliminate the scale's discriminant ability:

> By process of successive item removal it was found that the significant mean difference between the 2 patient groups disappeared after the 3 most discriminating items had been removed. Taken together, these 3 items were shown to provid *a strikingly mundane insight* into the "cause" of the characteristically significant elevation of alcoholics on Scale 4, viz., alcoholics say they have used alcohol excessively, have been in trouble with the law, and and have not lived the right kind of life (emphasis added).[50]

Further doubt about the excessive reliance on standardized self-report inventories to uncover a sociopathy–alcoholism connection is cast by the fact that although the MMPI scores suggest that both alcoholics and sociopaths display a psychopathic trend (a trend that may be invalid), alcoholics differ from sociopaths in other personality dimensions, such as guilt.[22] Other problems that arise when self-report inventories are used to select sociopathic persons have been discussed by Hare and Cox,[48] who noted that (1) given the nature of the sociopath, there is reason to doubt his responses to potentially incriminating questions and (2) many inventories were not developed (and are not continuously evaluated) with the use of well-defined criterion groups.

Lately, as attempts to define the alcoholic and prealcoholic personality types have met with continued failure, efforts to uncover the sociopathy–alcoholism link also have diminished. Rather than trying to establish the existence of a uniform personality type, current efforts appear to be focused on uncovering and clarifying the correlates of these psychiatric syndromes for purposes of making more refined and useful diagnoses, prognoses, and treatment regimens.

Although a clear connection between sociopathy and alcoholism has not been definitively established (ie, there is not a unitary sociopathy–alcoholism syndrome), there is certainly a strong association between antisocial activities and alcohol abuse. Several generalizations can be made: First, by definition, sociopathy is considered to emerge prior to the age of 15. It has also been suggested that alcoholics who engage in significant antisocial behavior start drinking at an earlier age than other alcoholics.[28,29] Whether the young person who drinks and is antisocial is primarily sociopathic or primarily alcoholic has been determined in part by the behavior which occurred first. Schuckit[20] suggests that the primary sociopath is characterized by an early onset of antisocial activities which both precede his alcohol abuse and are more severe than the antisocial behaviors of primary alcoholics. Further, the research of Edwards et al[9] indicates that alcoholic offenders on average have a higher likelihood for recidivism and are offenders of late onset (ie, their first offense occurs later than the first offense of other prisoners), findings that are congruent with the notion that alcoholism contributes to the "genesis of crime" in these individuals.

Secondly, although statistics on sex indicate (1) that for both alcoholic and sociopathic classifications males are overrepresented, (2) that males have both more school problems and more antisocial problems than females *before* developing alcoholism,[51] and (3) that they have more alcohol-related police difficulties than women.[51,52] Schuckit and Morrissey[53] assert that the "antisocial backgrounds" of sociopathic alcoholics "are probably quite similar for the two sexes." Goodwin[8] supports the notion that male and female alcohol abusers who exhibit antisocial behaviors may be more alike than dissimilar by noting that studies[54,55] "indicate that women are as likely as men to be drinking at the time they become homicide offenders or victims." It is possible that differences in the sexual incidence of the conditions can be attributed to secondary factors such as the fact that women usually start drinking later than men (thus minimizing the probability that they will become enmeshed in a total life-style—a life-style associated with the early onset of any forms of antisocial activity).[16] However, it is likely that these sexual differences will be reduced if the age of onset is controlled. For example, Gomberg[56] states that research on delinquent girls and hospitalized alcoholics suggests that early-onset female alcoholics will manifest significantly more sociopathic characteristics than will older, later-onset female alcoholics. In short, they will be more like early-onset male alcoholics.

Thirdly, there are remarkable familial associations between antisocial personality disorders and alcohol abuse. Whether or not a causal process is operating, it is apparent that alcohol abusers who are antisocial have a higher incidence of both alcoholism and sociopathy among their family members. It is unclear whether these associations are due to heredity, genetics, parental disciplinary practices, socioeconomic status, differential law enforcement practices, or some combination of these factors. For example, regarding the variable of socioeconomic status, lower-class samples differ from upper- and middle-class samples on characteristics like place of drinking, arrest record, and grade completed in school (among others)[53]; each of these characteristics may, in part, explain the increased incidence of alcoholic and sociopathic diagnoses in this group.

Finally, there is some evidence[16,40] that both sociopathy and the early development of alcoholism may be part of a generalized deviant behavior syndrome or pattern. In her comprehensive study of the "roots" of antisocial behavior, Robins found that, while children referred to a child guidance clinic for problems other than antisocial behaviors rarely emerged as sociopathic adults, a large proportion of the antisocial children became antisocial, alcoholic, and/or drug addicted adults. Only a small number were considered healthy and trouble-free as adults. These proportions compare to a 60% healthy rate and a 2% sociopathic rate for a control group. The argument that a generalized deviant behavior syndrome or pattern may be present among these individuals receives further support by two additional facts: (1) The tendency toward adult deviant behavior among children referred for antisocial behavior pervaded "every area in which society sets norms . . . [with] no clear connections . . . between *type* of deviance in childhood and *type* of deviance in adults," and (2) "None of the symptoms used to diagnose sociopathic personality failed to occur in at least some of the subjects with other diagnosis, [while] . . . the symptoms most common among the sociopaths were not the ones that best discriminated them from all other diagnostic groups."[16]

Based on the overlap in behavior and symptomatology in the two diagnostic groups, it seems safe to conclude that we are dealing with a subgroup of alcoholics and sociopaths who are more similar to each other than they are to other primary alcoholics and primary sociopaths. Within this subgroup are (1) individuals who can be called alcoholic sociopaths,[20,22] characterized by early antisocial behavior that antedates their alcohol abuse and exhibiting a more severe antisocial behavior pattern,[16,29] and (2) individuals who can be referred to as sociopathic alcoholics,[22] characterized by a later developing and less severe pattern of antisocial activity that may have resulted from their increasing alcohol abuse.[2,29]

The prognosis for any individual exhibiting both sociopathy and alcoholism is poor.[16,20,22,46,57] In a study of a 90-day in-patient alcoholism rehabilitation program, Wilkinson et al[57] found that program dropouts, when compared to program completers, started drinking at an earlier age, had less stable job and marital histories, were more aggressive and hostile, and less often endorsed MMPI items indicating greater emotional control. Both Goodwin et al[27] and Edwards et al[9] found that being alcoholic increased the probability of recidivism among prisoners. Finally, Schuckit et al[29] stated that the person who is both sociopathic and alcoholic is highly susceptible to alcoholic relapse, which, when it occurs, is usually accompanied by assaultive behavior toward the spouse and other family members.

Ross,[58] in a study cited by Schuckit,[20] found that among a group of imprisoned alcoholics "routine treatment methods for alcoholism were ineffective." Cloninger,[46] on the basis of his review of the antisocial personality, concluded that "as an adult, the sociopath is an unsatisfactory patient for either the specialist or the primary physician. To the mental health specialist, he poses an almost insoluable problem in treatment." The sociopath tends to present a number of physical and psychological symptoms which are not amenable to pharmacotherapy, since the sociopath—especially the alcoholic/sociopath—has a high potential for drug abuse and dependence. The situation is further complicated by the sociopath's low level of cooperation and lack of remorse, which is used often as a means of mobilizing the new patient.

In a study of medical treatment for alcoholics, Panepinto et al[59] found the poorest outcomes (as measured by maintained treatment contacts) in alcoholics who had diagnoses of personality disorders. In discussing their results, they described the treatment regimen as one in which contacts were with internists, were fairly brief (about ten minutes), were symptom/complaint-oriented, were highly predictable, and were accompanied by rather lengthy waiting periods (45 minutes to an hour). In commenting on these results, Kissin[60] later observed that this type of medically-oriented treatment did not seem appropriate for personality-disordered, asymptomatic patients. So far as a suitable subcategory of personality disorders is concerned, these cautions would appear to apply to antisocial personality-disordered persons. As Rada[22] comments, "Few treatment strategies have been regularly successful with this patient population. In each instance, an individualized treatment program must be planned." Cloninger[40] adds that "given the pronounced socioeconomic component in antisocial personality, the most effective prophylactic measures may well prove to be socioeconomic." Unfortunately, due possibly to the conceptual and diagnostic confusion, there appears to be no treatment approach which has demonstrated remarkably effective results with this group of individuals. It remains for clinicians and other professionals (eg, social workers, probation officers, prison officials, primary care physicians) to develop treatment procedures that can be tested and implemented for this population.

This paper has presented a discussion of sociopathy and alcoholism, highlighting points of convergence and divergence between the two syndromes. Throughout the discussion, we have pointed out that conceptual and diagnostic confusion persists about these conditions as researchers and professionals devote large amounts of energy to attempts to discriminate the sociopathic alcoholic from the alcoholic strength and both states from other psychiatric conditions. From the studies reviewed, it seems apparent that antisocial behavior is more common and more severe among younger-onset alcoholics than older-onset alcoholics; there is a higher than normal familial coincidence of the two syndromes; although both conditions are more common among men than women, female sociopathic and alcoholic individuals may be more similar to their male counterparts than they are to female primary alcoholics; the conditions may be more prevalent among lower socioeconomic groups; the prognosis for persons diagnosed as alcoholic and sociopathic is very poor; and no effective treatment interventions appear to have been developed for the conditions.

Some of the confusion and resultant failure to develop innovative treatment approaches for the conditions may be due to the fact that there is still a tendency to try to locate an alcoholism–sociopathy personality type; further confusion may result from a misinterpretation of research findings. Regarding the latter point, for example, it has been suggested that researchers have misinterpreted scores on standardized self-report inventories (eg, the MMPI's Pd Scale), that crime and deviancy rates too often have been equated with sociopathy, and that alcohol use and alcohol abuse too often have been equated with alcoholism.

The more important issue, however, may lie with the persistent efforts to uncover an alcoholism–sociopathy personality type. There is ample evidence that such efforts are misguided and/or premature. Both conditions have been shown to be influenced greatly by contextual and environmental variables which interact with any individual vulnerability in the syndromes' emergence. The focus on personality types may cause researchers and clinicians to overlook important environmental and contextual factors that are germane to the syndromes' development, maintenance, and arrest. Alcohol, for example, impacts sharply on the person's perceptions and actions. However, how the person acts, even when intoxicated, is influenced greatly by cultural norms and social sanctions. The aggressive behavior of an individual is influenced by the aggression of others and the consequences of their aggression for the individual. Finally, societal reactions often influence the subsequent careers and actions of persons who engage in any form of deviance. These, and other factors, are strongly supportive of the notion that an interactive phenomenon is operating in the case of sociopathy and alcoholism. The sensitive researcher and clinician, it would seem, should be cognizant of these interactions as he attempts to understand the syndromes and develop innovative and effective treatment and investigative strategies.

References

1. Bennet RM, Buss AH, Carpenter JA: Alcohol and human physical aggression. *Q J Stud Alcohol* 30:870–876, 1969.
2. Carpenter JA, Armenti NP: Some effects of ethanol on human sexual and aggressive behavior, in Kissin B, Begleiter H (eds): *The Biology of Alcoholism,* vol 2, *Physiology and Behavior.* New York, Plenum Press, 1972, pp 509–543.
3. Boyatzis RE: The effect of alcohol consumption on the aggressive behavior of men. *Q J Stud Alcohol* 35:959–972, 1974.
4. Mendelson JH, Mello NK: Alcohol, aggression and androgens, in *Aggression.* Res Publ vol 52. Association for Research in Nervous and Mental Disease, 1974, pp 225–247.
5. Taylor SP, Gammon CB: Aggressive behavior of intoxicated subjects: The effect of third-party intervention. *J Stud Alcohol* 37:917–930, 1976.
6. Shupe LM: Alcohol and crime: A study of the urine alcohol concentration found in 882 persons arrested during or immediately after commission of a felony. *J Crim Law Criminol* 44:661–664, 1954.
7. Wolfgang ME: *Patterns of Criminal Homicide.* Philadelphia, University of Pennsylvania Press, 1958.
8. Goodwin DW: Alcohol in suicide and homicide. *Q J Stud Alcohol* 34:144–156, 1973.
9. Edwards G, Kyle E, Nicholls P: Alcoholics admitted to four hospitals in England, III. Criminal records. *J Stud Alcohol* 38:1648–1664, 1977.
10. Haberman PW, Baden MM: *Alcohol, Other Drugs and Violent Death.* New York, Oxford University Press, 1978.
11. Haberman PW, Baden MW, Alcoholism and violent death. *Q J Stud Alcohol* 35:221–231, 1974.
12. Guze S, Wolfgram E, McKinney J: Psychiatric illness in the families of convicted criminals: A study of 519 first degree relatives. *Dis Nerv Syst,* 28:651–659, 1967.
13. Winokur G, Reich T, Rimmer J, *et al:* Alcoholism III. Diagnosis and familial psychiatric illness in 259 alcoholic probands. *Gen Psychiatrist* 23:104–111, 1970.
14. Goodwin, DW: Family and adoption studies of alcoholism, in Mednick S, Christiensen KO (eds): *Biosocial Bases of Criminal Behavior.* New York, Gardner Press, 1977, pp 143–157.
15. *Diagnostic and Statistical Manual of Mental Disorders,* ed 3 (DSM-III). Washington, DC, American Psychiatric Association, 1980.
16. Robins LN: *Deviant Children Grown Up.* Baltimore, Williams and Wilkins, 1966.
17. Hoffman H, Jackson DN, Skinner HA: Dimensions of psychopathology among alcoholic patients. *J Stud Alcohol* 36:825–837, 1975.

18. Barnes GE: The alcoholic personality: A reanalysis of the literature. *J Stud Alcohol* 40:571–634, 1979.

19. Barnes GE: Characteristics of the clinical alcoholic personality. *J Stud Alcohol* 41:894–910, 1980.

20. Schuckit MA: Alcoholism and sociopathy-diagnostic confusion. *Q J Stud Alcohol* 34:157–164, 1973.

21. Podolsky E: The sociopathic alcoholic. *Q J Stud Alcohol* 21:292–297, 1960.

22. Rada RT: Sociopathy and alcohol abuse, in Reid WH (ed): *The Psychopath: A Comprehensive Study of Antisocial Disorders and Behaviors.* New York, Brunner/Mazel, 1978, pp 223–234.

23. *Criminal Offenders and Drinking Involvement.* Publ No 3, State of California Department of Public Health, Division of Alcohol Rehabilitation, 1960.

24. Bartholomew AA: Alcoholism and crime. *Aust N Z J Criminol* 1:70–99, 1968.

25. Gibbens TC, Silberman M: Alcoholism among prisoners. *Psychol Med* 1:73–78, 1970.

26. Guze SB, Tuason VB, Gatfield PD, et al: Psychiatric illness and crime with particular reference to alcoholism: A study of 223 criminals. *J Nerv Ment Dis* 134:512–521, 1962.

27. Goodwin DW, Crane JB, Guze SB: Felons who drink: An 8 year follow-up *Q J Stud Alcohol* 32:136–147, 1971.

28. Rosenberg CM: Young alcoholics. *Br J Psychiatry* 115:181–188, 1969.

29. Schuckit M, Rimmer J, Reich T, et al: Alcoholism: Antisocial traits in male alcoholics. *Br J Psychiatry* 117:575–576, 1970.

30. Rimmer J, Reich T, Winokur G: Alcoholism V. Diagnosis and clinical variation among alcoholics. *Q J Stud Alcohol* 33:658–666, 1972.

31. Sutherland E, Cressey D: *Principles of Criminology,* ed 7. Philadelphia, JB Lippincott, 1966.

32. Lemert EM: *Social Pathology.* New York, McGraw-Hill, 1951.

33. Becker HS: *Outsiders: Studies in the Sociology of Deviance.* New York, The Free Press, 1963.

34. Orford J, Waller S, Peto J: Drinking behavior and attitudes and their correlates among university students in England. *Q J Stud Alcohol* 35:1316–1374, 1974.

35. Blane HT, Overton WF, Chafetz ME: Social factors in the diagnosis of alcoholism. I. Characteristics of the patient. *Q J Stud Alcohol* 24:640–663, 1963.

36. Wolf I, Chafetz ME, Blane HT, et al: Social factors in the diagnosis of alcoholism. II. Attitudes in physicians. *Q J Stud Alcohol* 26:72–79, 1965.

37. Wuthrich P: Social problems of alcoholics. *J Stud Alcohol* 38:881–890, 1977.

38. Wolfgang ME: Criminal homicide and the subculture of violence, in Wolfgang ME (ed): *Studies in Homicide.* New York, Harper & Row, 1967, pp 3–12.

39. Glueck BC: Psychodynamic patterns in the sex offender. *Psychiatr Q* 23:1–21, 1954.

40. Robins LN, Bates W, O'Neal P: Alcohol drinking patterns of former problem children, in Pittman DJ, Snyder CR (eds): *Society, Culture, and Drinking Patterns.* New York, John Wiley & Sons, 1962, pp 395–412.

41. Glueck S, Glueck E: *Unraveling Juvenile Delinquency.* New York, The Commonwealth Fund, 1950.

42. Amark C: A study in alcoholism: Clinical, social-psychiatric, and genetic investigations. *Acta Psychiatr Scan,* suppl no 70, 1951.

43. Frances R, Timms S, Bucky S: Studies in familial and nonfamilial alcoholism. I. Demographic studies. *Arch Gen Psychiatry* 37:564–566, 1980.

44. Brugger C: Familienunterschungen bei Alkoholdeliranten. *Z Gesamte Neurol Psychiatr* 151:740, 1934.

45. Bleuler M: Psychotische Belastung von körperlichen Kranken. *Z Gesamte Neurol Psychiatr* 142:780, 1932.

46. Cloninger CR: The antisocial personality. *Hosp Pract,* August 1978, pp 97–103, 106.
47. Dahlstrom WG, Welsch GS: *An MMPI Handbook.* Minneapolis, University of Minnesota Press, 1960.
48. Hare RD, Cox DN: Psychophysiological research on psychopathy, in Reid WH (ed): *The Psychopath: A Comprehensive Study of Antisocial Disorders and Behaviors.* New York, Brunner/Mazel, 1978, pp 209–222.
49. Miller WR: Alcoholism scales and objectives assessment methods: A review. *Psychol Bull* 83:649–674, 1976.
50. MacAndrew C, Geertsma RH: An analysis of responses of alcoholics to Scale 4 of the MMPI. *Q J Stud Alcohol* 24:24–38, 1963.
51. Rimmer J, Pitts FN, Reich T, *et al*: Alcoholism. II. Sex, socioeconomic status and race in two hospitalized samples. *Q J Stud Alcohol* 32:942–952, 1971.
52. Lisansky ES: Alcoholism in women: Social and psychological concomitants. I. Social history data. *Q J Stud Alcohol* 18:588–623, 1957.
53. Schuckit MA, Morrissey ER: Alcoholism in women: Some clinical and social perspectives with an emphasis on possible subtypes, in Greenblatt M, Schuckitt MA (eds): *Alcoholism Problems in Women and Children.* New York, Grune & Stratton, 1976, pp 5–35.
54. Cole KE, Fisher G, Cole SS: Women who kill: A sociopsychological study. *Arch Gen Psychiatry* 19:1–3, 1968.
55. Metheson JCM: Alcohol and female homicides. *Brit J Inebr* 37:87–90, 1939.
56. Gomberg ES: Problems with alcohol and other drugs, in Gomberg ES, Franks V (eds): *Gender and Disordered Behavior.* New York, Brunner/Mazel, 1979, pp 204–240.
57. Wilkinson AE, Prado WM, Williams WO, *et al*: Psychological test characteristics and length of stay in alcoholism treatment. *Q J Stud Alcohol* 32:60–65, 1971.
58. Ross CFJ: Comparison of hospital and prison alcoholics. *Brit J Psychiatry* 118:75–78, 1971.
59. Panepinto WC, Higgins MJ, Keane-Dawes WY, *et al*: Underlying psychiatric diagnosis as an indicator of participation in alcoholism therapy. *Q J Stud Alcohol* 31:950–956, 1970.
60. Kissin B: Patient characteristics and treatment specificity in alcoholism, in *Recent Advances in the Study of Alcoholism.* Exerpta Med, Int Cong Series No 407, Amsterdam, 1977.

CHAPTER 10

Hidden Psychiatric Diagnosis in the Alcoholic

FREDERIC M. QUITKIN, MD, and JUDITH G. RABKIN, PhD

With a complex, poorly understood disorder such as alcoholism, etiological insights and treatment strategies may be generated by identifying another frequently associated illness. If temporal sequence can be defined, then causal or precipitating roles of one disorder in relation to the other may be suggested. Since alcoholism and other psychiatric disorders all have unclear etiologies, analysis of their association may prove fruitful. Understandably, the clinician would be most enthusiastic if alcoholism were found related to a psychiatric disorder (Axis I diagnosis)[1] rather than a personality disorder (Axis II diagnosis),[1] since the latter are resistant to change. It would be particularly helpful if the psychiatric disorder is one known to be responsive to a specific treatment or to preventive intervention.

We do not think that most patients with alcoholism have additional psychiatric disorders, either covert or obvious. However, there is some evidence that several psychiatric syndromes, including anxiety and depressive disorders, may contribute to or provoke alcohol abuse. Because the manifestations of alcohol abuse and/or withdrawal usually dominate the clinical picture, all symptoms may be thus attributed and other diagnoses remain unrecognized. Since the relationship of primary depressive disorder to alcoholism is reviewed elsewhere in this volume, we will focus on alcoholism and two subtypes of anxiety disorder to which it seems related: panic disorder and posttraumatic stress disorder. In addition, we will consider the association between alcohol abuse and a subtype of affective disorder, not always identified as such, that we refer to as hysteroid dysphoria. Evidence for

FREDERIC M. QUITKIN • Director, Depression Evaluation Service, New York State Psychiatric Institute; Associate Professor of Clinical Psychiatry, Columbia University College of Physicians and Surgeons, New York, New York 10032.   **JUDITH G. RABKIN** • Research Scientist, New York State Psychiatric Institute; Adjunct Assistant Professor of Public Health in Psychiatry, Columbia University College of Physicians and Surgeons, New York, New York 10032.

the association of each with alcohol abuse and treatment implications will in turn be discussed.

Panic Disorder

The essential criteria for this disorder as defined in third edition of the *Diagnostic and Statistical Manual of Mental Disorders* (DSM—III)[1] include recurrent panic attacks which impair functioning and occur in the absence of severe physiological or psychological stress. They consist of discrete episodes of intense fearfulness accompanied by sympathetic nervous system discharge such as sweating, palpitations, trembling, fear of dying, and feelings of unreality. Over time, anticipatory anxiety develops between these acute episodes. In our experience, this symptom constellation often precedes the development of agoraphobia; that is, patients with panic disorder often avoid situations in which they may feel trapped or closed in, such as subways, elevators, and crowds; this may progress to a fear of leaving home. However, panic disorder can also occur in the absence of specific phobias.

Historically, patients who now receive the diagnosis of panic disorder with or without agoraphobia previously received a variety of labels including anxiety neurosis, effort syndrome, and neurocirculatory syndrome.[2,3] We use data from studies of such patients to support the hypothesis that what we now call panic disorder is complicated by alcoholism more frequently than would be expected by chance. Three types of evidence suggest this association: studies of psychiatric patients, studies of alcoholic patients, and studies of treatment of patients with panic disorder complicated by alcoholism.

Studies of Patients with Panic Disorder

Woodruff and colleagues[3] studied 62 outpatients given diagnoses of anxiety neurosis. Anxiety attacks were reported by 81% of them. About a quarter were "heavy drinkers" and 15% met criteria for alcoholism. Approximately one third also had a family history positive for alcoholics.

Noyes and his group[4] studied 129 patients diagnosed as having anxiety neurosis, based on the presence of either anxiety or anxiety attacks as well as a group of associated symptoms such as trembling, sweating, and palpitations. It is not clear how many actually had anxiety attacks. A control group was chosen from patients hospitalized for surgical procedures. The risk for both anxiety neurosis and alcoholism was found to be greater among relatives of patients with anxiety neurosis than among relatives of controls.

Sims[5] reevaluated 146 patients who received diagnoses of "neurosis" 12 years following hospital discharge. Established drug or alcohol abuse was diagnosed in 10% of these patients. On the basis of their clinical descriptions, five appear very likely to have had panic disorder, and two others probably did.

TABLE I. DSM-III Field Trial Data Showing Patients With Subtypes of Anxiety Disorder Who Also Have Alcoholism Diagnosis

Anxiety subtype	Anxiety diagnosis[a]	Alcoholism diagnosis	Percentage with both diagnoses
Agoraphobia with panic attacks	70	12	17%
Panic disorder	90	7	8%
Combined	160	19	12%
Simple phobia	29	0	0
Social phobia	38	0	0
Agoraphobia without panic attacks	19	0	0
Generalized anxiety disorder	264	21	5%
Obsessive-Compulsive	123	3	2%
Atypical	48	4	10%
Combined	521	28	5%

[a] All patients in this subset were selected because they have either a primary or secondary diagnosis of anxiety disorder. When appearing concurrently with an alcoholism diagnosis, either may be primary.

A fourth data set shows the relationship between subtypes of anxiety disorder and alcoholism in a national patient sample. These data, provided by Spitzer and Williams,[6] are from the DSM-III Field Trial Study of 12,488 psychiatric patients. A total of 5% or 681 patients in the study had either primary or secondary diagnoses of one of the subtypes of anxiety disorder enumerated in DSM-III.* Excluding patients with panic attacks, 5% also had diagnoses of alcohol abuse or dependence. None of the patients with diagnoses of simple phobia, social phobia, or agoraphobia *without* panic attacks had alcoholism diagnoses. In contrast, 12% of patients diagnosed as having either panic disorder or agoraphobia with panic attacks also had a simultaneous diagnosis of alcoholism, as seen in Table I.

These four studies[3-6] suggest an association between alcoholism and panic disorder. Noyes' study suggests a familial relationship while the others more simply describe their simultaneous presence. A very rough estimate of the prevalence of this association can be made from the data available. Woodruff suggests that 5% of the general population has anxiety neurosis, or what we call panic disorder. The reports of Sims and Woodruff suggest that 10% of these patients also abuse alcohol, a figure close to the 12% found among panic disorder patients in the DSM-III Field Trials. If these estimates

*Post traumatic stress disorder was not so classified in the first phase of the Field Trials and so is not listed in this analysis.

are approximately accurate, then about one half percent of the population may have panic disorder complicated by alcoholism.

Panic Disorder in Alcoholic Populations

Mullaney and Trippett[7] studied 102 consecutive admissions to a regional alcoholism center in England. Patients were assessed with several instruments including the Present State Examination, which is a structured psychiatric interview, and the SCL–90, a self-report symptom checklist. From these instruments, composite agoraphobia and social phobia scores were derived and a judgment made concerning the presence of these disorders. The authors report that one third of their sample were "clinically rated as having disabling agoraphobia and/or social phobia, and a further third as having less disabling symptoms of either or both kinds."[7(p565)] Both of these are remarkably high proportions. For 44 of the patients judged full or borderline phobic, the age of onset of both phobias and problem drinking could be ascertained. In 36 of the 44 patients, the onset of the phobias preceded the onset of severe alcohol abuse. This supports the possibility that some of these patients may have used alcohol to deal with the anxiety associated with these phobias.

In the course of group therapy with male hospitalized alcoholics, Curlee and Stern[8] observed that four out of seven had strong fears of heights. All reported that they attempted to deal with this fear by using alcohol. This led the investigators to a more systematic assessment of phobias in 100 male alcoholics using MMPI items and profiles. Their responses were compared to those of normal and psychiatric comparison groups. Whereas 5% of the normal controls feared closed spaces and 6% open spaces, 27% of the alcoholics feared closed and 14% open spaces. The authors do not report whether these patients had panic attacks. However, it is our clinical experience that patients with a fear of open and closed spaces frequently have panic attacks, and it seems likely that some of these patients may have had panic disorder.

Depending on the criteria utilized, the proportion of agoraphobics in the Mullaney and Trippet study is between 16% and 43% and is somewhat smaller in that of Curlee and Stern. Both groups of alcoholics appear to include more patients with phobias then would be expected by chance. It is unclear how many of these patients would meet DSM–III criteria for panic disorder.

The number of alcoholic patients found to have panic disorders is apt to vary widely depending on the socioeconomic status, age, and sex of the sample. Panic disorder has a wide range in age of onset. Many patients do not develop significant morbidity until after they have established careers and families. Therefore, samples of middle-class alcoholics may contain the highest percent of patients with panic disorder. In addition, panic disorder is more common in females than males so that a middle-class adult female alcoholic population is most likely to contain covert cases of panic disorder.

Treatment of Patients with Panic Disorder Complicated by Alcoholism and/or Drug Abuse

A complete review of psychopharmacologic treatment of panic disorder is beyond the scope of this presentation. It is worth emphasizing, however, that since Klein and Fink's[9] first uncontrolled clinical report of the utility of imipramine in this disorder, at least four independent double-blind studies of tricyclic antidepressants[10–13] and four of monoamine oxidase inhibitors[13–16] have clearly established the efficacy of these drugs in its treatment.

My colleagues and I observed that, in a general psychiatric hospital, a majority of patients with histories of severe alcohol and/or drug abuse had panic disorder as well.[17] This was clearly related to the prevailing admissions policy, which excluded most uncomplicated alcoholism patients. Nonetheless, the relevant issue is whether the presence of panic disorder offers a lead in treating these alcohol–sedative addicted patients. Our understanding of panic disorder suggests that patients with this disorder have two basic psychopathologic features, as noted earlier. First, there are anxiety attacks of abrupt onset accompanied by a sudden discharge of the sympathetic nervous system. Anticipatory anxiety regarding these panic attacks constitutes the other component of the syndrome. Most patients find the panic anxiety markedly more unpleasant than the anticipatory anxiety. They find alcohol, sedatives, or minor tranquilizers somewhat useful in alleviation of the anticipatory anxiety, but utterly ineffective for the panic attacks. In a futile attempt to get some results, they resort to increasing doses of these agents. After a period of time, the signs and symptoms of substance abuse become more clinically obvious than those of the panic disorder, which in this context can be misdiagnosed as alcohol withdrawal signs.

The course of five alcohol- and barbiturate-dependent patients whom we treated with imipramine was contrasted with five patients who were not maintained on imipramine. The patients on imipramine did well and did not return to drug or alcohol abuse, but those not maintained on imipramine tended to return to drug abuse, were rehospitalized, and responded poorly to ECT and phenothiazines. Clearly, this anecdotal report of the efficacy of imipramine in alcohol- and barbiturate-dependent patients represents no more than an interesting lead requiring confirmation in properly controlled studies.

Imipramine is not addictive, and we know of no case of imipramine abuse. This is probably because there is no immediate reinforcing alteration in mood or consciousness associated with its intake. Tolerance to imipramine is not developed, and patients can work while taking it, contrary to the effects of large doses of barbiturates, alcohol, and minor tranquilizers. Depending upon individual tolerance and intensity of symptoms, most patients can be maintained on doses ranging from 100 to 300 mg of imipramine hydrochloride daily while they are overcoming their phobias, without its interfering with social or vocational functioning. We believe one should suspect this treatable syndrome in all sedative and alcohol-abusing patients who have histories of anxiety attacks or evidence of phobias, or both. Careful clinical assessment may reveal its presence.

Most convincing would be a properly controlled study conducted in a group initially identified as alcoholic but subsequently discovered also to meet criteria for panic disorder. We have attempted this type of study in two settings. In the first clinic there were plenty of alcoholic patients who also met criteria for panic disorder. However, the majority of them were social class V males with no family or economic ties in the community. This patient group had a treatment drop-out rate of 70% to 90%. We found it futile to conduct a controlled trial in such a population. A second attempt was made in a clinic with a more reliable patient group. We had little difficulty identifying alcoholics who also met criteria for panic disorder. In fact, the clinic psychiatrist had been treating a small group of these patients with tricyclic antidepressants. However, the staff of the clinic was opposed to the possibility of a drug study which would prohibit the use of disulfiram in order to assess the utility of the tricyclics. Since there appeared to be no design which would test their utility if other drugs such as disulfiram were used, the project was halted. In general, staffs of alcoholic treatment centers frequently have a negative view about all medication other than disulfiram, even if the drug in question is one with an extremely small likelihood of abuse. This anti-medication orientation limits the testing of a variety of potentially useful agents.

Hysteroid Dysphoria

Although there continues to be controversy about the nosological validity of this syndrome, and it is not included in DSM–III as a separate category, we believe those whom we so classify have distinctive behavioral characteristics and treatment responses. In one of his early descriptions of the syndrome, Klein[18] observed:

> Hysteroid dysphorics are fickle, emotionally labile, irresponsible, shallow, love-intoxicated, giddy, and short-sighted. They tend to be egocentric, narcissistic, exhibitionistic, vain, and clothes-crazy. They are seductive, manipulative, exploitative, sexually provocative, and think emotionally and illogically. They are easy prey to flattery and compliments. Their general manner is histrionic, attention-seeking, and may be flamboyant. In their sexual relations they are possessive, grasping, demanding, romantic, and foreplay centered. When frustrated or disappointed they become reproachful, tearful, abusive, and vindictive, and often resort to alcohol (p 152).

In short, hysteroid dysphoric patients, who are predominantly female, seem to be almost caricatures of femininity, and the syndrome is probably a good example of the way cultural role expectations and pressures shape the form of symptomatic manifestations.

Klein has suggested that the primary defect of hysteroid dysphorics is their affective vulnerability. He believes that these patients have a pathologically heightened emotional reactivity to approval or disapproval and that other aspects of their behavior are expressions of this defect or attempts to compensate for it. Their impulsivity reflects the domination of thinking and judgment by mood; their sexual provocativeness and manipulativeness are an attempt to elicit attention and approval; and their lack of depth and consistency in personal relationships seems secondary to the use of others as mood-adjusting agents.[19]

Most American psychiatrists, influenced by psychoanalytic or psychodynamic theory, focus on the character pathology of this group. Such patients are commonly viewed as oral hysterics, hysteroids, narcissistic, or borderline personalities. Their difficulties are conceptualized as Axis II personality disorders, and the treatment often consists of psychoanalysis or another form of long-term psychotherapy.

Not all of the patients described as borderline or oral hysterics meet our operationalized criteria for hysteroid dysphoria. However, we consider those who do meet the criteria to have an affective disorder (Axis I) as well as a personality disorder (Axis II). The classical endogenous form of depressive disorder is characterized by weight loss, difficulty with sleeping often associated with early morning awakening, and autonomy of mood—that is, unresponsiveness to events. In contrast, patients with atypical depressive disorder overeat and oversleep and in addition may be hypersensitive to interpersonal rejection. We regard hysteroid dysphoria as a form of atypical depressive disorder.

At present, evidence regarding treatment for either the character pathology or the personality–affective disorder is largely anecdotal. Our clinical experience suggests that mood fluctuation in these patients is effectively modified by monoamine oxidase inhibitors but not by tricyclic antidepressants or placebo. Empirical confirmation of these clinical impressions would provide support for the proposition that hysteroid dysphoria is indeed a form of affective disorder. We are currently testing this hypothesis in a prospective controlled study. In addition, preliminary data[20] show an apparent increased incidence of affective disorder in the families of hysteroid dysphorics. This is another kind of evidence suggesting an association between hysteroid dysphoria and affective disorder.

Evidence supporting the relationship of alcoholism to hysteroid dysphoria is also anecdotal. We have observed a link between increased alcohol use and illness both during the mood crashes of these patients and the occasional hypomanic swings that have been observed following phenelzine administration. When they feel depressed and rejected, hysteroid dysphoric patients often resort to alcohol or amphetamines as forms of self-medication. With return to a euthymic mood following treatment with phenelzine, the alcohol abuse stops. However, among the small percentage of patients who become hypomanic while receiving phenelzine, increased alcoholic intake may also be found. Winokur and his colleagues[21] observed a rise in alcohol consumption in 42 of 100 patients during a manic episode. It is possible, therefore, that the increased alcohol intake demonstrated by hypomanic hysteroid dysphorics may not be related to their personality disorder, but merely to a ubiquitous complication observed in some manic or hypomanic states. Whether alcohol abuse among hysteroid dysphorics is precipitated by depressed mood or hypomanic swings or both remains to be clarified.

A pilot project to assess psychiatric diagnoses in female admissions to an alcohol treatment ward has been initiated. We have assessed 11 patients; of these, 2 were hysteroid dysphorics, 1 had panic disorder, 1 had atypical depression, and 7 had no evidence of covert psychiatric illness. Certainly data from 11 patients warrant no firm conclusions.

A complete discussion of the toxic interaction of alcohol and monoamine oxidase inhibitors is beyond the scope of this paper. Using MAOIs in alcohol-abusing populations is dangerous. However, many of these patients have failed to respond to extensive trials of psychotherapy and use of "safer" medications. We think judicious use of MAOIs is indicated. It may be wise to initiate this treatment in the hospital unless there is a family member who can responsibly supervise the patient in the early stages of treatment when the abuse potential is greatest.

An overview of the relationship of hysteroid dysphoria, alcohol abuse, and the utility of MAOI should leave the objective observer in a skeptical state. A fair summary of the currently available evidence is that this is at best a clinical hunch requiring a series of controlled studies to establish that these relationships do exist.

Post Traumatic Stress Disorder

Although traumatic (actual) neuroses were recognized by Freud and his contemporaries at the time of World War I, the syndrome has had an uneven history in American psychiatry. It was included in the DSM–I under the heading of "gross stress reaction," dropped from the second edition, and reinstated and renamed "post traumatic stress disorder" in DSM-III, where it is classified as a subtype of anxiety disorder. Its essential feature is the development of characteristic symptoms following a traumatic event outside the range of ordinary experience. The characteristic symptoms include reexperiencing the traumatic event either in the form of recurrent flashbacks or nightmares, psychic numbness, and a variety of autonomic, dysphoric, or cognitive features. Under the heading "Complications" in DSM–III, it is noted that "substance use disorders may develop."

It is not feasible to calculate the community prevalence of post traumatic stress disorder, since no records are kept of at-risk populations (those who experience natural or manmade disasters). Cases are, however, easy enough to identify retrospectively from relevant historical material or concurrently on the occasion of such events as floods or major fires.

Follow-up studies of survivors of disaster provide rather limited evidence regarding the development of subsequent disorder when the events include massive biological as well as psychological insult. This is notably the case for survivors of prisoner of war and concentration camps and of wartime experiences of civilian populations such as the Leningrad seige or the Dutch famine of World War II. Some data are provided by follow-up studies of natural disasters. For example, Logue[22] reported that in the months after a major flood, 24% of those whose homes were flooded but only 5% of matched controls in adjacent areas described alcohol as "helpful." In this and similar retrospective studies, the design precludes causal interpretations. In general, the richest data source is furnished by studies of combat veterans for whom prestressor records are available, and most research concerning post traumatic stress disorder is based on military samples.

The first major empirical study of combat reactions was conducted in World War II by Grinker and Spiegel.[23] Alcoholism was found to be one of the commonly encountered sequelae of combat exposure. The most prevalent symptoms, in this and other major studies,[24,25] are recurrent intrusive flashbacks, nightmares, insomnia, apprehensiveness, and anxiety. It seems plausible to regard the use of alcohol following the manifestations of such symptoms as an effort, albeit an ineffective one, to reduce subjective distress.

In a recent paper, Lacoursiere and his colleagues[26] present this position, based on clinical experience with Vietnam combat zone veterans. They note that self-medication with alcohol initially relieves the symptoms of post traumatic stress disorder, especially the recurrent nightmares, since alcohol usually suppresses REM sleep. But tolerance develops which leads to an increase in alcohol use. Attempts to cut back on drinking can lead to withdrawal symptoms that resemble and even exacerbate the initial post traumatic stress disorder symptoms, culminating in resumption of alcohol use and abuse. The authors report that treatment with antianxiety medication and focused psychotherapy for the symptoms of post traumatic stress disorder, in conjunction with disulfiram, led to amelioration of the alcoholism which was the presenting complaint. This paper is noteworthy not for the treatment proposed, which is not really described or systematically evaluated, but for its confirmation of the role of psychiatric disorder in precipitating alcohol abuse.

A longitudinal strategy in the study of post traumatic stress disorder and alcoholism is illustrated by assessment of their concordance in veterans with and without combat experience. Strange and Brown[27] studied 50 veterans admitted to a neuropsychiatric ward within a year of completing their tour of duty in the Vietnam combat zone. Compared to matched psychiatrically ill veterans without war zone experience, fewer combat veterans had pre-enlistment histories of antisocial behavior or psychiatric disorder, but more had postdischarge records of legal difficulties and alcohol abuse.

These studies represent several converging lines of evidence which together tentatively suggest an association between post traumatic stress disorder and alcoholism. They raise the possibility that amelioration of the psychiatric disorder can facilitate treatment of alcohol abuse.

Until now, treatment approaches have consisted largely of psychotherapeutic techniques popular at the time. After World War I, emphasis was placed on the methods of abreaction and catharsis; more recently, crisis intervention and behavioral techniques have been employed.[26] Horowitz et al[28] have developed therapeutic techniques based on a psychoanalytic model which are intended to address the core symptoms for patients with different personality styles. Their relevance for patients with concurrent alcoholism is limited, since such patients have been systematically excluded from Horowitz's studies, but they may be shown to be useful in future work.

More generally, psychotherapeutic approaches are believed to be helpful in the acute period of illness if they are focused, problem-oriented, and brief. Nonspecific psychotherapy is seen as not useful.[29] No empirical evidence is available to support these impressions, but they seem to be accepted as clinical guides. With the passage of time, the syndrome becomes increasingly difficult to treat, or even to diagnose, and prognosis is generally considered poor.[29,30]

Barbiturates and hypnotics have been used to reduce the anxiety of patients with post traumatic stress disorder, and chemically induced prolonged sleep and insulin were once thought to be useful. However, other psychopharmacological interventions have not been reported in the literature. Very recently, preliminary evidence has been generated by Hogben and Cornfield[30] which suggests that monoamine oxidase inhibitors are effective in treating this syndrome. They administered phenelzine to five treatment-refractory chronically ill patients with post traumatic stress disorder characterized by spontaneous panic attacks. All had failed to respond to previous trials with psychotherapy and other medication. The patients showed significant reduction of anxiety, agitation, and dysphoria. Most important, nightmares and flashbacks were eliminated for four of the five. Cornfield is planning a formal study of phenelzine and post traumatic stress disorder to confirm these promising results. It will be important to distinguish post traumatic stress disorder characterized by spontaneous panics from other syndromes.

Future Research

For all three of these psychiatric disorders, basic descriptive data are needed to assess the frequency and nature of their association with alcohol abuse. Epidemiological studies are required to determine the prevalence of each among alcoholic patients, their temporal relationship to onset of alcohol abuse or dependence, precursors of each, and interactions with regard to course and outcome of both the anxiety disorder and the alcohol problem. Although interesting psychotherapeutic and pharmacological strategies have been proposed for each syndrome in the presence of alcoholism, major research remains to be conducted to determine their efficacy for either condition.

The extensive background which has clearly established the therapeutic utility of tricyclic antidepressants in panic disorder leads us to conclude that controlled studies of tricyclics with panic-alcohol patients are indicated. Evidence for the utility of psychopharmacologic treatment in hysteroid dysphoria and post traumatic stress disorder is less robust but warrants further study in patients with these diagnoses who abuse alcohol.

References

1. *Diagnostic and Statistical Manual of Mental Disorders,* ed 3 (DSM III). Washington, DC, American Psychiatric Association, 1980.
2. Gorman J, Fyer A, Gliklich J, *et al*: Mitral value prolapse and panic disorders: Effects of imipramine, in Klein DF, Rabkin JG (eds): *Anxiety: New Research and Changing Conceptions.* New York, Raven, 1981.
3. Woodruff RA, Guze SB, Clayton PJ: Anxiety neurosis among psychiatric outpatients. *Compr Psychiat* 13:165–170, 1972.
4. Noyes R, Clancy J, Crowe R, *et al*: The familial prevalence of anxiety neurosis. *Arch Gen Psychiatry* 35:1057–1059, 1978.
5. Sims A: Dependence on alcohol and drugs following treatment for neurosis. *Br J Addict* 70:33–40, 1975.
6. Spitzer R, Williams J: Personal communication, 1980.
7. Mullaney JA, Trippett CJ: Alcohol dependence and phobias: Clinical description and relevance. *Brit J Psychiatry* 135:565–573, 1979.
8. Curlee J, Stern H: The fear of heights among alcoholics. *Bull Meninger Clinic* 37:615–623, 1973.
9. Klein DF, Fink M: Psychiatric reaction patterns to imipramine. *Am J Psychiatry* 119:432–438, 1962.
10. Klein DF: The importance of psychiatric diagnosis in prediction of clinical drug effects. *Arch Gen Psychiatry* 16:118–126, 1967.
11. Klein DF, Gittelman R, Quitkin F, *et al: Diagnosis and Drug Treatment of Psychiatric Disorders: Adults and Children.* Baltimore: Williams and Wilkins, 1980.
12. Zitrin CM, Klein DF, Woerner MG: Behavior therapy, supportive psychotherapy, imipramine and phobias. *Arch Gen Psychiatry* 35:307–316, 1978.

13. Sheehan DV, Ballenger J, Jacobsen G: Treatment of endogenous anxiety with phobic, hysterical and hypochondriacal symptoms. *Arch Gen Psychiatry* 37:51–59, 1980.
14. Tyrer P, Candy J, Kelly DA: A study of the clinical effects of phenelzine and placebo in the treatment of phobic anxiety. *Psychopharmacologia* 32:237–254, 1973.
15. Lipsedge JS, Hajjoff J, Huggins P, *et al*: The management of severe agoraphobia: A comparison of iproniazid and systematic desensitization. *Psychopharmacologia* 32:67–80, 1973.
16. Solyom L, Heseltine GFD, McClure DJ, *et al*: Behavior therapy versus drug therapy in the treatment of phobic neurosis. *Can Psychiat Assoc J* 18:25–31, 1973.
17. Quitkin FM, Rifkin A, Kaplan J, *et al*: Phobic anxiety syndrome complicated by drug dependence and addiction. *Arch Gen Psychiatry* 27:159–162, 1972.
18. Klein DF: Drug therapy as a means of syndromal identification and nosological revision, in Cole JO, Freedman AM, Friedhoff AJ (eds): *Psychopathology and Psychopharmacology*. Baltimore, Johns Hopkins University Press, 1973, p 143.
19. Liebowitz MR, Klein DF: Hysteroid dysphoria. *Psychiat Clinics of No Amer* 2:555–575, 1979.
20. Stone M: Assessing vulnerability to schizophrenia or manic depression in borderline states. *Schizophrenia Bull* 5:105–110, 1979.
21. Winokur G, Clayton P, Reich T: *Manic Depressive Illness*. St Louis, Mosby, 1969.
22. Logue JN: *Long-term Effects of a Major Natural Disaster: The Hurricane Agnes Flood in the Wyoming Valley in Pennsylvania, June, 1972*. Doctoral dissertation, Columbia University School of Public Health, New York, 1978.
23. Grinker K, Spiegel S: *Men Under Stress*. Philadelphia, Blakiston, 1945.
24. Hocking F: Extreme environmental stress and its significance for psychopathology. *Am J Psychotherapy* 24:4–26, 1970.
25. Horowitz MJ: *Stress Response Syndromes*. New York, Jason Aronson, 1976.
26. Lacoursiere RB, Godfrey KE, Ruby LM: Traumatic neurosis in the etiology of alcoholism: Viet Nam combat and other trauma. *Am J Psychiatry* 137:966–968, 1980.
27. Strange RE, Brown DE: Home from the war: A study of psychiatric problems in Viet Nam returnees. *Amer J Psychiatry* 127:488–492, 1970.
28. Horowitz MJ, Wilner N, Kaltreider N, *et al*: Signs and symptoms of post traumatic stress disorder. *Arch Gen Psychiatry* 37:85–92, 1980.
29. Van Putten TV, Emory WH: Traumatic neuroses in Vietnam returnees: A forgotten diagnosis? *Arch Gen Psychiatry* 29:695–698, 1973.
30. Hogben G, Cornfield RB: The treatment of traumatic war neurosis with phenelzine. *Arch Gen Psychiatry* 38:440–445, 1981.

CHAPTER 11

Psychiatric Aspects of Alcohol Intoxication, Withdrawal, and Organic Brain Syndromes

DONALD M. GALLANT, MD

Alcohol Intoxication

When a patient arrives in a physician's office or an emergency room with symptoms of slurred speech, difficulty with coordination, ataxia, loquaciousness, and difficulty with attention, there may be a natural tendency by the physician to attribute the patient's symptoms to alcohol intoxication. However, similar symptoms may be caused by certain neurological diseases such as multiple sclerosis, cerebellar dysfunction, or intoxication due to other sedative substances such as barbiturates or benzodiazepines. Metabolic diseases such as diabetes mellitus may also be associated with impairment of central nervous system function and subsequent development of the above signs and symptoms. Even if the diagnostic impression is supported by a relatively high blood level of alcohol, it would be wise for the physician to follow the patient carefully in order to be sure that these symptoms clear as the alcohol disappears from the blood. It should be emphasized that the alcohol intoxication may be masking underlying physical sequelae of alcoholism. A careful history and physical examination should evaluate the possibility of trauma.

Evidence of acne rosacea (dilation of vessels with thickening of skin) palmar erythema, spider nevi, cigarette burns, cheilitis, skin bruises, evidence of multiple trauma, and poor nutrition may all suggest past history of very heavy alcohol intake and thus contribute toward establishing a diagnosis.

DONALD M. GALLANT • Professor, Department of Psychiatry, Adjunct Professor of Pharmacology, Tulane University School of Medicine, New Orleans, Louisiana 70112.

If the patient is cooperative, careful inquiry into recent meals and amount of alcohol ingested may help the physician to formulate an educated guess about the present level of the blood alcohol. Food does inhibit alcohol absorption. If the patient has started his drinking less than one hour after his last heavy meal, the blood alcohol level should be somewhat modified as compared to drinking on an empty stomach.[1] The blood alcohol peaks within 30 minutes to three hours after rapid ingestion ceases. Each ounce of whiskey, glass of wine, or a 12-ounce bottle of beer raises the blood level by approximately 15 to 25 mg.

Severity of the symptoms of intoxication depends upon the rapidity of the blood alcohol level ascent and upon the peak level of blood alcohol concentration attained as well as the patient's acquired tolerance and the presence of other drugs. Sexual differences in absorption and metabolism of alcohol should also be considered in development of intoxication symptomatology. It has been demonstrated that women become more rapidly intoxicated than men, exhibiting an increase of blood levels between 35% to 45% higher than men, after receiving the same amount of alcohol per unit of weight, regardless of body build.[2] Peak levels of alcohol occur even more rapidly during the premenstrual phase with higher absorption rates at this time as compared to other phases of the menstrual cycle. It should be noted that oral contraceptives contain compounds such as estrogen that do inhibit the metabolism of alcohol, thus resulting in higher peak levels and more sustained blood levels.[3]

If the patient does not display typical signs and symptoms of alcohol intoxication, as detailed in Table I, at blood levels of 150 mg%, this display of very high tolerance indicates a strong possibility of alcohol dependence. If the blood alcohol level is 300 mg% and the patient is still walking around, the diagnosis of alcohol dependence can be confirmed. From a medical and legal viewpoint, it is essential for the physician to obtain a blood alcohol level because the unreliability of the alcoholic's history of alcohol consumption has been well established. In a study at a medical clinic associated with the Toronto Addiction Research Center, only 17% of the alcoholic patients in the clinic were honest about their drinking at all times; these data were confirmed by the evaluation of 24-hour urine collections for alcohol content prior to the day of clinical appointment.[4] The patients did not realize that their urine was being surveyed for the presence of alcohol. The denial mechanism utilized by the patient, who fools himself as well as the people around him, can be exaggerated in a most inappropriate manner when he is intoxicated, particularly as to the amount that he drank prior to the clinic visit.

The clinician should be particularly cautious with elderly people who become intoxicated more quickly because of lean body mass, decreased quantity of functioning organ tissue, and decreased efficiency of mitochondrial activity.

TABLE I. Signs and Symptoms of Alcohol Intoxication and Overdose

Signs	Symptoms	Diagnostic aids
Mild to moderate intoxication impaired attention poor motor coordi- nation dysmetria ataxia nystagmus slurred speech prolonged reaction time flushed face orthostatic hypotension hematemesis stupor	Mild to moderate intoxication alcohol on breath loquacity impaired judgment inappropriate behav- ioral responses inappropriate emotional responses euphoria dizziness blurred vision	In low dose intoxication, blood alcohol level is about 100 mg% or higher (if level is greater than 300 mg% and patient is alert and relatively well-coordinated, then this highly tolerant person may be an alcoholic and experience withdrawal symptoms as the blood level decreases).
Severe intoxication and overdose respiratory rate decreased bruises or scars from analgesia and lack of coordination shock coma	Severe intoxication irrational angry out- bursts with violent acts progressively sluggish responses to environ- mental stimuli "dry heaves"	In high dose coma, the blood level of alcohol should be greater than 300 mg%. Otherwise, the etiology of the coma may not be alcohol. Diabetic acidosis and hypoglyce-mia may be easily ruled out.

Management of Acute Alcohol Intoxication

In most cases of mild alcohol intoxication, it is essential for the physician to remember that his attitude will be most important in determining whether or not the patient follows up with therapy. The physician must show the patient that he cares, is concerned about the patient's welfare, is nonjudgmental, and genuine in his statements to the patient. Although the intoxicated patient may be revealing some of his innermost sober feelings, these feelings usually come out in an inappropriate manner while he is under the influence of alcohol. Any anger or defensiveness on the part of the physician will usually result in the patient's discontinuing efforts at follow-up therapy for his drinking problem. A firm but kind therapeutic approach offers the patient some confidence in developing a trusting relationship which is the key for future constructive efforts in follow-up treatment.

In more severe cases of alcohol intoxication, particularly in those individuals who have been on a poor diet with a resultant glycogen-depleted liver and impaired gluconeogenesis, hypoglycemia may be an additional medical problem. If the patient is semicomatose or comatose, immediate steps should be taken to sustain the airway, assure a regular respiratory rate, and maintain the circulatory system. Besides checking vital signs every 15 to 30 minutes, one must explore the possibility of occult bleeding and other causes of coma such as central nervous system disturbances. In those patients with very poor nutrition, severe pulmonary infection can occur with little increase in white blood cell count or temperature, indicating a deficit in the patient's immune response. Not only is the blood alcohol concentration useful as a diagnostic aid, but the osmolality may be of some help, for it is known that a blood alcohol concentration of 100 mg% increases the serum osmolality by 28 to 30 milliosmols per kg of water. If the osmolality is normal or only slightly increased, alcohol intoxication can be excluded as the cause of coma.[5] High serum osmolality correlates with high blood level of alcohol. Significant respiratory depression and death have occurred at concentrations as low as 400 mg%.[6]

In those patients who are comatose and are already showing impairment of respiration on admission, several emergency steps can be initiated while awaiting the results of the laboratory tests. In order to rule out severe hypoglycemia, 50 ml of 50% glucose solution can be given intravenously with 100 mg of thiamine. If the patient's skin shows needle marks indicative of narcotic drug use, the administration of naloxane in a dosage of 0.4 mg intravenously and repeated at two to three minute intervals two or three times may prove to be lifesaving and reverse ethanol-induced coma.

In those patients who are conscious and have had other causes of intoxicated behavior ruled out, medical observation and adequate nursing care should be sufficient. The patient should be placed on his side with the head down in order to avoid aspiration of vomitus. An infusion should not be started unless the patient is dehydrated from vomiting or diarrhea; routine use of infusions in this type of patient may offer more iatrogenic risks than benefits.

Another emergency procedure for the comatose patient with impaired respiration is the use of edrophonium (Tensilon) chloride, which is relatively safe but only rarely indicated. If the history of progressive muscle weakness and other indications of myasthenia are elicited from friends or family, the injection of edrophonium chloride at a dosage of 0.2 ml or 2 mg followed 45 seconds later with 0.8 ml or 8 mg of the drug will help to make the diagnosis and restore the respiratory rate to normal. The very short duration of action of this drug helps to avoid any serious pharmacologic side effects.

The use of gastric lavage and activated charcoal are not indicated on a routine basis unless the ingestion of alcohol has taken place shortly prior to the patient's admission to the emergency room. The rapid absorption of alcohol is a contraindication for using these procedures in a routine manner. However, if the blood level of alcohol is greater than 600 mg%, hemodialysis may then be useful in those patients with impaired liver function. The use of analeptics is of no value.

Alcohol Idiosyncratic Intoxication

The criteria for the diagnosis of this disorder stress the behavioral changes displayed by the patient while under the influence of alcohol and considered to be unusual or atypical behavior for him. Therefore, the lay diagnosis of "alcoholic blackout" and previous diagnosis of "pathological intoxication" belong in this category. The alcoholic blackout would be defined as an amnesic incident that occurs while the patient is drinking moderately or heavily and which he cannot recall when he sobers up. In obtaining carefully detailed histories, it is not unusual to find that the amnesic behavior was only routine nonsignificant speech or action which the patient cannot recall. However, those incidents in which the patient becomes assaultive or violent are so impressive to the interviewer that many physicians believe that the typical incident of an alcoholic blackout involves very peculiar or very unusual behavior. When one sees a patient during an alcoholic blackout, it is impossible to say whether or not this is an episode for which he or she will be amnesic the next day. In fact, some patients actually appear to act less intoxicated during some of these episodes. It should be emphasized that although the patient is responsible for attaining the state of intoxication in which this type of amnesic behavior occurs, he is not truly responsible for his actions or words during the actual incident. If the patient has had a previous history of violent behavior during an alcoholic blackout, (for example, pathological intoxication), he is much more likely to repeat this behavior during another blackout. Psychotic as well as violent behavior can occur during these blackouts. If the clinician is unaware of the history of alcohol intake, the patient can be misdiagnosed as a schizophrenic and placed on neuroleptic drugs which can further confuse the diagnosis and be potentially harmful for the patient. In those episodes of pathological intoxication when the patient shows dangerous behavior during his drinking episodes for which he is amnesic the next day, Maletsky showed that there is a very high incidence of abnormal EEGs in these patients during such periods of behavior.[7]

In an extensive evaluation of 220 alcoholics admitted to a treatment program, it was found that 43% had a history of psychotic symptomatology, usually during heavy alcohol or drug use and associated with prior history of antisocial problems or drug use.[8] Therefore, the severely abnormal episodic behavior often displayed by these patients during alcohol consumption can be confused with other neuropsychiatric diagnoses such as temporal lobe epilepsy, schizophrenia, and drug intoxication.

These abnormal behavioral reactions with alcohol can also be confused with phencyclidine (PCP) reactions. Complaints of analgesia, cerebellar dysfunction with ataxia and slurring of speech, nausea, and diaphoresis can all be seen with PCP intoxication as well as with alcohol intoxication. Therefore, careful elicitation of drug history as well as urine survey for phencyclidine may be necessary, particularly in those young intoxicated patients who come into the emergency room with very assaultive or suicidal behavior.

Management of Idiosyncratic Intoxication

As we mentioned before, it is sometimes quite difficult to realize when a patient is in the middle of an alcoholic blackout or pathological intoxication and thus not responsible for this actions at this time. As we have described it previously, the behavior, frequently routing and not significant, can at other times be violent and unpredictable. If the therapist senses that the patient is exhibiting symptoms of pathological intoxication, he should then regard the patient as dangerous and approach him as carefully as he would any other patient who was totally incompetent and potentially violent. The guidelines for this type of situation are:

1. One should never disagree with the patient about anything he says. An individual who is on the verge of an explosion can be set off by any discord in the environment.
2. One should use the voice and body movements as therapeutic tools. The voice should always be calm and slow, with a monotone and no sudden changes of pitch. The motor movements should be kept to a minimum and initiated in a very slow manner. Thus, both voice and movement should serve as calming instruments of therapy.
3. Although in most situations, one should call the patient by his or her title and last name out of respect for the person, in this type of precarious situation, it may be wise to find out the patient's first name and start using it in a calm, familiar, and friendly manner. The patient will, one hopes, be made to feel more comfortable by the familiar form of address.
4. In talking to the patient, one should always remember that there is little likelihood of violence while a dialogue is going on. At the same time, one must try to find out personal facts about the patient that have a positive affective charge to them, such as the names of one or two people to whom he feels closest and for whom he has positive feelings. If this type of information can be elicited, the next step is to attempt to get his permission to call them on the telephone in order to bring someone with a positive affective change to see him. The longer the conversation progresses, the less chance there is for violence. Additionally, having the patient verbalize about positive affective rela-

tionships in the past or talk to a close friend or relative on the phone may help bring him out of this amnesic episode by bringing back events that are familiar to him.

Alcohol Withdrawal Syndromes

Mild to Moderate Alcohol Withdrawal

Diagnostic criteria of this syndrome include such symptoms as gastro-intestinal distress, asthenia, anxiety, irritability, and autonomic hyperactivity. According to the third edition of the *Diagnostic Statistical Manual of Mental Disorders* (DSM–III), the patient should show at least one of these symptoms within the first 24–48 hours after cessation of reduction of heavy, prolonged ingestion of alcohol.[9] Other diagnoses which may resemble this syndrome are hypoglycemia, ketoacidosis, short-acting sedative withdrawal syndromes, and familial or essential tremor.

For the majority of patients displaying the syndrome of alcohol withdrawal, outpatient treatment can be sufficient and one need not resort to hospitalization. The blood alcohol can be used as one of the more reliable guidelines for making decisions about placing the patient on an alcohol withdrawal unit with specialized care or in a medical ward for more intensive treatment of severe withdrawal symptoms, or following the patient at home with proper supervision. For example, if the alcohol level is 150 to 200 mg% and the patient appears to be alert and not dysarthric, then the physician should be on guard about the possible appearance of withdrawal symptoms as the blood alcohol level decreases. In this type of patient, the tolerance for alcohol is far too high and suggests chronic alcohol abuse with an increased predisposition to develop withdrawal symptoms upon cessation of the alcohol.

In a study by Pattison, only 45 of 564 patients or 8% of acute alcohol outpatient admissions required hospitalization.[10] In another extensive study of alcohol detoxification by Whitfield, less than 10% required medical detoxification and the remainder of the 1,024 patients in the study received "non drug detoxification."[11] Seizures occurred in only 1%, hallucinations in 3.7%, and delirium tremens in less than 1%. However, 8% of the original sample of 1,114 subjects did require medical referral to a hospital emergency room for further evaluation. While Whitfield's treatment team was specially trained to deal with nondrug detoxification and instructed on how to "talk the patient down" and give him reality testing in a therapeutic manner, it is important to recognize that the use of benzodiazepines was required only in less than 10% of the entire patient population. It appears that most detoxification programs refer patients to inpatient facilities, where they are automatically placed on medication; this step makes it difficult eventually to withdraw them from the sedative hypnotics. If Pattison's and Whitfield's patient populations are representative of alcoholism populations in general, then it would not be an exaggeration to state that the majority of alcoholic patients should be able to withdraw from alcohol without the use of habituating minor tranquilizers.

Therapeutic management of acute withdrawal is not necessarily the first step in treatment. One may help the patient to titrate the decrease of alcohol with family aid and then change over to a short-acting hypnotic for sleep for the next five to seven days (eg, chloral hydrate). The use of muscle-relaxation exercises and even self-hypnosis may help the patient to decrease his discomfort as he goes through the process of a mild withdrawal stage. In this manner, one may be able to avoid the automatic pharmacologic approach used by some detoxification units in the place of psychologic management. Thiamine, 50 to 100 mg per day, in addition to multivitamins, may be of some help in replenishing the vitamin deficiency and certainly is quite safe to include in the therapeutic armamentarium of outpatient treatment. Shortly after the patient's blood alcohol reaches zero, disulfiram should be seriously considered unless there are definite medical contraindications.

The signs and symptoms of alcohol withdrawal are detailed in Table II. If the patient shows a combination of symptoms that suggests the withdrawal symptoms are causing too much discomfort, hydroxyzine or a benzodiazepine may be used on a temporary basis and administered by a relative or friend in order to be sure the patient does not misuse the medication. Of course, the more severe the symptoms and signs of withdrawal, the more difficulty the patient will experience in abstaining from alcohol and the more frequently he should be seen at the office. It is not unusual to have patients come in on a daily basis when they are started on disulfiram and to give them only enough tranquilizers to last until they return to the clinic the next day. Dependency-producing medication such as benzodiazepines should not be used for more than one to two weeks, for patients with problems of alcohol abuse are more likely to misuse these tranquilizers as well.

In those alcoholic patients displaying tremor, the physician must learn low to distinguish between the "alcoholic tremor" of withdrawal and the benign essential or familial tremor which is readily relieved by alcohol and seen frequently among alcoholics. In the latter case, the patient's drinking to relieve the tremor may have subsequently led to increased alcohol consumption. The benign essential tremor is rhythmic, usually at a rate of four to ten per second, and worsens with fatigue, extreme cold, and observation or social stress. The use of adrenergic blockers such as propranolol or metroprolol are most efficacious in treating this condition. It is not unusual to see an alcoholic patient who uses this essential tremor as one of the reasons for

TABLE II. Signs and Symptoms of Alcohol Withdrawal

Signs	Symptoms	Diagnostic aids

Mild to moderate signs
  malaise or weakness
  muscle tension
  tremor
  hyperreflexia
  elevated blood pres-
    sure
  tachycardia
  diaphoresis
hyperacuity of all sen-
  sory modalities
flushed face
	Mild to moderate symptoms
	  fluctuation of symptoms
	    during the course of a day
	  irritability
	  anxiety and agitation
	  overalertness
	  extreme fatigue
	  disturbance of sleep–wake-
	    fulness cycle
	  anorexia
	  vomiting
	  headache
	  diarrhea
	  expressions of strong crav-
	    ing of alcohol
		EEG showing bursts of high ampli-
		  tude slow waves with random
		  spikes
		electrolyte depletion
		hypoglycemia may be present
		association of high laboratory
		  values commonly found in alco-
		  holics (e.g. macrocytosis, ele-
		  vated levels of uric acid, SGPT,
		  GGPT, alkaline phosphatase,
		  bilirubin and triglycerides) with-
		  out any other known cause

Severe withdrawal signs
  respiratory alkalosis
    with hyperventila-
    tion
fever
grand mal seizures
	Severe withdrawal symptoms
	  incoherent speech
	global confusion with
	  clouding of consciousness
	illusions
	hallucinations with lack of
	insight	

increasing alcohol consumption show a most impressive positive personality change after the tremor has been inhibited by propranolol.

The use of antipsychotic agents or neuroleptic agents for either moderate or severe withdrawal is questionable, since these agents can lower the convulsive threshhold as well as potentiate orthostatic hypotension or cause atropine-like side effects which may be uncomfortable for the patient. Among the safer agents to use on a *temporary* basis are sedative antihistamines for sleep, paraldehyde, and benzodiazepines. If emesis occurs, then prochlorperazine, 10 mg subcutaneously, can be used to control it on a temporary basis. The oral dosage of chlordiazepoxide for the management of withdrawal symptoms should not have to exceed 200 mg daily. If a higher dosage is necessary, this usually means that moderate to severe withdrawal symptoms are developing and the patient should be placed in a detoxification unit or hospitalized. If the patient has a past history of convulsions during withdrawal from alcohol, then the drug of choice may be one of the benzodiazepines, since they do have anticonvulsive as well as sedative properties. In addition, with the oral administration of these agents, a peak blood level can be attained within four to seven hours, while it takes a longer period of time with phenytoin. However, as stressed by Whitfield,[11] reassurance and reality orientation are the basis of the therapeutic approach for withdrawal symtomatology.

The time required for the practicing physician to deal effectively with the alcoholic outpatient is not wasted because early adequate treatment may decrease the number of repeated visits to the office or hospital for recurrences of the alcoholism and its medical complications. While the treating psychiatrist should not assume total authoritative control of the patient, the need for abstinence during treatment has to be emphasized. Otherwise, the mental and social effects of continued drinking distort the evaluation of important aspects of the patient's life. While a patient continues to drink, it is impossible to evaluate how much of the patient's nervousness, depression, insomnia, impotence, domestic difficulty, and other psychological and social distress is exclusively a reflection of the excessive use of alcohol. It then becomes too confusing for the therapist to deal with the patient's underlying problem; at times therapy can become a farce if one allows the patient to continue arriving at the office with alcohol on his breath. If this behavior does continue, it may be necessary to institute inpatient detoxification even though the patient may only experience mild to moderate withdrawal symptoms. From a therapeutic viewpoint, it may be necessary to interrupt the self-destructive cycle of heavy drinking followed by withdrawal symptoms which are then followed by relief of these symptoms through resumption of alcohol intake. In an outpatient therapeutic relationship, the use of disulfiram may represent a symbol of the patient's commitment not only to abstinence but also to dealing with his psychiatric problems in a serious manner within the therapy setting.

Alcohol Withdrawal Delirium (Including the Diagnosis Formerly Known as Delirium Tremens)—Severe Withdrawal

Diagnostic criteria for alcohol withdrawal delirium include a clouding of consciousness, difficulty in sustaining attention, disorientation, and autonomic hyperactivity, with these symptoms occurring within the first several days after complete cessation of drinking or reduction of extremely heavy alcohol ingestion. With adequate treatment, these symptoms should disappear by the end of the first week.

Although other diagnoses can be confused with alcohol withdrawal delirium, a diagnostic problem arises when the history of alcohol intake is unknown and there is no family available to offer additional information. Such diagnosis as schizophrenia, schizophreniform disorder, other psychotic disorders, or dementia can be confused with this diagnosis if there is no history of alcohol intake. Several decades ago, the teaching in many medical schools emphasized the visual hallucinations as being predominant in delirium tremens, while auditory hallucinations were thought to be more common in schizophrenia. It should be noted that, in those years, many of the alcoholic patients came into detoxification units late in the course of their withdrawal syndrome, and thus the visual hallucinations were most impressive to the clinician and overshadowed the auditory hallucinations that frequently occur earlier in the course of the withdrawal syndrome. Studies such as the one by Goodwin et al[12] give a more objective view of the significance of hallucinations in various psychiatric disorders. In a study of specific hallucinatory experiences in 117 patients, no clinical significance could be attributed to the type of hallucinations reported by the patients. The following disorders were evaluated: alcohol withdrawal syndrome, primary affective disorders (bipolar and unipolar), acute and chronic schizophrenia, hysteria, senile brain disease, and drug-induced psychosis. Visual and auditory hallucinations were common in all these disorders and did not help to differentiate between any of these illnesses. The clinician has to be very much aware that the illusions and hallucinations which frequently occur in the alcohol withdrawal delirium as well as the previously mentioned diagnostic categories may be masking head trauma, space-occupying lesions, metabolic abnormalities, or even hypoxia associated with congestive heart failure in a person who has a diagnosis of alcoholism. In one study of patients presenting with this type of delirium, 13 patients referred to a psychiatric clinic in a delirious state after prolonged intoxication were found to have a chronic subdural hematoma.[13]

If the diagnosis of alcohol withdrawal delirium is correct, then immediate hospitalization is indicated, for the diagnosis infers that the patient is unable to care for himself and is seriously ill. The use of benzodiazepines on a temporary basis may be of considerable help in those alcoholics who have experienced recent alcohol withdrawal convulsions because these compounds possess anticonvulsant activity as well as sedative properties. If the patient is suspected of having a moderate amount of liver damage, the most appropriate benzodiazepine may be oxazepam, which does not require hydroxylation by the liver and therefore does not accumulate. Chlordiazepoxide, diazepam, and chlorazepate are all metabolized in the liver and thus can accumulate in the patient who has a fair degree of liver damage, particularly since they do have a relatively long half-life. Hydroxyzine is a safer sedative from the viewpoint of dependence, but its anticholinergic activity may confuse the patient if the drug is administered in high dosages. It also has no anticonvulsant properties. The adequate use of sedative-hypnotic therapy for the severe withdrawal symptoms, good nursing care, absence of restraints, a well-lighted room, and the use of thiamine and multivitamins can help to alleviate the symptomatology. As we mentioned above, the use of neuroleptics or antipsychotic agents is not suitable for the treatment of delirium tremens, and some patients have been reported to develop prolonged unconsciousness following the use of these medications.[14] These compounds can also potentiate seizure activity, while the benzodiazepines can control and prevent the development of withdrawal seizures.[15] However, there is no indication for the use of intramuscular benzodiazepines because they are absorbed very poorly following intramuscular injection. For example, 50 mg of oral chlordiazepoxide results within two hours after ingestion in plasma levels which are significantly higher than those following a 50 mg intramuscular dose administered to an abstinent alcoholic subject.[16] If the patient is vomiting profusely and unable to tolerate oral medication, then the use of an intravenous benzodiazepine such as diazepam would be indicated. It should be stressed that intravenous infusions should only be used in patients who are definitely dehydrated from excessive vomiting or diarrhea. Even in these cases, the clinician has to be quite careful with those glycogen-depleted patients who might be thiamine-deficient, for the patient may be converted to Wernicke's encephalopathy by glucose infusion.

For those patients displaying classical symptoms of the early phase of withdrawal such as hyperreflexia, vomiting, diarrhea, blood pressure and pulse increase, diaphoresis, asthenia, and tremor, institution of immedate medical treatment is indicated. Without adequate therapy, the second phase of delirium tremens may be severe and appear on the third or fourth day after abstinence.[17] The latter phase manifests itself with motor and autonomic hyperactivity, fever, and disorientation with possible hallucinations and even development of grand mal seizures. The onset of this phase is more likely to occur among those patients who have other medical complications such as infectious process and/or poor nutrition.

One very reliable indicator of the appearance of delirium tremens or severe withdrawal symptoms is the potassium level.[18] A study of 37 chronic alcoholics displaying no evidence of gross cirrhosis or diabetes and no alkalosis, who had been well fed for one to two days before the appearance of delirium tremens, showed a continuing decrease in serum potassium with a resultant typokalemia in all of the 26 patients who proceeded to develop delirium tremens. The decrease in potassium level was observed in the first several hours to one day before the appearance of delirium tremens. None of the 111 patients whose serum potassium remained unchanged or increased developed delirium tremens. The decrease in serum potassium was not associated with any other variation in serum electrolytes or acid–base balance. In two patients, potassium infusion did not inhibit the development of delirium tremens, and in six patients who were evaluated for urine potassium the level of potassium excretion did not change. Therefore, the apparent change in serum potassium was related to an intracellular shift. Serum magnesium levels and measures of other electrolytes showed no relationship with the onset or clinical severity of delirium tremens.[18,19] The value of measuring serum potassium levels twice daily in those patients newly admitted to detoxification units appears to be greater than evaluation of any other laboratory tests in predicting the severity of the withdrawal phase.

The dosage range of the benzodiazepines should vary with the duration and intensity of the alcohol consumption prior to withdrawal, the weight of the patient, and other pharmacokinetic variables if the data are available. In mild to moderate cases of the alcohol withdrawal syndrome without delirium, the dosage of oxazepam may vary from 15 mg QID to 30 mg QID, or a dosage of chlordiazepoxide may vary from 25 mg QID to 50 mg QID. In those severe cases of the alcohol withdrawal syndrome with delirium, a dosage of oxazepam as high as 45 mg QID may be needed, and the dosage of chlordiazepoxide may have to be as much as 100 mg or 150 mg QID. However, it is extremely important to decrease and discontinue the benzodiazepine agent prior to discharge from the hospital. It has been our experience that those patients discharged on benzodiazepines are more likely either to become habituated to the medication or else to return to alcohol. An interesting analogy of this experience has been reported as occurring in mice. After chronic involuntary administration of alcohol, mice have been shown to have an increased tendency to continue self-administration of the alcohol when offered free choice between alcohol and tap water.[20] Diazepam administered during the period of withdrawal served to maintain the alcohol self-administration. Without diazepam, the tendency to self-administration of alcohol returned to control levels. Thus, one sees similar examples in mice and human subjects concerning the return to alcohol consumption after using diazepam as a means of withdrawal.

There are many patients who abuse habituating drugs in association with alcohol. The combined alcohol–barbiturate patient presents an additional medication problem withdrawal since he is more likely to have seizures. A fairly reliable rule of thumb in calculating the dosage of medication used during withdrawal for this type of patient is substitution of 15 mg of phenobarbital for each ounce of 100 proof alcohol. Administration of 200 mg of pentobarbital may help the physician determine the extent of the addiciton. The appearance of ataxia with slurred speech at this dose suggests that the patient is not severely physically dependent and should not require too large a dosage of the long-acting barbiturates for withdrawal purposes.[21]

Although propranolol has been used to decrease the clinical manifestations of the alcohol withdrawal syndrome, inhibiting delirium tremens and modifying the blood pressure increase, the clinician should proceed cautiously with the use of this drug, for it may potentiate the hypoglycemia that can occur within the first 36 hours after ingestion of large amounts of alcohol by malnourished alcoholics.[22] Without a specific negative history of asthma, propranolol should not be administered to a severely ill patient.

The possible biochemical transition between alcohol addiction and narcotic addiction has been demonstrated in a most interesting manner.[23] Nalorphine administration during alcohol ingestion in alcoholic patients produced alcohol withdrawal symptoms of anorexia, tremor, disorientation, insomnia, and weakness; similar symptoms were seen in these patients after discontinuation of alcohol following two weeks of constant ingestion.[23] These data suggested that an accumulation of morphine-like compounds may play a role in the mediation of alcohol withdrawal symptoms in chronic alcoholic patients, despite the fact that the withdrawal symptoms following nalorphine administration were more typical of alcohol withdrawal than narcotic withdrawal symptomatology.

Alcohol Hallucinosis

Alcohol hallucinosis can be a very confusing diagnosis if there is no history of alcohol intake and no family available to give a history. The patient will usually show an affect that correlates with the type of hallucinations and there is no clouding of consciousness as in delirium tremens syndrome. These symptoms may be quite dramatic and the patient can be misdiagnosed as a schizophrenic if there is no adequate history available, which is frequently the case in the hospital emergency room. An evaluation of the hallucinations of functional psychotics and alcoholics found only a higher incidence of auditory and taste hallucinations in the functional group.[24] In regard to visual, olfactory, tactile, and sexual aspects of the hallucinatory material, there were no significant differences in the two groups.

Usually, the onset of this type of withdrawal syndrome occurs only after many years of heavy drinking; therefore, the average age of onset is approximately 40. This diagnosis cannot be applied to those individuals who have had prior psychotic episodes without any relationship to alcohol or drug intake. The hallucinatory content can be accompanied to severe paranoid delusions with the voices either discussing the patient in the third person or else talking directly to him. However, even when the patient is displaying paranoid delusions as well as hallucinations, the sensorium still has to be clear in relation to orientation for one to make a definitive diagnosis.

The appearance of these symptoms is due solely to the phenomenon of alcohol withdrawal and should not persist beyond two weeks. Therefore, the use of neuroleptics is not indicated, as it will only confuse the diagnostic problem. The appearance of extrapyramidal side effects with masked facies secondary to neuroleptic drug administration can only result in the patient's appearing even more "schizophrenic" to the interviewer. Temporary sedation may be necessary, but follow-up evaluation of these patients does not show any evidence of a trend toward development of a chronic hallucinatory process.

The Protracted Withdrawal Syndrome

While the protracted withdrawal syndrome is not listed in DSM–III (g), it has been adequately described in the literature.[25] Symptoms attributable to the protracted withdrawal syndrome are such physiological variations as respiratory irregularity, labile blood pressure and pulse, impairment of slow wave sleep, decrease in cold-stress response, persistence of tolerance to sedative effects, and tremor. Subjective complaints of spontaneous anxiety, depression episodes for no reason, and even transient psychotic reactions have been reported in relation to this syndrome, which apparently persists in some patients after the acute withdrawal syndrome has terminated. Biochemical changes including diminished tryptamine metabolism, lowered norepinephrine, and a decrease in testosterone and growth hormone response have been reported. This syndrome has been described as lasting anywhere from one month to more than one year. To diagnose this syndrome, the therapist should ascertain that the patient has not had a combination of these symptoms prior to alcohol abstinence. No other metabolic, physiological, or psychological cause for these behavioral and emotional abnormalities should be apparent other than the abstinence from alcohol.

It does appear that the syndromes of mild to moderate acute withdrawal, as well as those of severe withdrawal (see Table II), can gradually blend into the protracted withdrawal syndrome. It has been shown that the drug-free alcoholic tested at 7 days, 17 days, and 21 days after the last drink exhibited very little improvement in neuropsychological testing of cognitive performance.[26] The therapist should, therefore, move more slowly in therapy with such patients; abrupt confrontation therapy should be avoided until cognitive abilities show maximal improvement. Instead, stress should be placed on the approaches that are used in developing a trusting relationship with the patient at this stage.

In addition to the physiologic and behavior changes already described, the patient shows an increased irritability and impatience with family members and friends. He often complains of fatigue and lower stress tolerance. Some patients can panic and believe they are slipping back and may suddenly resort to the use of alcohol in an attempt to alleviate these symptoms. Complaints of emotional lability are also not unusual.[27] Forgetfulness occurs with periods of loss of concentration, and minor problems become major crises. There is a high level of distractibility, and the patient may be unconsciously setting himself up for return to alcohol because of these symptoms. As Budenz[27] has stated, the patient says to himself "Is this what life is going to be without alcohol?"

A fully detailed explanation to the patient, by helping him to understand what these symptoms represent and realize that they may be a normal part of the withdrawal phase of alcohol, can thus help him temporarily to accommodate to the discomfort and maintain his abstinence. Premature use of psychopharmacologic agents during this phase can result in the patient's becoming psychologically dependent on these drugs. In addition, use of the psychopharmacologic agents during these periods may cause uncomfortable reactions such as anticholinergic or sedative side effects which may further confuse the patient. Full explanation of the possibility of protracted withdrawal to both the patient and the family may help psychologically to alleviate some of these symptoms and enable the family to assist the patient in a more knowledgeable manner. It can also help to decrease the anxiety of the unknown and aid the patient in surviving and surmounting the symptoms of this syndrome. It is important to emphasize that the emotional and physical reactions during this phase are not unusual and that the patient will do well as long as he realizes that these symptoms are not a sign of relapse or of psychological illness. While antianxiety agents may be helpful during the acute phase of the withdrawal syndrome, the use of psychopharmacologic agents during this phase of abstinence is rarely indicated except for the use of antidepressant medication in those patients with a known history of affective illness who are undergoing a recurrent episode at this time.

The help of Alcoholics Anonymous (AA) can be essential at this time. AA uses the phrase the "dry drunk" to refer to some of these symptoms. Inclusion of the spouse in married couples group therapy,[28] as well as in Al-Anon, is crucial during this phase. It is all-important for the spouse and family to understand the implication of the symptoms and to be in a position to help the patient modify them. The ultimate goal of therapy is to learn how to enjoy life while sober and how to increase one's own sense of self-worth or self-respect. Volunteer and other community activities may be just as important as AA and therapeutic counseling. Abstinence must be regarded as only the first step in treatment, and the patient should understand that his initial sobriety now allows him to make positive changes in his life while he simultaneously sees his problem more clearly.

As we noted earlier, psychopharmacologic agents, particularly the benzodiazepines, have no place in the treatment of alcoholic anxiety or the anxiety seen in the protracted withdrawal syndrome. In addition to the data from mice in the study by Deutsch and Walton,[20] which indicated that in mice diazepam administration during alcohol withdrawal may lead back to subsequent preference to alcohol over water, there is even more disturbing data about the benzodiazepines in the literature. In the study of chronic pain patients, using the Wechsler Adult Intelligence Scale (WAIS), the memory quoteint, and Bender–Gestalt, patients using benzodiazepines alone demonstrated alterations of cognitive function.[29] These patients were compared with patients receiving narcotics alone and a nonmedicated group. The latter two groups did not show cognitive impairment on the previously mentioned tests. The cortical effects of these benzodiazepine compounds emphasize the importance of a recent suggestion by the Food and Drug Administration that the benzodiazepines be limited to short-term use. As we noted in the description of the protracted withdrawal syndrome, these patients already have difficulty with anxiety, depression, distractibility, and attention span as well as certain physiological abnormalities. Increasing the problems of attention span by impairing cognition via benzodiazepines can only hinder the patient's attempts to rehabilitate himself in therapy.

Organic Mental Disorders

The ability of alcohol to induce semipermanent and permanent organic mental changes is clearly demonstrated in the study by Lee and his associates.[30] In this neurophysiologic evaluation of 37 alcoholic patients, all of them less than 35 years of age, drinking a minimum of 50 gm of alcohol daily for the previous year and abstinent for four weeks prior to testing, the results showed that the prevalence of brain damage was far greater than liver damage; 59% were intellectually impaired and only 19% had cirrhosis by biopsy. At times, routine psychological testing will not detect the early organic mental changes. More discrete testing (eg, the Halstead Category Subtest) will show impairment on these more demanding tests, even though alcoholics without memory complaints may not differ from controls on standard clinical memory tests.[31] Alcoholics who complain of memory deficits will be more impaired on both the standard and more specific memory tests, overlapping the performance of the more severely impaired Korsakoff patients, thus showing evidence for continuum of impairment from chronic alcoholism to the full Korsakoff syndrome.[32]

Dementia Associated with Alcoholism

The differential diagnosis of this disorder is Alzheimer disease, alcohol amnestic disorder (which does not include loss of intellectual abilities which interfere with social and occupational functioning), and chronic subdural hematoma which has been frequently misdiagnosed as chronic dementia as well as acute mental disorder.[13] The state of consciousness is not clouded in this chronic organic mental disorder. The prognosis of alcoholic dementia is obviously better than that of Alzheimer disease, which is one of progressive deterioration, and unlike Alzheimer's, this syndrome does not include aphasia. In addition, functioning deficit is somewhat more specific, with constructional difficulty in drawing, stick design, copying geometric designs, and behavioral disturbances, in addition to moderately severe amnesia. If the alcoholic dementia patient is able to maintain abstinence, it is not unusual to see improvement occurring as late as six to 12 months after he has initiated his sobriety. The same observations are valid for Korsakoff syndrome, which is a more circumscribed illness, structually and functionally, and less incapacitating, since the remaining intellectual functions are relatively intact except for memory changes.

Wernicke encephalopathy, also included under dementia associated with alcoholism in DSM–III, appears to be associated with progressive degeneration, particularly in the periventricular area of the brain. Wernicke encephalopathy is a diagnosis that may be made only at autopsy.[33] In an autopsy review at a large hospital in Perth, Austrialia, 1.7% of all autopsies showed Wernicke encephalopathy to be present. Of the 51 patients with this disease at death, 45 were alcoholics and only 7 had been diagnosed as alcoholics prior to death. Many of the patients died suddenly as a result of hemorrhage into the brain stem, involving the cardiac and respiratory nuclei. Cerebral atrophy and ventricular dilatation were commonly associated with the autopsy findings. One major recommendation resulting from the data of this study was the routine use of large dosages of prophylactic thiamine in alcoholic patients, particularly those with clinical evidence of cerebral damage. Recent research into the etiology of the Wernicke–Korsakoff syndrome has indicated that thiamine pyrophosphatase (TPP)-dependent tranketalase activity may be decreased in those patients who develop the syndrome.[34] Transketalase activity was evaluated in five patients with this illness; four of them showed a low transketalase activity in the blood cells even in the presence of an excess of TPP. It was suggested that some alcoholics may have more of a genetic-metabolic tendency than others for the development of the Wernicke–Korsakoff syndrome.

Alcohol Amnestic Disorder

The diagnoses that must be considered in the differential diagnoses of alcohol amnestic disorder are delirium of metabolic of other causes, dementia of the Alzheimer type, and discrete cerebral vascular lesions secondary to thrombotic episodes. This syndrome is a result of circumscribed neuropsychiatric symptomatology characterized by anterograde and retrograde amnesia, with fairly good preservation of other intellectual abilities. In this category is the former diagnosis known as Korsakoff syndrome, which is characterized by an anterograde amnesic deficit greater than retrograde amnesia. If the patient is using a great deal of denial about his drinking problem or other problems prior to the onset of this discrete neurophysiological dysfunction, he may then tend to deny his memory defects in a rather pathetic way. For example, he may make an inappropriate guess about the month or year to try to cover up his memory deficit. While trauma and anoxia as well as cerebral vascular accidents can cause this type of syndrome, the most common cause in alcoholism. The major pathology appears to be in the diencephalon or mesial temporal structures. There is no clouding of consciousness as in delirium and intoxication and no general loss of intellectual abilities as in Alzheimer disease. There is no definite constructional dysfunction as noted in dementia associated and alcoholism.

Management of Organic Mental Disorders Associated with Alcoholism

Although the brain damage that is associated with alcoholism does resemble premature aging of adaptive abilities, the alcohol-induced atrophy may be a reversible process that is associated with a normalization of functional impairment with abstinence.[35] Tests that may detect long-term residual central nervous system damage after 12 months of abstinence are the Trail Making Test and Block Design of the WAIS.[36]

It is important to realize that approximately 35% to 50% of alcoholics in different rehabilitation settings show demonstrable neuropsychological impairment on the previously mentioned tests as well as on the Halstead–Reitan Category Subtest and the Wisconsin Scoring Test. The degree of impairment appears to be associated with the duration of drinking history.[36,37]

Realizing the nature and degree of impairment can help the therapist to establish realistic guidelines and goals for the patient, thus avoiding early failure in treatment. At this time, the type of neuropsychological impairment in the dementias associated with alcoholism as measured by such tests as the Halstead Category Subtest and Picture Arrangement indicate a deficit in ability to adapt to new situations as well as new abstraction problems. Therefore, vocational rehabilitation and other aspects of therapeutic guidance should not involve any marked departure from the former occupation or social habits of the patient.

The types of brain damage described under the alcoholic dementias are more widespread than generally thought. In an evaluation of the extent of alcoholic brain damage in Ireland, Draper estimated that of approximately 6,000 alcoholic admissions to Irish psychiatric hospitals each year, 2,000 or one third have brain damage.[38] If this one-third figure were applied to United States psychiatric hospitals, then more than 10% of all admissions (33% of all psychiatric admissions are for alcoholism) to these hospitals each year would have neuropsychological impairment due to alcohol abuse. Draper has described such patients who remain untreated:

> Even when sober and indeed when abstinent, these cases will be responsible for more traffic accidents, more personal injury, more industrial accidents, poorer work performance, especially on skilled tasks or problem solving, than their non-damaged colleagues.

Early brain damage has to be recognized by the physician and the family and treated appropriately, or else relapse will almost certainly occur as a result of impaired judgment.

An invaluable part of treatment of the organic mental disorder is helping the patient and his family to recognize the problem and meaning of alcohol-induced brain damage. It is important for the patient and the family to realize that there is a possibility that many of the organic mental changes are reversible with time, abstinence, and good nutrition. It is essential to give them an optimistic viewpoint and appropriate instructions on how to manage the daily behavior of the patient while he is waiting for some of the organic symptoms to resolve. Short training sessions concentrating on visual-motor coordination with appropriate exercises and attention span can be performed on a daily basis. Since the patient does have problems with attention span, these sessions should probably not last more than thirty minutes at any one interval. They can be repeated twice daily. Abstract thinking tasks such as creating three-dimensional figures and abstracting from categories should also be part of these training sessions. For memory tasks, the use of mnemonics can be a most useful technique for those patients displaying moderate to marked memory impairment. Utilizing these procedures in association with developing routine habits for the patient has proved to be most useful. We encourage the patient to get out of bed at the same time every day, eat his meals at the same time every day, and try to stay with the same schedule, including sleep time, on a daily basis. In addition, we have the patient keep a little notebook in his shirt pocket with time of his appointments for that day, times for phone calls, times for other types of social engagements, and professional or work schedules. The patient utilizes these notes to compensate for his short-term memory deficit, which is the major problem in most of our patients with alcohol-induced brain damage when they are admitted to our rehabilitation program. We had one case of an outstanding land-lease lawyer who was involved in many important oil exploration contracts in south Louisiana. Despite the fact that the combination of alcoholism and diabetes had seriously interferred with his recent memory, by the use of note-taking habits developed in our training sessions he was still able to maintain a very large and profitable law practice after discharge from the alcoholism rehabilitation unit. His knowledge of the law, which he had acquired many years before and had practiced over and over again in courtroom settings, still enabled him to be one of the most skillful lawyers in the state of Louisiana, despite the fact that he could not remember to whom he talked on the telephone one hour before. On a 12-month follow-up with this man, his recent memory impairment showed marked improvement and he was functioning at an even higher capacity. It is essential to emphasize to the patient and the family that in a significant number of these alcohol-induced brain damaged cases the prognosis can be quite good, and perhaps it may be just as important to emphasize this fact to the treating physician.

References

1. Lin Y-J, Weidler DJ, Garg DC, *et al*: Effects of solid food on blood levels of alcohol in man. *Res Commun Chem Path N Y* 13:713–722, 1976.
2. Jones BM, Jones MK: Alcohol effects in women during the menstrual cycle. *Ann N Y Acad Sci,* 1975, pp 576–587.
3. Hatcher R, Jones BM: Inhibition of alcohol dehydrogenase with estrogen. *Alc Tech Rep* 6:39–41, 1977.
4. Orrego H, Blake JE, Blendis LM, *et al*: Reliability of assessment of alçohol intake based on personal interviews in a liver clinic. *Lancet* Dec 22:1354–1356, 1979.
5. Redetzki HM: Ethanol intoxication, in Remack BH, Temple AR (eds): *Management of the Poisoned Patient*. Princeton NJ, Science Press, 1977.
6. Sellers EM, Kalant H: Alcohol intoxication and withdrawal. *New Eng J Med* 294:757–762, 1976.
7. Maletzky BM: The alcohol provocation test. *J Clin Psychiatry* 39:407–411, 1978.
8. Schuckit MA: *The history of psychotic symptoms in alcoholics.* Paper presented at the Annual Meeting of the American Psychiatric Association in San Francisco, Calif., May 3–9, 1980.
9. Diagnostic and Statistical Manual of Mental Disorders, ed 3 (DSM–III). Washington, DC, American Psychiatric Association, 1980.
10. Pattison ME: Management of alcoholism in medical practice. *Med Clinic N Am* 61:797–809, 1977.
11. Whitfield CL, Thompson G, Lamb H, *et al*: Detoxification of 1,024 alcoholic patients without psychoactive drugs. *JAMA* 239:1409–1410, 1978.
12. Goodwin DW, Alderson P, Rosenthal R: Clinical significance of hallucinations in psychiatric disorders. *Arch Gen Psychiatry* 24:76–80, 1971.
13. Reisner H: Das chronische subdurale Hämatom-Pachymeningeosis haemorrhagica interna. *Nervenarzt* 50:74–78, 1979.
14. Holzback E, Buhler KE: Die Behandlung des Delirium tremens mit Haldol. (Treatment of delirium tremens with haloperidol). *Nervenarzt* 49:405–409, 1978.
15. Guerrero-Figueroa R, Rye MM, Gallant DM, *et al*: Electrographic and behavioral effects of diazepam during alcohol withdrawal stage in cats. *Neuropharmacology* 9:143–150, 1970.
16. Perry PP, Wilding DC, Fowler RC: Absorption of oral and intramuscular chlordiazepoxide by alcoholics. *Clin Pharmacol Ther* 23:535–541, 1978.
17. Gessner PK: Drug therapy of the alcohol withdrawal system, in Majchrowicz E, Noble EP: *Biochemistry and Pharmacology of Ethanol*. New York, Plenum Press, 1979, vol 2.
18. Wadstein J, Skude G: Does hypokalemia precede delirium tremens? *Lancet* Sept 9:549–550, 1978.
19. Majumdar SK: Serum magnesium in delirium tremens. *Am J Psychiatry* 136:1343, 1979.
20. Deutsch JA, Walton NY: Diazepam maintenance of alcohol preference during alcohol withdrawal. *Science* 198:307–309, 1977.
21. Wesson DR, Smith DE: A conceptual approach to detoxification. *J Psychedel Drugs* 6:161–168, 1974.
22. Majumdar SK: Danger of using beta-adrenergic antagonists in the management of withdrawal reactions in chronic alcoholics. *Brig J Alc Alcoholism* 14:127–128, 1979.
23. Markley HG, Mazey E: Induction of alcohol withdrawal symptoms by nalorphine in chronic alcohol patients. *Int J Addict* 13:395–402, 1978.
24. Deiker T, Chambers HE: Structure and content of hallucinations in alcohol withdrawal and functional psychosis. *J Stud Alcohol* 39:1831–1840, 1978.
25. Kissin B: Biological investigations in alcohol research. *J Stud Alcohol* Nov 1979 supp, pp 146–181.

26. Eckardt MJ, Parker ES, Noble EP: Changes in neuropsychological performance during treatment for alcoholism. *Biol Psychiatry* 14:943–954, 1979.
27. Budenz DT: *Relapse to Alcohol/Drug Addiction.* Middleton Wis, Progressive Lit, 1979.
28. Gallant DM, Rich A, Bey E, *et al*: Group psychotherapy with married couples: A successful technique in New Orleans alcoholism clinic patients. *J La State Med Soc* 122:41–44, 1970.
29. Hendler W, Cimini C, Terrence MA: A comparison of cognitive impairment due to benzodiazepines and to narcotics. *Am J Psychiatry* 137:828–830, 1980.
30. Lee K, Moller L, Hardt F: Alcohol-induced brain damage and liver damage in young males. *Lancet* Oct 13:759–762, 1979.
31. Ryan C, Butters N: Further evidence for a continuum of impairment encompassing male alcoholic Korsakoff patients and chronic alcoholic men. *Alcoholism Clin and Exp Res* 4:190–198, 1980.
32. Knox WJ: Objective psychological measurements and alcoholism: Survey of the literature 1973. *Psychol Rep* 42:439–480, 1978.
33. Harper C: Wernicke's encephalopathy: A more common disease that realized: A neuropathological study of 51 cases. *J Neurol Neurosurg Psychiatry* 42:226–231, 1979.
34. Blass JP, Gibson GE: Genetic factors in Wernicke-Korsakoff syndrome. *Alcoholism Clin Exp Res* 3:126–134, 1979.
35. Epstein PS, Pisani VD, Fawcett JA: Alcoholism and cerebral atrophy. *Alcoholism Clin Exp Res* 1:61–65, 1977.
36. Parsons OA: Neuropsychological deficits in alcoholics: Facts and fiction. *Alcoholism Clin and Exp Res* 1:51–56, 1977.
37. Smith JW, Burt DW, Chapman RF: Intelligence and brain damage in alcoholics. *Q J Stud Alcohol* 34:414–422, 1973.
38. Draper RJ: The extent of alcoholic brain damage in the Republic of Ireland. *J Irish Med Assoc* 71:356–360, 1978.

CHAPTER 12

Alcohol and Adolescent Psychopathology

ROBERT B. MILLMAN, MD, and ELIZABETH T. KHURI, MD

Most people begin drinking alcohol during the adolescent years and, just as their parents do, use and abuse alcohol more than any other psychoactive drug. Most of them do not get into trouble, and the alcohol use may be considered appropriate for their age and sociocultural milieu. At the same time, the alcohol use does have profound impact on many young people, and behavior patterns are often developed that will be destructive in later years.[1,2]

It is during these years that individuals progress from the safety and insularity of childhood to an appreciation of their relationship to an adult world, with its attendant pleasures, pain, and responsibilities. It is a time of intense change and turmoil occurring incident to unique biological, psychological, cultural, and economic realities. Young people lack an adult indentity and often feel powerless. Few believe that they will measure up to the demands of society, and many have a realistic and profound dread of the future. Whereas testing and experimentation are critical elements in a young person's search to discover himself, the rules of behavior remain those of the adult society, with curiosity, spontaneity, and initiative frequently mistaken for aggressiveness or impulsiveness. The family, the educational system, and other societal institutions are often perceived as unresponsive or hostile.[3-5]

Their sense of themselves depends in part upon peer affiliation and acceptance. They need to compare what they think and feel they are to what they seem to be in the eyes of others, although many of them do not have the necessary confidence or experience to develop productive relationships.[4] It is a period of emotional upheaval marked by intense yearnings for approval and often a wish for an idealized supportive relationship. Narcissistic crises

ROBERT B. MILLMAN • Clinical Professor of Public Health, Associate Professor of Clinical Psychiatry, Cornell University Medical College, New York, New York 10021. ELIZABETH T. KHURI • Clinical Associate Professor of Public Health, Cornell University Medical College, New York, New York 10021.

commonly occur, in which self-esteem is severely impaired and overwhelming feelings of despair, shame, or rage are experienced.[6,7] Early sexual activity is frequently undertaken; yet many of these experiences are found to be unsatisfactory or a source of intense anxiety and further demoralization by these frightened and unprepared young people.[8]

The problems of being young are further compounded by poverty or minority-group status. Families are often disrupted and legitimately successful adult role models may be unknown or distant. In fact, role models are often drawn from criminal or alcohol-abusing sectors.[5] Many of these youngsters, particularly those who live in inner-city ghettos, are intelligent, sophisticated observers of people and situations; they have often acquired a remarkable array of survival skills on the street.[9] At the same time, they are unable to cope with the educational system and find classes boring, irrelevant, or demeaning. They have few skills that are appreciated by society, and a sense of resentment, hopelessness, and inevitable failure often results.[3–5,10]

In this context, the inability of some young people to focus on long-range goals, their desire for immediate gratification, and their lack of appreciation for the consequences of behavior are not surprising. Drinking alcohol or taking other psychoactive drugs remains one of the few pleasurable options for many adolescents; it may be a predictable, reliable method to enhance or punctuate an otherwise unrewarding life. The youthful alcohol user may obtain peer acceptance and a pharmacological effect that relieves tension and anxiety and enhances self-esteem.[8,11,12]

Patterns of Abuse

Researchers, funding agencies, and treatment personnel tend to be parochial in their concerns. They are interested in alcohol or in other drugs, rarely both. Patients, on the other hand, and adolescents in particular, are less insular in their interests; they take both alcohol and other psychoactive substances. In contrast to adults, for whom sociocultural factors may limit substance use to alcohol, young people often view alcohol as one of the depressants to be used in varying combinations with other drugs.[8]

Accurate assessment of alcohol and other drug use patterns among adolescents is difficult, given the stigmatized or illegal nature of the phenomena, the marked cultural and geographical variation, and the rapidity of change.[13,14] Since many surveys are school-sponsored, responses will be biased by attitudes toward the school as well as by the fact that many students do not attend school regularly, often for alcohol- or drug-related reasons.[15,16] An additional problem devolves from the general conceptual difficulty of defining adolescence. The age range of some surveys includes only people between the ages of 14 and 18 years; others include all who fall in the 12- to 20-

year range.[17] Many surveys do not sufficiently distinguish between the intermittent, controlled use of alcohol and other drugs and more compulsive abuse syndromes.[18] It is also likely that some surveys exaggerate the prevalence or severity of drug-taking behaviors to emphasize the need for expansion of research and treatment programs. Despite these limitations of the data, it is possible to outline some of the broad trends in adolescent alcohol use patterns.

Young people typically begin drinking alcohol at age 13–14, with beer and wine and occasionally hard liquor. They drink in association with parents or other family members or with friends at social functions. During this initial period, cigarette-smoking and, somewhat later, marijuana use may begin. Other drug use may then occur, in large measure depending on sociocultural factors such as drug availability and current styles. Use of depressants, stimulants, and hallucinogens usually occurs before there is any opiate use, though this progression is complex and nonlinear.[19,20]

Most adolescents stop at particular points in this sequence, perceiving that the drug use is unpleasant and/or dangerous. Many young people will use only alcohol or another drug during a particular period. More often, a variety of drugs will be used in a so-called polydrug abuse pattern. This pattern varies in severity from the intermittent use of alcohol and drugs on special occasions to the compulsive, disorganized, dangerous, multiple-drug abuse of severly disabled young people. It is not unusual for highly functioning, well-adjusted teenagers to take alcohol, marijuana, methaquaalone, and cocaine in preparation for a concert. They believe themselves to be sophisticated drug-takers and disdain those who cannot handle their drugs.[8,16,21] The compulsive abuser of alcohol or other drugs who is unable to function in school or in society is so considered. It is reassuring to note that as young people give up more dangerous abuse, they often return to the alcohol, marijuana, and perhaps nicotine which they had used earlier.

Young people first learn about alcohol and the pattern of its use from friends or family. This process of anticipatory socialization includes learning to associate alcohol-drinking with psychoactive and physiological effects which they learn to identify as pleasurable. The experience is then repeated.[22] Physiologically and behaviorally induced craving and withdrawal symptoms may then occur, resulting in a compulsive abuse syndrome. This sequence is, of course, importantly influenced by a myriad of complexly intertwined factors.[23-25]

During the 1960s and early 1970s, little attention was paid to adolescent alcohol use. The spectre of illicit drug use increasing to epidemic proportions captured public attention and media focus.[26] Recently there has been public and professional concern that drinking and alcohol-related problems have increased significantly. It is clear that the prevalence of alcohol use by adolescents increased significantly from World War II to the mid-1960s.

There is little evidence that the proportion of young drinkers has increased since then. Approximately 70% of today's teenagers have had alcohol experiences. [1,2] Three quarters of a sample of male high-school seniors and two thirds of females reported use in the past month. Daily use was reported by approximately 7% of samples. [16]

According to several surveys, drinking to intoxication increased from 15% to 20% of teenagers studied prior to 1966, to 45% to 70% in the 1970s. Fifty-two percent of male high-school seniors and 31% of females reported having taken five or more drinks in a row during the preceding two weeks. The prevalence of problem drinking has varied from 19% to 28% in different surveys. [1,2,16]

According to a study of 7,000 students at 34 New England colleges, more than 90% of undergraduates reported at least occasional drinking. Twenty per cent of the men and 10% of the women said getting drunk was important to them. Heavy drinkers included 29% of the men and 11% of the women. [27]

Whether heavy drinking has increased or whether it will lead to problem drinking in later years is unclear. According to one study, and not surprisingly, those who were nondrinkers in college were most likely to have remained nondrinkers 25 years later. Those who were problem drinkers in college were most likely to be problem drinkers and least likely to be abstinent 25 years later. At the same time, the predictability of later drinking patterns from earlier drinking patterns was found to be slight. [28]

There is evidence to suggest that heavy alcohol use is increasing in younger adolescent populations and in females. There is little question that the percentage of problem drinkers increases rapidly throughout late adolescence and the young-adult years, and there is a greater chance than at any other time of life for incurring the negative consequences associated with the *acute* effects of alcohol. These include deterioration in school and work performance, violent behavior, including suicides and homicides, and automobile accidents. Lowering the legal drinking age to 18 years has apparently led to an increase in the number of fatal automobile accidents in some areas. [2]

It is often difficult to distinguish "social" drinking from "problem" drinking in the young, and the term "alcoholism" is similarly less meaningful than it is with adults. Young people drink less regularly than do older people but tend to consume a larger amount on a drinking occasion. In some social or cultural situations, heavy drinking to intoxication is the norm. [2] Perhaps the social sanctions and rituals associated with controlled drinking in adults are less important in young people. [18] Young people tend to be impulsive and may have acquired little tolerance or other adaptive resources to the effects of alcohol.

Certain subsets of young people do experience more excessive drinking. Delinquent adolescents drink more and develop more pathological symptoms [29,30]; children of alcoholic parents, particularly of an alcoholic father, are more likely to be problem drinkers.[31] American Indian children also get into more trouble with alcohol. Whereas surveys show that black and Hispanic youths use alcohol less than do whites, it is possible that there are more problem drinkers in these populations.[32]

Determinants of Alcohol Abuse Behavior

Multiple determinants of alcohol abuse behavior in the young have been cited in the literature; these include psychological, biological, sociological, and pharmacological factors.[2,6,16,17,33-36] Despite numerous and costly attempts at separating these out, it should be recognized that they are often inextricably intertwined. As our colleagues have described elsewhere in this volume, an association between these characteristics and the abuse of alcohol does not necessarily represent a causal relationship. In fact, none of these determinants and no psychological or other sort of examination has been shown to be predictive for the development of problem drinking or alcoholism.[8,18,23]

Sociocultural

Adolescence itself must be considered a risk factor in the incidence of alcohol and other drug abuse. Other frequently cited determinants include truancy, school performance, number of evenings out for recreation, delinquency, religious commitment, and parental control and support.[2,16,20,21,37,38] These variables all have to do with the degree to which a young person is under the influence or supervision of adult-run institutions, including the school, the home, and the church. Interestingly, there is a positive relationship between alcohol and drug abuse and hours worked on a job. It is probable that the increased income, the enhanced ability to buy drugs, and the associations developed on the job are responsible for this association.[16]

Parents often violently condemn the occasional and controlled use of marijuana and other illicit drugs when they themselves abuse alcohol. Often adolescents have been convinced that alcohol is the drug of choice for mature, ambitious adults.[8,18] Sexual experiences are frequently unsatisfactory for young people, due to lack of experience and feelings of anxiety and inadequacy. Many find that low doses of alcohol or sedatives increases desire, relieve inhibitions, and improve performance; some young men are able to achieve and sustain an erection only with this assistance. The great vogue methaqualone has had in recent years attests to this phenomenon. The development of tolerance to the alcohol necessitates increased amounts, resulting in decreased ability and recurrence of the anxious, depressed feelings. Some young people escalate their drinking, effectively decreasing their sexual desires and the associated conflicts. The compulsive use of any of the psychoactive drugs is generally associated with decreased sexual interest and impaired performance.[8,39]

Psychobiological

Young people who abuse alcohol and other drugs have been described from the vantage of a wide variety of psychological perspectives. Many of these data are based on retrospective formulations, after people have already become compulsive abusers. There are no data from prospective studies that have characterized specific symptom complexes, psychodynamic constellations, or well-defined personality types as being etiologic in the alcoholic abuse behavior. Whereas certain of these psychological characteristics may be risk factors for the development of alcoholism, the psychopathology noted may in part be a reaction to the pharmacology of alcohol or its pattern of use in a society that condemns the drug-dependent life. There is no good evidence for the existence of a well-defined preaddictive or alcoholic personality type.[8,23,24,40]

An additional conceptual problem derives from the general difficulty of distinguishing normal from abnormal adolescents. It is often stated that adolescent turmoil is normal and that it is abnormal to be relatively conflict-free during this period. These diagnostic difficulties are further compounded by the fact that many of the data on normal development are derived from studies of psychopathology. Current knowledge suggests that adolescent alcoholics may suffer from the full spectrum of psychiatric disorders, or they may be normal. It is necessary to define the meaning of the alcohol or other drug use in each youngster.[8,39,41]

Alcohol abuse may be seen as *self-medication* of painful affects of depression, guilt, shame, rage, and loneliness in some young people.[6,36,42] Depression is often particularly difficult to diagnose in this population. A so-called masked depression has been invoked to explain the boredom, restlessness, apathy in school, wanderlust, continual philosophizing, sexual promiscuity, and frantic seeking of new activities that are seen in certain adolescents.[43] Suicide is, in fact, a leading cause of death in the young; it is often associated with alcohol use; and suicide rates appear to be increasing in youthful populations. Some young people use alcohol in an attempt to control or satisfy unacceptable drives, particularly sexual longings, security needs, or primitive sadistic and aggressive impulses. It has been suggested that there may be an impairment in affect or drive defense in some adolescents, such that these desires are experienced as overwhelming.[6,36] Alcohol is also used as antipsychotic medication by a subgroup of alcoholic populations.[42]

The diagnoses of narcissistic and, particularly, borderline personality disturbances are increasingly applied to adolescent alcoholics. Multiple phobias, conversion symptoms, dissociative reactions, and hypochondriacal and paranoid trends are often seen. Anxiety states, perverse sexual trends, infantile and hysterical personalities, and chaotic and impulse-ridden behavior may be present. When stressed, as during the alcohol withdrawal syndrome, these young people often develop psychotic symptoms as well. Characteristic ego pathology marked by splitting, the inability to synthesize contradictory self- and object-images, and the inability to recognize, tolerate, and master separation, loss, or narcissistic injury, are considered critical to the diagnosis.[44] Whereas the borderline conceptualization may be quite useful for the diagnostician and therapist, it is possible that it is being overused in young people in general, but particularly for youthful alcohol and drug abusers.

The literature of several decades ago made much of the contribution of so-called latent or overt homosexuality to the development of alcoholism. This view has been in large part discredited for complex and often valid reasons. At the same time, there are a significant number of youthful alcoholics who exhibit prominent anxiety symptoms related to unacceptable sexual desires. In some cases alcohol allows young people to act out these forbidden desires; in other cases they are able to dissociate themselves from the actions, or at least tolerate them. The recently described, but apparently quite common, syndrome of the panic disorders may also be etiologic in some cases of alcohol abuse in the young. True panic attacks are described as spontaneous attacks of anxiety in association with autonomic signs, such as shortness of breath, hyperventilation, paresthesias, palpitations, chest pain, nausea, and dizziness, characteristically accompanied by feelings of impending doom. These attacks may be related to depressive illness.[45]

A history of childhood hyperactivity, poor school performance, and easy distractability might suggest the diagnosis of minimal brain dysfunction. Also called "attention deficit disorders," or hyperkinesis, this rather poorly defined syndrome is known to persist into adolescence and adulthood. A family history of this disorder is often obtained as well. It is probable that some young people are self-medicating this disorder with alcohol.[45]

There is preliminary, though quite provocative, evidence that the pharmacologic effects of chronic use of alcohol and other psychoactive drugs may be important in the development of psychopathology. Chronic use of alcohol or other depressants may result in chronic depressive or anxiety states.[40] These findings are consistent with findings related to protracted abstinence syndromes from alcohol or opioids.[23] The recent work on endogenous morphine-like substances and high-affinity binding sites for benzodiazepines in the brain are also supportive of this conceptualization. It is possible that chronic use of alcohol depletes the body of critical neurotransmitters or otherwise alters receptors, such that long-term or even permanent affective changes occur. Perhaps the chronic anxiety and other changes seen in some long-abstinent recovering alcoholics are a model for naturally occurring anxiety or depressive states.

It should again be emphasized that many of the other drugs may be used alone or in combination with alcohol in association with these psychobiologic disorders. In fact, the choice of drugs may offer diagnostic information as to the underlying psychodynamic patterns. Many severely disturbed young people will use only alcohol, opiates, or depressants and will not use marijuana, hallucinogens, and stimulants. The latter drug group further diminishes their hold on reality and enhances anxious or paranoid feelings. Stimulant abusers may be self-medicating minimal brain dysfunction.[8,45,46]

Patterns of abuse may also reflect personality characteristics and psychopathology.[35] A depressed obsessive character may use alcohol compulsively but in an organized, structured pattern. Borderline or psychotic youngsters may drink large quantities of alcohol and take a wide variety of other drugs in a disorganized, chaotic manner, such that they experience frequent adverse reactions or overdoses. Some of these people take great pride in their abuse patterns, calling themselves "garbage heads" or worse.[8] In Erickson's terms, they have little else of which to be proud and they rely on a "negative identity" for self-definition and self-esteem.[4]

There is evidence to suggest that premorbid psychopathology varies directly with the distance, cultural or geographic, one has to travel to get illicit drugs. Thus, a middle-class heroin addict from the suburbs is likely to be more disturbed than a young black or Hispanic male from the inner city. The situation with alcohol is somewhat different, since this drug is easily available in all societal sectors. At the same time, young people growing up in a culturally deprived atmosphere where there are a great many highly visible alcoholics, such as in some poor inner-city areas, are less likely to have significant psychopathology than is the suburban youngster who has had much less exposure to alcoholism and less social deprivation. As a group, adolescent alcoholics exhibit more psychopathology than do compulsive abusers of other drugs. This may be due to the fact that in recent years it has been more socially acceptable for teenagers to compulsively abuse drugs than alcohol.[10,41]

Prevention and Treatment

Prevention

Given the varied and complex determinants of alcohol abuse in adolescents, prevention approaches have not been particularly effective. In contrast to drug use, alcohol use and even abuse is to a large extent sanctioned by society. The drinking behavior is often associated with maturity and poise, and a myriad of social functions are organized around an alcohol focus. Educational campaigns that stress the dangers of alcohol abuse or the goal of responsible drinking have not had significant impact. Articulate and apparently successful recovering alcoholics who are invited to schools or community groups to recount the horrors of their alcoholism may sometimes even stimulate additional experimentation. Young people do not believe that it can happen to them. They often feel that even if they do get into trouble with alcohol or other drugs, they will conquer the problem and become as successful as the invited speaker.

Carefully planned, well-organized programs that teach adolescents to cope with stress and anxiety and that suggest the rewarding emotional, educational, vocational, and recreational alternatives to drug use have shown promise. Optimally, these programs should require active participation and discussion and encourage the development of productive relationships. Sex education should be an integral part of prevention programs. These approaches are not without liabilities, institutional mandates in regard to sex education or the acquisition of coping skills may be overly manipulative and inadequately presented by unskilled and insensitive agents of the school or the community.[8,47]

General Treatment Considerations

Adolescents often perceive their drinking and drug-taking behavior to be safe, under control, and enjoyable. They may take pride in their capacity for alcohol or in how drunk they become on occasion. The alcohol use is likely to be sufficiently short-term and free of adverse consequences so that they may not appreciate the abuse and its implications. They are also wary of seeking help from conventional authorities. They are uncomfortable revealing themselves to adults with whom they believe they have no rapport. They believe they will not be understood or appreciated by even well-meaning authority figures, including the teacher, doctor, and parent. They are also often intensely concerned with confidentiality.[48-52]

Behavior patterns and psychobiologic sequelae of alcohol use may be sufficiently short-term as to render this population likely to do better in treatment than do adults. In contrast to adult patients, the young are more likely to develop the skills and discipline necessary to live reasonably contentedly without alcohol or drugs. At the same time, despite these clinical impressions, there are few data supporting this idea that the provision of early treatment to compulsive alcohol abusers during the adolescent years will ensure better results.

Individual therapists, including family physicians, psychiatrists, and other health personnel, continue to be an important treatment resource for adolescent alcohol abusers. They may be the only resource available in certain areas. Then, too, the youngsters' alcohol abuse behavior may still be sufficiently benign so that admission to an alcohol treatment program would be inappropriate. Unfortunately therapists often do not know as much about the alcohol abuse behavior as do some of their young patients, and they often find them undesirable as patients. Also, the economics of private practice preclude the provision of educational, legal, vocational, and recreational services.[53]

It is often difficult to engage adolescents in regularly scheduled therapy or counseling sessions. They may be uncomfortable in one-on-one encounters with a therapist, and they are loath to discuss the intimate details of their lives, particularly their failures. This difficulty is compounded if the therapist assumes the traditional stance of neutrality and reserve. It is often necessary, particularly at the outset of treatment, to schedule short informal sessions, with the therapist actively discussing practical issues of survival. Often discussions of music, sports, or clothing will be valuable in establishing a therapeutic alliance. Issues of alcohol use must, of course, be discussed, but the therapist should exercise care that he does not assume a critical parental role of exhortation and threats. Most of these young people have heard it all before; they will benefit most from a dignified, supportive relationship with an accepting, interested, knowledgeable adult. Optimally, they will come to appreciate their own worth and potential in this relationship.[8]

As with adult patients, adolescent patients will often deny the extent of their alcohol use or in other ways distort historical data so as to create a desired effect. Direct confrontation of these failures to tell the truth, particularly at the outset of treatment, may lead to increased resistance or power struggles. At the same time, if the therapist accepts the information without reservation, he may undermine the sense of trust and respect that is the basis of the therapeutic alliance. This may also increase the patient's already intense guilt feelings. If possible, the therapist must act as an ally, so that the responsibility for behavior and improvement rests on the patient. An attitude of gentle but persistent curiosity is more effective than an approach as an adversary. It may be necessary to listen carefully but neutrally and gloss over questionable issues at different stages. Confirmed problems and behaviors may be considered in more depth with a view to returning to the possible inaccuracies at a later treatment stage.[8]

There is controversy as to whether young people should be treated within the family group. Family therapy is essential in some cases to identify and attempt to alter patterns of familial interaction that provoke alcohol abuse behavior. In other instances, it may be more useful for the therapist or the treatment team to see the youngster separately and allow him to feel that the therapist is his advocate and worthy of trust. In this situation, the therapist should see the parents or other family members only when the patient is present, and all familial contacts, including telephone conversations, should be accurately reported to the patient. It may sometimes be necessary to encourage the separation of the patient from a family situation that is destructive, particularly one in which there are other drug abusers present. On other occasions, families must be encouraged to protect themselves from the antisocial or violent behavior of a compulsively drinking adolescent.

Group or milieu therapy is highly useful for adolescents, particularly when supervised by therapists who have shared similar cultural experiences. The general focus should be on common problems, methods of coping, the establishment of trusting relationships with each other, and sexual problems. Optimally, these groups should be well structured, though informal and flexible in nature.

Treatment of the psychopathology that led to or resulted from the drug abuse behavior will obviously depend on the individual personality patterns. This is discussed in detail elsewhere in this volume. Certain general considerations deserve emphasis. These people have often felt inadequate and helpless in the face of the real problems of living. Treatment personnel must be sensitive to this profound lack of self-esteem as well as to the various modes of denial they employ.[3,4] Careful work and firm intervention are necessary to help them better assess the risks of particular self-destructive behaviors.

Compulsive alcohol abusers are often unable to recognize the extremes of emotion, particularly anxiety and depression. These mood states may have become the conditioned stimulus for the craving for alcohol or drugs. Protracted abstinence symptoms may also be so conditioned. It is often useful to repeatedly identify these mood states with the patient so that they may be separated from the alcohol abusing behaviors.[8]

Treatment Programs

Treatment programs generally focus on either alcohol or drug abuse, rarely both. Alcohol treatment programs are often aimed at adults; they are frequently not geared to the needs of the youthful alcohol abuser. Then, too, they are often unwilling to undertake the treatment of an adolescent who takes drugs in addition to alcohol. Drug abuse treatment programs are more often focused on the youthful patient but may not be knowledgeable or interested in the treatment of his alcoholism.

Age-oriented treatment programs focused on both alcohol *and* drug abuse appear to be the most efficient and effective means of providing treatment and preventive services to adolescent populations. Comprehensive medical services, educational resources, psychosexual counseling, recreational facilities, and legal help should optimally be integral parts of the rehabilitation program.[54] Adolescents should be encouraged to identify with the center, attend programs daily and in the evening, and utilize it as a significant life resource. THE DOOR in New York is quite innovative in this regard, though it is aimed at youngsters who have not yet become overwhelmingly involved with drugs or alcohol.[50,52]

School-based programs are a critical resource for the prevention, casefinding, and early treatment of some young people. Impaired school performance, lateness, or truancy may be the first sign of an alcohol problem. A wide variety of programs of generally undocumented effectiveness exist to serve these functions. There is generally an educational-preventative component that publicizes the dangers of alcohol or drug use. These programs are sometimes organized in a peer-group format, supervised by teachers or counselors with some substance abuse knowledge. Many of these programs tend to focus on drug use and have not considered alcohol abuse in any depth. Some are unrealistically stringent and attempt to contravene all psychoactive drug use. This may discourage troubled youngsters from seeking help. School-based programs should probably not attempt to treat severely alcoholic or drug-dependent students. These young people should be referred to specialized programs, but the school should attempt to maintain follow-up. Every effort should be made to keep these people in school or to facilitate their reentry into school after a period of absence related to intensive treatment or hospitalization. It makes little sense merely to expel them from the school environment without proper referral; they will maintain relationships with other less alcohol-involved students and perhaps spread the disease.[8,48,55]

Inpatient programs based on the therapeutic community model are widely used in the treatment of drug abusers, but less often with alcohol abusers. These are tightly organized programs, generally supervised by former drug abusers, that seek to create a milieu serving to discourage drug use and other self-destructive or antisocial behaviors. Role models for responsible behavior are provided by staff and residents, and the sense of isolation that many young people feel may be reduced. Many of these facilities rigorously emphasize the breaking down of unhealthy behavior patterns through confrontation and an intricate system of rewards and punishments. They are often unprepared to handle adolescents with significant psychopathology. Moreover, their focus is often on minorities and the poor, so that middle-class people may feel uncomfortable. Young people are often unwilling to leave family and friends to enter these facilities and, once in, many leave precipitously.[8,50]

A model that might be useful for adolescent alcohol abusers combines an inpatient and outpatient therapeutic community structure with extensive medical and psychiatric backup. In lieu of rigorous confrontation, a warm, supportive environment might be provided with emphasis on the alternatives to drug use. Clients would enter the system at any point, depending on their needs, and progress through it at their individual rates. They might enter at the inpatient phase, for example, move to an intensive day-care center phase, and then to a more limited clinic phase as they developed ties to societal institutions such as school, work, or family and have less need for program support. If difficulties arose with any patient at any level, more supportive care would be availiable.[8,56]

Self-help groups on the Alcoholics Anonymous model, including Alanon and Alateen, have not been widely accepted by adolescent alcoholics. This may derive in large part from sociocultural factors. The concerns and style of many AA groups are not those of the youthful, nor is the language. Many of these youngsters do not feel comfortable in that milieu. Perhaps adolescent groups based on the AA model but incorporating the language and styles of the adolescent sector might be developed. At the same time, adolescents often require and will benefit from a structure that places more emphasis on stable authority figures than do self-help groups.

As with adult patients, there are few good data on the effectiveness of different treatment approaches or programs for adolescents. There is a paucity of follow-up studies on young people who have been in treatment. This may be due to generally insufficient funds and personnel and lack of expertise in treatment programs to accomplish this task. It is critical that this information be gathered to determine which people do well in which programs. Perhaps more importantly, continued follow-up may provide support and encouragement to young people who are doing well and facilitate the readmission of adolescents who have returned to alcohol use.[8,35]

Some alcohol-abusing adolescents who are referred to treatment programs, therapists, or psychiatric facilities are not in need of intensive treatment. Their alcohol use or any other drug use may be normal within their social or cultural milieu and may represent benign experimentation. The disruption of the lives of some of these young people as a result of treatment, or the attitudes of treatment personnel, may be worse than the consequences of their drug use. After a comprehensive evaluation has determined that an adolescent is developing reasonably well and that the alcohol use does not represent a serious danger, it may be useful to attempt to provide reassurance as to his/her sanity and prospects for the future. Warm reassurance and encouragement in a few sessions with provision for follow-up care may be all that is required.[8,17,49,57]

References

1. Fishburne PM, Adelson HI, Cisin IH: *National Survey on Drug Abuse: Main Findings 1979.* US Government Printing Office, 1980.
2. Blane HT, Hewitt LE: *Alcohol and Youth: An Analysis of the Literature 1960–75.* Washington, DC, National Institute on Alcohol Abuse and Alcoholism, March 1977.
3. Blos P: *On Adolescence.* Glencoe, The Free Press, 1962.
4. Erikson EH: *Childhood and Society,* ed 2. New York, Norton, 1963.
5. Millman RB: Drug abuse in adolescence: Current issues, in Senay, E, Shorty V (eds):

Developments in the Field of Drug Abuse, Proceedings of the First National Drug Abuse Conference, 1974. New York, National Association for the Prevention of Addiction to Narcotics, 1974.

6. Wurnser L: Psychanalytic considerations of the etiology of compulsive drug use. *J Psychoanal Assoc* 22:820–843, 1974.

7. Mechanic D: Development of psychological distress among young adults. *Arch Gen Psychiatry* 36:1233–1239, 1979.

8. Millman RB: Drug and alcohol abuse in Wollman BB, Egan J, Ross AC (eds): *Handbook of Mental Disorders in Childhood and Adolescence.* Englewood Cliffs, Prentice-Hall, Inc. 1978.

9. Preble E, Casey JJ, Jr: Taking care of business: The heroin user's life on the street. *Internat J Addictions* 4:1–24, 1969.

10. Millman RB, Khuri ET: Drug abuse and the need for alternatives, in Schoolar J (ed): *Current Issues in Adolescent Psychiatry.* New York, Brunner/Mazel, 1973.

11. Weil A: *The Natural Mind.* Boston, Houghton Mifflin, 1972.

12. Wider H, Kaplan EH: Drug use in adolescents. *Psychoanal Study Child* 24:399–431, 1969.

13. Hunt LG: Incidence and prevalance of drug use and abuse, in DuPont, RI, Goldstein A, O-Donnell J (eds): *Handbook on Drug Abuse.* National Institute on Drug Abuse, US Department of HEW, and Office of Drug Abuse Policy, 1979.

14. *Project DAWN V: Phase Five Report of the Drug Abuse Warning Network, May 1976-April 1977.* DHEW Publ No (ADM) 78–618 1977.

15. *A Survey of Substance Use Among Junior and Senior High School Students in New York State.* Report No 1: Prevalence of Drug and Alcohol Use, Winter 1974/75. New York, New York State Office of Drug Abuse Services, 1975.

16. Bachman JG, Johnston LD, O'Malley PM: Smoking, drinking and drug use among American high school students: Correlates and trends 1975–1979. *Am J Public Health* 71:59–69, 1981.

17. Schnoll SH: Alcohol and other substance abuse in adolescents, in Gottheil EL, McLellan AT, Druley KA, Alterman AI (eds): *Addiction Research and Treatment: Converging Trends.* New York, Pergamon, 1979.

18. Zinberg NE, Jacobson RC, Harding WM: Social sanctions and rituals as a basis for drug abuse preventation. *Am J Drug and Alcohol Abuse* 2:165–183 1975.

19. Kandel D, Single E, Kessler RC: The epidemiology of drug use among New York State high school students: Distribution, trends, and change in rates of use. *Am J Public Health* 66:43–53, 1976.

20. Hamburg BA, Kraemer HC, Jahnke WA: Hierarchy of drug use in adolescence: Behavioral and attitudinal correlates of substantial drug use. *Am J Psychiatry* 132:1155–1167, 1975.

21. Kamali K, Steer RA: Polydrug use by high school students: Involvement and correlates. *Internat J Addictions* 11:337–343, 1976.

22. Becker HS: History, culture and subjective experience: An exploration of the social basis of drug-induced experiences. *J Health Soc Behav* 8:163–176, 1967.

23. Dole VP: Narcotic addiction, physical dependence and relapse. *N Engl J Med* 206:988, 1972.

24. Meyer RE, Mirin SM: The Heroin Stimulus: Implications for a Theory of Addiction. New York, Plenum Medical, 1979.

25. Millman RB: Drug abuse, addiction and intoxication, in Beeson, PB, McDermott W (eds): *Textbook of Medicine,* ed 14. Philadelphia, WB Saunders Co, 1975.

26. Brecher EM, Editors of Consumer Reports: *Licit and Illicit Drugs: The Consumers Union Report on Narcotics, Stimulants,* Depressants, *Inhalants, Hallucinogens, and Marijuana, including Caffeine, Nicotine, and Alcohol.* Mount Vernon, Consumers Union, 1972.

27. Getting back to the booze. *Time Magazine,* November 5, 1979.

28. Fillmore KM, Bacon SD, Hyman M: *Alcohol Drinking Behavior and Attitudes.* Rutgers Panel Study Report prepared for National Institute on Alcohol Abuse and Alcoholism. New Brunswick, NJ, Rutgers Center of Alcohol Studies, June 1977.

29. Blacker E, Demone HW, Jr, Freeman HE: Drinking behavior of delinquent boys. *Q J Stud Alcohol,* 26:223–237, 1965.

30. Simonds JF, Kashani J: Drug abuse and criminal behavior in delinquent boys committed to a training school. *Am J Psychiatry* 136:1444–1448, 1979.

31. Schuckit MA, Goodwin DA, Winokur G: A study of alcoholism in half-siblings. *Am J Psychiatry* 128:1132–1136, 1972.

32. Robins LN, Murphy GE: Drug use in a normal population of young negro men. *Am J Public Health* 57:1580–1596, 1967.

33. Tennant FS, Detels R, Clark V: Some childhood antecedents of drug and alcohol abuse. *Am J of Epidemicology* 102:377–385.

34. Blum R, Richards L: Youthful drug use, in Dupont RI, Goldstein A, O'Donnell J (eds): *Handbook on Drug Abuse.* US Dept of HEW and Office of Drug Abuse Policy, National Institute on Drug Abuse, 1979, pp 257–267.

35. Bihari B: Drug dependency: Some etiological considerations. *Am J Drug and Alcohol Abuse* 3:409–423, 1976.

36. Fenichel O: *The Psychoanalytic Theory of Neurosis.* New York, Norton, 1945.

37. O'Donnell JA, Voss HL, Clayton RR, et al: *Young Men and Drugs: A Nationwide Survey.* NIDA Research Monograph 5. Rockville, National Institute on Drug Abuse, 1976.

38. Burkett SR: Religion, parental influence and adolescent alcohol and marijuana use. *J of Drug Issues* 7:263–273, 1977.

39. Zinberg NE: Addiction and ego function, in Eissler RS, Freud A, Kris M, Solnit AJ (eds): *The Psychoanalytic Study of the Child.* New Haven, Yale Univ Press, 1975.

40. McLellan AT, Woody GE, O'Brien CP: Development of psychiatric illnesses in drug abusers. *N Engl J Med* 301:1310–1314, 1979.

41. Kaufman E: The psychodynamics of opiate dependence: A new look. *Am J Drug and Alcohol Abuse* 1:349–370, 1974.

42. Khatzian EJ, Mack JE, Schatzberg AF: Heroin use as an attempt to cope: Clinical observations. *Am J Psychiatry* 131:160–164, 1974.

43. Gallemore JL, Wilson WP: Adolescent maladjustment or affective disorder? *Am J Psychiatry* 129:608–612, 1972.

44. Kernberg OF: *Borderline Conditions and Pathological Narcissism.* New York, Jason Aronson, 1975.

45. Pope HG: Drug abuse and psychopathology. *N Engl J Med* 301, 1341–1343, 1979.

46. Milkman H, Frosch WA: On the preferential abuse of heroin and amphetamine. *J Ner Ment Dis* 156:242–248 1973.

47. Jacobson R, Zinberg NE: *Social Basis of Drug Abuse Prevention.* Washington, DC, Drug Abuse Council, Inc, 1975.

48. Bernstein B, Shkuda AN: *The Young Drug User. Attitudes and Obstacles to Treatment.* New York, Center for New York City Affairs, New School for Social Research, 1974.

49. Offer D, Ostrov E, Howard KI: The mental health professional's concept of the normal adolescent. *Arch Gen Psychiatry* 38:149–152, 1981.

50. Lecker S, Hendericks L, Turanski J: New dimensions in adolescent psychotherapy: A therapeutic system approach. *Pediatric Clinics of North America* 20:883–900, 1973.

51. Litt IF, Cohen MI: The drug-using adolescent as a pediatric patient. *J Pediatr* 77:195–202, 1970.

52. *Institute of Medicine, A Conference Summary: Adolescent Behavior and Health.* Washington, DC, National Academy of Sciences, 1978.

53. Chappel JN, Schnoll SH: Physician attitudes: Effect on the treatment of chemically dependent patients. *JAMA* 237:2318–2319, 1977.

54. Litt IF, Cohen MI: Prisons, adolescents, and the right to quality medical care: The time is now. *Am J Public Health* 64:894–897, 1974.
55. Hughes PH, Crawford GA: A contagious disease model for researching and intervening in heroin epidemics. *Arch Gen Psychiatry* 27:149–155, 1972.
56. Millman RB, Khuri ET, Nyswander ME: Therapeutic detoxification of adolescent heroin addicts, in Kissin B, Lowinson J, Millman, RB (eds): *Recent Developments in Chemotherapy of Narcotic Addiction*. New York, Annals of the New York Academy of Sciences, vol 311, 1978.
57. Hunt LG, Zinberg NE: *Heroin Use: A New Look*. Washington, DC, Drug Abuse Council, Inc, 1976.

CHAPTER 13

Psychiatric Problems of Alcoholic Women

SHEILA B. BLUME, MD

Women and Alcohol

Strong feeling, and particularly strong disapproval of drinking by women has been part of the Western culture for centuries. In the early days of ancient Rome the drinking of alcohol by women was strictly prohibited. [1] A law of Romulus provided the death penalty for women who drank as well as for those who committed adultery. There are records of women having been put to death for the offense of having drunk wine or having been caught with the keys to the family wine cellar. The idea that drinking by women was abhorrent in itself and would lead to lascivious behavior was already established in the ancient world.

In 1798, Immanuel Kant expressed an opinion about the sobriety of both Jews and women. He stated that both groups do not get drunk and avoid all appearance of drunkenness because their position in the community rests upon the belief of other in their piety and chastity:

> All separatists, that is, those who subject themselves not only to the general laws of the country but also to a special sectarian law, are exposed through their eccentricity and alleged chosenness to the attention and criticism of the community, and thus cannot relax in their self-control, for intoxication, which deprives one of the cautiousness, would be a scandal for them. [2]

Jews and women have been compared in one other respect related to drinking problems. Since both groups are thought to have a relatively low incidence of alcoholism, it is argued that any individual alcoholic from either group must be more deviant from the norm than would be true for a member of

---

SHEILA B. BLUME • Director, New York State Division of Alcoholism and Alcohol Abuse, Clinical Associate Professor, Department of Psychiatry, Albany Medical College, Albany, New York 12229.

a group with a higher incidence of alcoholism. Therefore, Jewish and female alcoholics should show more underlying psychopathology. This "sicker" hypothesis has been questioned for both Jews and women.[3,4] The belief, however, persists, and adds to the special problems of stigma faced by women who drink to excess. This stigma and the double standard of drinking in Western society have been discussed by several authors.[5,6]

In spite of the strong feelings of our society toward women and alcohol, relatively little research into the physiological, psychological, and sociological aspects of women's drinking was performed prior to the mid-1970s, when a nation-wide movement encouraged by the National Council on Alcoholism and the National Institute on Alcohol Abuse and Alcoholism (NIAAA) focused attention on this problem. Nearly all of the classical studies done on the physiology, biochemistry, and metabolism of alcohol had been done in males. The initial studies on the nature and course of the disease alcoholism were also done in men, for example, Jellinek's classic study of the course of the illness in 1,000 members of Alcoholics Anonymous.[7] A recent NIAAA-sponsored research review[8] calls attention both to recent findings and unanswered research questions concerning alcohol problems in women. Recommendations of the NIAAA research group range from a proposal to specify the sex of subjects in the titles of project reports to programs to increase the participation of qualified women scientists and administrators in alcoholism research.

Recent interest in the effects of maternal drinking on the fetus in producing both the fetal alcohol syndrome (FAS) and other alcohol-related birth defects has further increased the level of public and professional interest in the use of alcohol by women.[9] Fetal alcohol syndrome is thought to be the third most common cause of mental retardation associated with birth defect in the United States. Of these three (Down's syndrome, spina bifida, and fetal alcohol syndrome), only FAS is preventable. Effective prevention of FAS must include both identification and treatment of the pregnant alcoholic woman.

The Alcoholic Woman

Recent reviews of literature present a description of the clinical characteristics of the alcoholic woman, as she is found in the community and as she presents for treatment.[10-13]

Clinical Characteristics

Diagnosis. There has been considerable dispute about the use of the terms "alcoholic," "problem drinker," "alcohol abuser," and so forth. The term "alcohol dependence syndrome," as defined by the World Health

Organization in its *International Classification of Diseases—9*[14] and the American Psychiatric Association in its *Diagnostic and Statistical Manual of Mental Disorders* (Third Edition), [15] can be applied to male and female alike. However, other definitions and diagnostic standards are based on average levels of alcohol intake which are thought to be "hazardous." These have usually used the same cut-off point for male and female drinkers in spite of the fact that both women social drinkers and female alcoholics presenting for treatment drink considerably less than men. For example, as reported in the so-called Rand Report, non-problem-drinking women averaged 0.44 ounces of absolute alcohol daily compared to the male average of 0.91. Women accepted for treatment in the NIAAA-sponsored alcoholism programs surveyed in the report averaged 4.5 ounces of absolute alcohol per day compared to the male average of 8.2 ounces.[16] These differences are related, at least in part, to differences in body weight and proportion of body water. Thus, any definition of a population at risk for alcohol problems based on quantity of drinking must have separate standards for males and females. Screening tests aimed to identify problem drinkers have also tended to be developed with male populations. It is important that they be validated for women before they are used for this purpose.

Family History. There is a high incidence of both alcoholism and depression in the close relatives of alcoholic women.[18] The studies of Goodwin *et al* on adopted-out children of alcoholic biological parents in Denmark present strong evidence for the existence of a genetic predisposition to alcoholism in males.[19] The women in Goodwin's study, however, did not show this trend as clearly as the men.[20] This result is partly a product of the low incidence of alcoholism among women in Denmark, which led to a small number of cases in the study. However, it also may reflect, in part, the greater relative importance of developmental and psychosocial factors in women's alcoholism.

Psychology and Behavior. Most psychological and social theories of the causation of alcoholism do not distinguish between the sexes. The few longitudinal studies that shed light on social and psychological factors which predispose to alcoholism show markedly different results for males and females. The Oakland Growth Study,[21] although it had few female problem drinkers, identified general feelings of low self-esteem and inability to cope in girls who later became problem drinkers when they were tested at the junior-high-school and high-school levels. This was not true of the males.[22] In a 28-year follow-up of a study of drinking among American college students, researchers found that factors predictive of problem drinking in later life differed considerably between males and females.[23] Analysis of the data made it necessary to construct different definitions of "alcohol involvement" at the college level and of "problem drinking" at follow-up for males and females. The best predictor of later problems for college women was a high score on the "feeling adjustment" scale, composed of such items as drinking to relieve shyness, drinking to get high, drinking to be gay, and drinking to get along better on dates. Among men, those with "incipient problems" in college were more likely to show up in the problem drinker group at follow-up. In neither sex was the presence of overt alcohol problems in college the best predictor of problem drinking 27 years later.

One psychological theory that has focused specifically on the alcoholic woman has been that of sex role conflict. The theory is based on socially accepted definitions of masculine and feminine behavior. It postulates that women who develop alcoholism have strong identification with feminine roles at the conscious level but strong unconscious masculinity. This disparity creates a conflict at least partially relieved by the ingestion of alcohol, which enhances feelings of femininity in both normal and alcoholic women.[24] The concept of sex role conflict has been further developed to include women with conflict between conscious masculine strivings and unconscious feminine identification.[25] A recent study from the University of California investigated conscious and unconscious masculinity and femininity in 120 female alcoholics, 119 nonalcoholic women, and 118 women in treatment for psychiatric and emotional problems.[26] The study concluded that although a sex role conflict between "unconscious masculinity" and "conscious femininity" was more prevalent among alcoholic women than among the normal controls, less than one quarter of the total alcoholic sample showed this pattern of conflict. When sex role conflict was defined to include both conscious femininity and unconscious masculinity and the reverse, there was no significant difference between the incidence of sex role conflict in the alcoholic women and the normal controls. Sixty-six percent of the alcoholic women, 72% of the treatment controls, and 71% of the normal controls scored feminine on both conscious and unconscious measures. Those alcoholic women who manifested sex role conflict differed from the remainder of alcohlic women in showing lower self-esteem and a higher incidence of having had an absent parent during childhood. Certainly identification of alcoholic women suffering from such conflict is an important consideration for psychiatric treatment.

Physiology. Recent studies have shown differences between the effects of single doses of alcohol in normal men and women. Given a standard dose of alcohol based on body weight, women showed both higher and more variable peak blook alcohol levels, with higher peaks obtained during the premenstrual phase.[27] Women taking exogenous hormones, for example, birth control pills or estrogen replacement, tended to metabolize alcohol more slowly. Such differences will have an influence both on the amount of alcohol consumed by women and the relative predictability of the effect of a given number of drinks. There is some evidence that women spontaneously drink less during pregnancy, when hormone levels are high.[28]

Course and Symptoms. Most researchers agree that women coming to treatment for alcoholism differ from their male counterparts in a number of ways. Women start drinking and begin their pattern of alcohol abuse at later ages but appear for treatment at about the same age as male alcoholics. This points to a more rapid development or "telescoping" of the course of the illness in women. Alcoholic women are more likely to be divorced when they enter treatment or to be married to or living with an alcoholic "significant other." They are more likely than the alcoholic man to date on the onset of pathological drinking to a particularly stressful event. Women are more likely to have histories of both suicide attempts and previous psychiatric treatment. Their motivations to enter treatment and the problems they perceive relating to alcohol are more likely to be health and family problems, whereas for the male, job problems and trouble with the law, particularly arrests for driving while intoxicated, are more prevalent. Women alcoholics have a high incidence of obstetric and gynecological difficulties and may be more likely to develop cirrhosis than the male. Various studies have shown that women more often present with histories of other substance abuse along with their alcoholism, particularly tranquillizers, sedatives, and amphetamines.[29] Female alcoholics are also more likely to report such symptoms of psychological distress as anxiety and depression, and have a lower self-esteem than their male counterparts.[30]

Subtypes of Alcoholism. There have been many attempts to develop systems for subtyping of patients suffering from alcoholism. The most useful of these subtypings, particularly in women, is the distinction between primary and secondary alcoholism. Secondary alcoholism is defined as alcoholism associated with either preexisting diagnosable psychopathological states, or with such states developing during a prolonged period of abstinence. Primary alcoholism arises without such a history.[31] When categorized in this way, most alcoholic patients appearing for treatment are of the primary type. Among men the most common secondary alcoholism is that associated with sociopathy. In women the most common type is "affective alcoholism," usually associated with unipolar depression. This latter pattern may be seen in one fifth to one quarter of a typical female treatment population. Diagnosis must be based on a careful life history, since the presence of depressive symptoms at the time of treatment will not differentiate between the two groups. Once a woman is diagnosed as a secondary alcoholic suffering from affective alcoholism, an appropriate long-term treatment plan would include continuing contact during sobriety with attention to possible recurrence of depression. Early treatment of such recurrent can help the patient maintain her sobriety and well-being.

Fetal Alcohol Syndrome

Women alcoholics in the childbearing years should be screened for pregnancy, and those with children born during heavy drinking periods should have these children screened for fetal alcohol syndrome and other related birth defects. Both animal and human research leads to the expectation that children of heavily drinking mothers are more likely to be growth-retarded, hyperactive, and slower to develop. Those with the full fetal alcohol syndrome present a combination of birth defects including both prenatal and postnatal growth retardation (small for gestational age with failure to "catch up" in spite of good postnatal nutrition), small head circumference, mild to moderate mental retardation, small eyes, often with strabismus and/or ptosis, hypoplasia of the maxilla, a long upper lip with a flattened philtrum and thinned vermillion, and a small upturned nose. In addition, there may be skeletal, joint, genital, renal, skin, and cardiac defects.[9,32] Although the full fetal alcohol syndrome has only been seen to date in women whose alcohol intake averaged six drinks or more per day throughout pregnancy, safe levels of alcohol intake both in terms of timing during pregnancy and pattern of drinking are as yet unknown. There is evidence, however, that interruption of excessive drinking during pregnancy leads to lower incidence of birth defects.[33]

The Alcoholic Woman as a Woman

Before considering the treatment of alcoholic women, it is important to note that they share many of the problems common to all women in contemporary society.[34,35] The recognition of these factors and their incorporation into a program of rehabilitation for the alcoholic woman will often make the difference between success and failure of treatment.

An important factor in the psychiatric treatment of women is both public and professional perceptions of mental health and of appropriate masculine and feminine sex roles.[36] A particularly enlightening study published in 1970[37] explored sex role stereotypes in 79 clinically trained psychologists, psychiatrists, and social workers. It was found that definitions of a healthy, mature, and socially competent adult matched those for a healthy, mature, and socially competent male, while traits thought to be characteristic of healthy women were perceived as significantly less healthy for an adult of unspecified sex. Such stereotypes are important underpinnings of theories of sex role conflict. They also are central to notions of mental health based on successful adjustment to social expectations. A competing concept of masculine and feminine traits in mental health is the concept of androgyny. Androgyny stresses a balance or mixture of traits considered stereotypically "masculine" of "feminine" by society, used in a flexible way. The University of California study quoted above[26] attempted to assess androgyny in the three study groups of women: women in treatment for alcoholism, women in treatment for other emotional disorder, and normal nonalcoholic women. The alcoholic women were significantly less androgynous than the normal controls but did not differ in this respect from the treatment controls. Androgynous rather than stereotype feminine behavior would seem a most appropriate treatment goal for the alcoholic women.

Since women alcoholics have difficulties with self-esteem, it is important to consider aspects of female identity. A common component of identity for both men and women is occupation: I am what I do. It is thus important to note that in contemporary American society "women's work" is afforded much lower status than work usually associated with the male. Although increasing numbers of women are part of the work force, they are concentrated in low prestige jobs and earn an average of only slightly more than half the average income for men.[38] Work performed in the home is assigned essentially no social or economic value. (Does your wife work? No, she is a housewife.) The vast majority of working women who are also married continue to carry the responsibility for all or almost all of the cleaning, laundry, cooking, shopping, and child care.[39] Women are often underpaid, underemployed, undervalued, and overstressed. Striving for perfection in these competing areas of life will produce problems in any woman. In a recovering alcoholic woman attempting to allay feelings of guilt and shame and to make up for lost time, the problems will be even more intense.

A role usually assigned to the woman in contemporary society is that of keeper of the family. In separation or divorce, a wife continues to be awarded custody of minor children in most cases, even when the separation is based in part on her problems with alcohol. Many alcoholic women presenting for treatment are heads of single parent families, struggling to provide financial support as well as household and child care. It has been noted previously that alcoholic women are often married to men who are also problem drinkers. Because of her role as keeper of the family, the wife of an alcoholic husband often feels guilty and responsible for her husband's drinking. If she does not have available to her an effective network of social and emotional support outside the home, such as an understanding family or membership in Al-Anon Family Groups, she may begin to use alcohol as a temporary solution to her marital distress and begin a pattern of alcoholism in herself. Thus, in the treatment of both married alcoholic men and women, the spouse should be considered at risk for alcohol problems. A careful drinking history should be taken, and preventive measures instituted in the form of family treatment wherever possible. Particularly in order to reach those women who are heads of single parent families, but also for all who have young children, arrangements for child care and other household assistance will often by critical. It is difficult or impossible for a women to concentrate on therapy when her children are unsupervised at home.

A third aspect of a woman's identity is that she often, in contrast to a man, derives her identity through her relationship to others. She takes her husband's name at the time of marriage and is often known as "Sam's wife" or "Pat's mother." Even after the relationship is ended, she may be identified as

"Joe's widow" or "Sid's ex-wife." Part of the rebuilding of self-esteem requires attention to the alcoholic women's feelings about herself as an individual.

A fourth component in women's identity is tied to sexuality. Much has been said about woman as sex object, and the association in the public mind between alcohol abuse and promiscuity has been part of Western culture for centuries. Although much study has been given to the effects of alcohol on sex hormones and sexual performance in the male, practically nothing is known about these factors in the female. One researcher recently reviewing the field wrote, "Most experts comment on human sexual behavior and alcohol as though only males drink and have sexual interests."[40] Clinicians have recognized a high incidence of obstetric and gynecological problems in populations of female alcoholics in treatment.[11,12] Alcoholic women often complain of anorgasmia and lack of sexual interest. Some have, in fact, engaged in sexual behavior of which they would not ordinarily approve, either in an attempt to find a solution to their sexual problem, or searching for an escape from loneliness, primarily while intoxicated. However, the majority of alcoholic women are solitary drinkers who do their drinking at home. Even women on skid row are more likely to be solitary drinkers than men. Thus, only a minority of alcoholic women are regularly exposed to men while drinking, and fewer fit the cultural stereotype of promiscuity. Homosexual women are said to have an unusually high incidence of alcohol problems.[17] Those women whose problems with identity center around their sexuality will need special consideration of this factor during treatment.

Lastly, a woman's identity is shaped by her socioeconomic status and the subcultural group to which she belongs. Cultural differences in attitudes and female roles may serve as a help or hindrance in casefinding and treatment, which should be tailored as much as possible to the ethnic background of the patient. It is of little value, for instance, to expect a woman to go out alone to evening Alcoholics Anonymous (AA) meetings at which both sexes are present, when her subculture proscribes such an activity. On the other hand, the therapist may take positive advantage of extended family systems by involving them in welding a support system for the newly-sober patient.

Psychiatric Problems

Mention has been made of the high incidence of reported anxiety, depression, and other symptoms of psychological distress in women alcholics coming to treatment. It has also been pointed out that women more often than men are able to pinpoint a specific stressful time in life when their abuse of alcohol began. These reports should not be looked upon as rationalizations, but as clues to the drinking patterns, alcohol dependencies, and treatment strategies that are best suited to each alcoholic woman. Although some secondary alcoholics will be suffering from schizophrenia, neurosis, and other psychiatric disorders, specific studies of the incidence of these combined disabilities in women have been few. Winokur and Clayton[18] were able to delineate specific sub groups of female alcoholics in part based upon psychiatric diagnosis.

Halikas et al[41] recently reported on 71 alcoholic women who were interviewed in a systematic structured psychiatric interview. Among these patients, 56% fulfilled criteria for some psychiatric diagnosis other than alcoholism.

The most common psychiatric diagnosis, in addition to alcoholism, was affective disorder. Twenty-eight percent of the total population fulfilled criteria for a diagnosis of either unipolar (24%) of bipolar (4%) affective disorder. Another 10% had a mixture of additional neurotic symptoms including anxiety, phobias, obsessions, and compulsions. A third group of 6% of the total population had manifest psychotic symptoms at some point in the past in addition to their alcohlism and affective disorder.

Nineteen percent of the total population fulfilled criteria for the diagnosis of antisocial personality. In the diagnosis of alcoholism and antisocial personality, 8% also had a variety of other psychiatric symptoms such as anxiety, depressive complaints, and obsessive-compulsive symptoms. It also has been assumed that the acute and chronic brain syndromes associated with alcohol withdrawal and prolonged alcohol use do not differ between men and women, although this is another area which awaits study.[42]

Treatment of Alcoholic Women

Casefinding. The three most effective early intervention programs available today, drinking-driver rehabilitation, public intoxicant intervention, and employee assistance programs, have one characteristic in common: they reach a far greater proportion of male problem drinkers than female ones.[17] Since the problems that motivate women to go into treatment are most likley to be health and family problems, and primary casefinders for the female will be physicians, other health professionals, social and family service agencies, and attorneys. These professionals require special training to enhance their abilities to identify and intervene effectively in women's alcohol problems. Because of the potential to prevent fetal alcohol syndrome, special attention must be given to women of childbearing age. The added motivation provided by the wish to bear a healthy child can be most helpful in treating the pregnant alcoholic. Wives of alcoholic husbands and mothers of children being evaluated or treated for mental retardation and/or behavioral and emotional problems should be considered target groups for casefinding.

Detoxification. In detoxifying the woman alcoholic, either on an inpatient or outpatient basis, special care must be given to the taking of a complete history of psychotropic drug use. Since women are more likely to be users as well as abusers of such substances, the clinician should be alert to the delayed symptoms that are associated with withdrawal from the benzo-diazepines. These symptoms are likely to begin between two and ten days after the abrupt discontinuation of alcohol and drug use and may include seizures as well as insomnia, tremor, anorexia, hallucinations, and disorientation.[43] Delayed convulsions in any alcohol withdrawal should lead the clinician to suspect drug dependence in the differential diagnosis along with head trauma and other causes for seizures.

Psychotherapy. Review of individual psychotherapy, the constructive use of typical alcoholic defenses, and the techniques of group therapy, family therapy, and psychodrama are available in this volume and elsewhere.[44] A few points specific to the treatment of women will be made in this section. Opinions differ regarding the relative efficacy of individual versus group therapy for alcoholic women, and of mixed-sex versus all-female groups.[17] In the absence of comparative studies, the best that can be said at present is that all three modes of therapy can be successful, provided that the therapist is sensitive to the special needs and problems of women.

Early in treatment, by whatever modality, emphasis is placed on two main factors. The first is the education of the patient and family in the disease concept of alcoholism and the necessity for a long-term treatment program for all involved. In dealing with an alcoholic women, there should be particular emphasis on the effects of drinking during pregnancy and the dangers of abuse of psychoactive drugs. Her children should be evaluated and helped in whatever way possible. Al-Anon and Alateen are widely available self-help groups which provide invaluable assistance to the families of such patients. The second emphasis early in treatment is on practical techniques for attaining abstinence. Contact with other alcoholic women who have recovered from the illness is of tremendous help in this endeavor. Such contact may be made in Alcoholics Anonymous or Women for Sobriety,[45] where such groups are available. A number of autobiographical works by recovering alcoholic women may also be helpful.[45–47] Key objectives during this phase are instilling hope and allaying guilt, a special problem with the alcoholic woman who faces a particularly strong societal stigma and often enters treatment with marked depression and reduced self-esteem. Teaching the techniques of deep relaxation and other nondrug measures for anxiety relief may also be very helpful at this stage.

With the relief of initial anxiety and depression, a great deal of buried anger may surface. The patient must be helped to evaluate this anger in terms of her own psychological, interpersonal, and social reality, bearing in mind the special problems in women outlined above. Channeling this anger and other energies and helping the patient structure time previously taken up by activities centered around drinking will be major issues in the second phase of treatment.

The use of psychoactive drugs should be kept to a minimum because of the danger of drug dependence. Many women recover from the depressive symptoms present during and immediately after detoxification without antidepressant drugs, in response to psychotherapy and group support as sobriety becomes established. In some cases, such drugs play an important role, as they may in the treatment of recurrent depression in the affective alcoholic woman. Disulfiram (Antabuse) may be helpful in the early stages of treatment of the nonpregnant women, although many patients prefer to try to maintain abstinence without it. In these patients, disulfiram is particularly helpful in treatment after relapse, when the patient may be amenable to this additional motivational aid.

Once abstinence has been established, psychotherapeutic attention will focus on remaining problems in the alcoholic patient's life. Each case must be handled differently, since no generalizations will apply to all women in this phase of treatment. Some, as we have mentioned above, will be suffering from affective alcoholism and will require prolonged contact with attention to possible recurrence of depression. Some will have predominantly sexual problems, either relating to sex role confict, to sexuality, or to specific marital problems. Assistance with parenting problems, assertiveness training, family therapy, vocational rehabilitation, and legal or spiritual counselling may be of considerable help in any individual case. Once sobriety is well established and new and constructive ways of handling the old problems previously dealt with by the use of alcohol have been developed, many women will have completed the formal part of their treatment. All should be encouraged to participate in long-term follow-up self-help groups, such as Alcoholics Anonymous or Women for Sobriety, and further professional help should be made available at times of particular stress. No patient should feel that he or she will receive help only if there is a return to active drinking. Some women, having attained a stable sobriety, will elect to continue psychotherapy in order to understand and alter residual neurotic or character defenses.

Among the pitfalls in psychiatric treatment of alcoholic women is the establishment by the patient of a hostile-dependent relationship on the therapist. The therapist must walk a thin line which includes a clear expression of the therapist's approval and expectation of sobriety, and at the same time makes clear that the responsibility for that sobriety is squarely in the lap of the patient. The patient may test the therapist's concern by a return to drinking. If she appears for an individual or group session under the influence of alcohol, care must be taken that neither overt nor subtle rewards for this behavior are provided. Such rewards might include being oversolicitous or allowing the patient to monopolize a group session. The therapist should clearly state the expectations that the patient will appear for the next session sober. The therapist must make sure realistic plans have been made to achieve that goal. Patients who miss a session should be pursued aggressively. Such a patient who, when contacted, states, that she feels she no longer needs help is likely to be heading for a relapse, whether or not she is consciously aware of that fact. Treatment should be terminated only after mutual discussion which includes plans for participation in a long-term self-help group. Particular attention must also be given to strict respect for patient confidentiality. Because the societal burdens of guilt and shame lie strongest on the alcoholic woman, she must be assured that statements made in group or individual treatment will not be repeated to others. The federal regulations for confidentiality of alcohol and drug abuse records go far to protect such information.[48]

Prognosis

Recent reviews of the literature[4,17] report that for unselected groups of alcoholic patients the prognosis in males and females is roughly the same. One study[49] followed a group of 103 alcoholic women ten years after treatment in a public and private mental hospital in St Louis. Control groups included 69 women treated for affective illness and 103 normal sisters of the probands. At ten years the differences in morality were striking. Thirty percent of the alcoholic group was dead, although their average age at treatment was only the mid-forties. The average age at death was 51 1/2 years, with 82% of the deceased alcoholic women dying under the age of 60 and half of these deaths associated with violence, suicide, or cirrhosis of the liver. In contrast, 16 1/2% of the depressed women had died, at an average age or 71 1/2 years. Only 10% of the depressed women died under the age of 60, and only 20% had causes of death that might have been connected with the depressive diagnosis.

This highly mortality rate points up the importance of making treatment available to all women in need. Treatment of relapses should be as vigorous as the initial episode. A positive attitude communicating an expectation of success on the part of the therapist is an important ingredient in such treatment.

Conclusion

This chapter has presented an overview of alcoholism in women with special attention to psychiatric problems and issues in treatment. We still have much to learn about alcohol problems, their causes, natural histories and outcomes, and the intervention and treatment approaches that work best with each problem type and subtype. Although this is true for all alcohol problems, it is especially true for women's problems, about which our knowledge is even less secure. Statistical estimates of numbers of female problem drinkers in the United States were purposefully omitted from the chapter. Such estimates vary widely depending on populations studied. Male to female ratios approaching equality are found in some private clinics, whereas 3:1 or 5:1 ratios are more characteristic of voluntary and public programs. Specialized treatment facilities such as those for drinking drivers or public inebriates often register ratios of 9:1 or 10:1. Household surveys present yet a different picture, as do studies of adolescents. It is sufficient for us at this point to know there are female alcoholics among us in all walks of life, all ethnic and all socioeconomic groups. Many of them are hidden drinkers; all of them destroying their own lives and the lives of those they love. Since alcoholics can and do recover, it is our duty and our privilege to assist these women in a manner most appropriate to the individual needs of each.

References

1. McKinlay AP: The Roman attitude toward women's drinking, in McCarthy RG (ed): *Drinking and Intoxication*. Glencoe, Ill, The Free Press, 1959.
2. Jellinek EM: Immanuel Kant on drinking. *Q J Stud Alcohol* 1:777–778, 1941.
3. Blume S, Dropkin D, Sokolow L: The Jewish alcoholic: A descriptive study. *Alcohol, Health and Research World* 4:21–26, Summer 1980.
4. Blume S: Women with alcoholism: The impact of treatment. *J Psychol Treatment and Evaluation* 2:225–229, 1980.
5. Lender M: *A Special Stigma*. Paper presented at the 1978 Alumni Institute, Rutgers University Summer School of Alcohol Studies, New Brunswick, NJ, 1978.
6. Youcha G: *A Dangerous Pleasure*. New York, Hawthorn Books, Inc, 1978.
7. Jellinek EM: Phases of alcohol addiction. *Q J Stud Alcohol* 13:673–684, 1952.
8. *Alcohol and Women*. NIAAA Reasearch Monograph 1. US Dept of Health, Education and Welfare no (ADM) 80–835, 1980.
9. Streissguth AP, Landesman-Dwyer S, Martin JC, *et al*: Teratogenic effects of alcohol in humans and laboratory animals. *Science* 209:353, 1980.
10. Beckman LJ: Alcoholism problems and women: An overview, in Greenblatt M, Schuckit MA (eds): *Alcoholism Problems in Women and Children*. New York, Grune & Stratton, 1976, pp 65–96.
11. Beckman LJ: Women alcoholics: A review of social and psychological studies. *J Stud Alcohol* 36:797–824, 1975.
12. Gomberg ES: Problems with alcohol and other drugs, in Gomberg ES, Franks V (eds): *Gender and Disordered Behavior: Sex Differences in Psychopathology*. New York, Brunner/Mazel, 1979, pp 204–240.
13. Homiller JD: Alcoholism among women. *Chem Dependencies* 4:1–31, 1980.
14. *International Classification of Diseases—9* (ICD-9). Ann Arbor, Mich, Commission on Professional and Hospital Activities, 1979.
15. *Diagnostic and Statistical Manual of Mental Disorders* (DSM-III). Washington, DC, American Psychiatric Association, 1980.
16. Armor DJ, Polich JM, Stambul HB: *Alcoholism and Treatment* New York, John Wiley and Sons, 1978.
17. Blume S: Researches on women and alcohol, in NIAAA Research Monograph 1: *Alcohol and Women*. US Dept of Health, Education and Welfare, 80–835, 1980, pp 121–151.
18. Winokur G, Clayton P: Family histories IV: Comparison of male and female alcoholics. *Q J Stud Alcohol* 29:885–891, 1972.

19. Goodwin D, Schulsinger F, Hermansen L, *et al*: Alcohol problems in adoptees raised apart from alcoholic biological parents. *Arch Gen Psychiatry* 28:238–243, 1973.
20. Goodwin D, Schulsinger F, Knop J, *et al*: Alcoholism and depression in adopted-out daughters of alcoholics. *Arch Gen Psychiatry* 34:751–755, 1977.
21. Jones MC: Personality antecedents and correlates of drinking patterns in women. *J Consult Clin Psychol* 36:61–69, 1971.
22. Jones MC: Personality correlates and antecedents of drinking patterns in adult males. *J Consult Clin Psychol* 32:2–12, 1968.
23. Fillmore KM, Bacon SD, Hyman M: *The 27 Year Longitudinal Panel Study of Drinking by Students in College.* Final Report 1979 to NIAAA contract ADM 281–76–0015. Washington, DC, NIAAA, 1979.
24. Wilsnack SC: Sex role identity in female alcoholism. *J Abnorm Psychol* 82:253–261, 1973.
25. Wilsnack SC: The impact of sex roles on women's alcohol use and abuse, in Greenblatt M, Schuckit MA (eds): *Alcoholism Problems in Women and Children.* New York, Grune & Stratton, 1976.
26. Beckman LJ: Sex-role conflict in alcoholic women: Myth or reality. *J Abnorm Psychol* 84:408–417, 1978.
27. Jones BM, Jones MK: Women and alcohol: Intoxication, metabolism, and the menstrual cycle, in Greenblatt M, Schuckit MA (eds): *Alcoholism Problems in Women and Children.* New York, Grune & Stratton, 1976.
28. Little RE, Schultz FA, Mandell W: Drinking during pregnancy. *J Stud Alcohol* 37:375–379, 1976.
29. Lyons J, Welte J, Hines G, *et al*: *Outcome Study of Alcoholism Rehabilitation Units.* Albany, NYS Division of Alcoholism and Alcohol Abuse, Nov 1979.
30. Beckman L: Self-esteem of women alcoholics. *J Stud Alcohol* 39:491–498, 1978.
31. Schuckit M, Morrissey ER: Alcoholism in women: Some clinical and social perspectives with an emphasis on possible subtypes, in Greenblatt M, Schuckit MA (eds): *Alcoholism Problems in Women and Children.* New York, Grune & Stratton, 1976.
32. Clarren S, Smith D: The fetal alcohol syndrome. *N Engl J Med* 298:1063–1067, 1978.
33. Rossett HL, Ouellette EM, Werner L, *et al*: Therapy of heavy drinking during pregnancy. *Obstet Gynecol* 51:41–46, 1978.
34. Seiden AM: Overview: Research on the psychology of women. I: Gender differences and sexual and reproductive life. *Am J Psychiatry* 133:995–1007, 1976.
35. Seiden AM: Overview: Research on the psychology of women. II: Women in families, work and psychotherapy. *Am J Psychiatry* 133:1111–1123, 1976.
36. Report of the task force of sex bias and sex-role stereotyping in psychotherapeutic practice. *Am Psychol* 1169–1175, December 1975.
37. Broverman D, Broverman I, Clarkson F, *et al*: Sex-role stereotypes and clinical judgments of mental health. *J of Consulting and Clinical Psychology* 34:1–7, 1970.
38. Women's Action Alliance: Women at Work Exposition 1978 Conference Report, 1978.
39. Schultz T: Does marriage give today's women what they really want? 30,000 Journal readers share their intimate lives. *Ladies' Home Journal*, June 1980, 89–155.
40. Carpenter JA, Ammenti NP: Some effects of ethanol on human sexual and aggressive behavior, in Kissin B, Begleiter H (eds): *The Biology of Alcoholism* vol 2. New York, Plenum Press, 1972.
41. Halikas JA, Herzog MA, Mirassou MM, Lyttle MD: Psychiatric diagnosis among female alcoholics, in Galanter M (ed): *Currents in Alcoholism*, vol 8. New York, Grune & Stratton, in press.
42. Hill SY: Introduction: The biological consequences, in *Alcohol and Women.* NIAAA Research Monograph 1. US Dept of Health and Welfare publ no (ADM) 80–835 1980, pp 45–62.

43. Benzer D, Cushman P: Alcohol and benzodiazepines: Withdrawal syndromes. *Alcoholism: Clinical and Experimental Research* 4:243–247, 1980.

44. Zimberg A, Wallace J, Blume SB, (eds): *Practical Approaches to Alcoholism Psychotherapy*. New York, Plenum Press, 1978.

45. Kirkpatrick J: *Turnabout: Help for a New Life*. Garden City, NY, Doubleday and Co, Inc, 1978.

46. Allen C: *I'm Black and I'm Sober*. Minneapolis, Comp Care publications, 1978.

47. Burditt JR: *The Cracker Factory*. London, Collier Macmillan Publishers, 1977.

48. *Confidentiality of Alcohol and Drug Abuse Patient Records*. Federal Register, Dept of Health, Education, and Welfare, 127. Washington, DC, July 1, 1975.

49. Smith E: *Alcoholism and Depression in Women: A Preliminary Report on Mortality at Ten Year Follow-Up*. Presented at the National Conference on Alcoholism, Alcoholism Forum, Washington, DC, April 29, 1979.

CHAPTER 14

The Contribution of Psychoanalysis to the Treatment of Alcoholism

AUSTIN SILBER, MD

This report represents the crystallization of knowledge derived from supervising the psychotherapy of alcoholic patients in a clinic setting. The therapists were psychiatric residents, social workers, and social work students. The therapy was once-a-week psychotherapy based on psychoanalytic concepts and principles and was, by design, supportive and informative.

The techniques for treating these alcoholic patients underwent a gradual evolution, and some of this material is abstracted from other papers which emphasize the formulation and application of these psychotherapeutic techniques.[1-5]

During the initial years of therapy conducted at our clinic, therapists were encouraged to concentrate, as early in treatment as was feasible, upon the expressed anxiety of their patients. Anxiety was a constant finding, and its intensity was frequently the most important factor leading to the selection of patients for treatment. It was decided to regard this manifest anxiety as representative of the alcoholic's fear and intolerance of internalized aggression.

Knowledge of the developmental histories of the patients emphasized excessive, phase-inappropriate, frustrating, and/or overstimulating behavior on the part of their parents. This noxious behavior was especially marked during the preoedipal years. One consequence of this was the activation during childhood of considerable latent aggression. However, patients consistently failed to appreciate this specific residue of aggression which was added to, and significantly amplified, other derivatives of their anger or rage. Instead, the patients were conscious of experiencing intense anxiety. It was

AUSTIN SILBER • Clinical Professor of Psychiatry, Training and Supervising Analyst, The Psychoanalytic Institute at the New York University Medical Center, New York, New York 10023.

these anxious feelings (signifying the festering rage) which demanded the therapist's prompt attention.

Early in treatment, the therapist would attempt to ascribe the increase of anxiety to a contemporary figure in the patient's present environment. A friend or superior could be seen as the person currently functioning in a thwarting capacity. The therapists were encouraged to focus on objects of secondary rather than primary significance, that is, a friend or boss rather than a mate or parent. The patient was told that he was fearful of experiencing rage directed at this person but instead felt anxious. The therapist used his knowledge of the general dynamics of the alcoholic patient in a manipulative and seductive fashion, quickly presenting himself as an all-knowing, omniscient figure. By interpreting the fear rather than the wish, the therapist functioned in consonance with the patient's ego. Since this exposition was initiated early in therapy, a magical element was rapidly introduced. The therapist's unique knowledge about what was transpiring in the patient's mind was offered in such a manner as to elevate the therapist into the role of an omniscient, powerful figure.

With this newly acquired authority, the therapist then pursued an educational approach. Patients were encouraged to experience, recognize, define, and accept their feelings. Any action as a response to feelings was regarded as a completely separate matter. It was stressed that action requires judgment. Behavior was thus clearly differentiated from affective experience. Feelings, wishes, fantasies, and thoughts were all given a positive valence. Actions, however, were to be avoided as an automatic response to feelings. Feelings must first be reflected upon and actions restrained until judgment deemed the activity appropriate.

Through this approach, some of the superego's generalized primitiveness and punitiveness was mitigated, and a better appreciation of reality was enhanced by making explicit the differences between feeling, thinking, and doing. Even though magic was invoked, developmentally significant knowledge was restitutively imparted.

In those therapeutic encounters where the depressive affect rather than anxiety was most prominent, the sense of guilt was initially highlighted. It was noted as a manifestation of the wish to be punished because of one's aggressive impulses and wishes. Once again it became necessary to differentiate between wishes and feelings on one hand and actions on the other. It was stressed again and again that all wishes need be regarded as acceptable, reasonable and desirable. It was only in relation to actions that guilt was acknowledged as an appropriate emotional response. If present, it had meaning but was most likely the consequence of the failure to differentiate among feeling, thinking, and acting and was the result of punishing oneself because of aggressive wishes.

Masochistically provocative behavior, a frequent finding in this therapy, is dealt with in much the same way. It is clearly defined as stemming from the patient's wish to be punished because of aggressive impulses. Once again the therapist reiterates the need to be accepting of all impulses, feelings, and thoughts. Actions, on the other hand, require careful deliberation. Behavior must be monitored so that it is realistic and reasonable. The patients are encouraged to experience more of their inner lives and exhorted to accept this aspect of themselves. This positive educational effort also helps to diminish the severity of the superego's demands and strengthens the ego's ability to be in control. The differences between inner and outer reality are more explicitly defined as these patients are encouraged and helped to separate and differentiate feelings from actions.

This opening approach, which is basically manipulative, using knowledge about dynamics in a magical vein, helps forge a strong early bond between patient and therapist. As treatment progresses, the therapist shifts from playing the role of the omniscient figure to that of a more benign, consistent, parental type—benevolent in so far as wishes and feelings are concerned, firm in avoiding unevaluated action, and consistent in clarifying the distinction between wishes, feelings and actions.

Over a period of years, it became more apparent that the therapist's attitudes toward both the alcoholic patient and his symptomatology frequently had a significant effect upon the course of the treatment. As a result, emphasis in supervision shifted from the delineation of the fears in regard to aggression and the resultant magical effect this recognition exerted in the therapy, to efforts to help the therapist quickly recognize and appreciate the essential helplessness of these patients. By attempting to modify the therapist's preconceived attitude, which frequently was latently antagonistic, it was hoped further to facilitate the successful treatment of these patients.

The therapist was urged to regard lack of sobriety as a symptom in a dynamic sense similar to other familiar symptoms, such as compulsive or phobic ones. These recognizable symptoms in all psychotherapies are generally approached with circumspection until their function in the psychological life of the patient is adequately appreciated. The therapists, in a series of lecture-seminars, were given an intellectual grasp of the function of symptoms, for example, a compromise formation between a drive derivative and the opposition to it in a situation of conflict, with the consequent binding of anxiety. Signal anxiety, the hierarchy of danger situations described from the genetic point of view,[6] and the hierarchy of responses available to the ego were also discussed. The importance of the ego's biphasic response to anxiety, that is, the evaluation of the danger and its magnitude, imminence, and pertinence, as well as the ego's reaction to this evaluation,[7] was sketched in for the therapists, and the differences between feeling and acting were reemphasized. It is in differentiating feeling from behaving that the ego's biphasic response (i.e., evaluation and reaction to evaluation) is of such importance and of such immediate clinical usefulness.

The symptom of alcoholism is frequently given a special significance in that it absorbs more and more of the attention and concern of the patient and assumes more and more importance in his life. Concurrent with this increased absorption in the process of drinking is the gradual impairment of certain ego functions which cease to operate autonomously and are caught up in the conflicting forces that in a dynamic and economic sense affect the structure of the symptom. The perception of reality and the interest in, meaning of, the constancy of this perception, can all be affected to varying degrees. The ego's integration and utilization of this percept is also compromised. Other autonomous ego functions affecting judgment, anticipation, thinking, object comprehension, recall, language, capacity for self observation, delay of action, and motility can also lose their autonomy in a similar way as they are embroiled in conflict. The manner in which the patient's ego will be able to handle functions dependent upon optimal ego autonomy is thus affected. Moreover, one frequent psychological consequence of the ingestion of alcohol is the *illusion* that impaired autonomous functions have been restored to optimal activity as a consequence of the drinking.

The loss of ego autonomy has an immediate effect upon any kind of psychotherapy because the autonomous functions are the medium through which the patient communicates with the therapist[8] and through which it is possible to make inferences about the functioning of the psychic apparatus. The psychotherapeutic situation, which by its very nature accentuates the importance of certain of these autonomous functions, for example, self-observation and verbalization, is dramatically altered as a consequence of impairment. Thus, it should become apparent that it is the therapist's task to recognize the deficits inherent in this psychotherapeutic situation and that the therapist's ego must supply the necessary reparative ingredients. He must be prepared to do more talking and make observations about the patient that one would ordinarily expect the patient to make unaided.

These elements are all emphasized so that the therapist will not initially concentrate all interest upon the drinking *per se*, but will begin to recognize that the drinking itself represents an attempt to deal with many conflicting ideas and impulses, as yet unknown to either the patient or the therapist. It is important to stress the fundamental interest in the need to understand the meaning of behavior, even if this goal is not attainable with the therapeutic means available.

The therapists were familiarized with alcoholic patients' general need to be cared for and with the fact that they often experience extreme emotional deprivation. These explanations are necessary to overcome the therapists' reticence in actively explaining to their patients the purpose of the psychotherapy, the particular methods being used, and the rationale implicit in this psychotherapeutic approach. Such an exposition by the therapist constitutes an early satisfaction given to the patient within the structure of the therapeutic situation; it is consonant with a psychologically sound initiation of therapy with the alcoholic patient.

In preliminary sessions, these ideas are discussed and, in a sense, rehearsed with the therapists, who are explicitly urged to share their understanding with their patients as early as possible.

The object of the psychotherapy is outlined in terms of helping the patient to function more comfortably and with greater awareness of himself and his surroundings. The patient is made aware that there are many determinants to his condition, and he will gradually become cognizant of the meanings and the effects they exert upon him. As the patient verbalizes his complaints and concerns, the therapist will, with time, help him view these concerns from different vantage points, many of them quite novel to the patient and helpful in alleviating some of his pain and discomfort. The more he is able to understand about his life and his difficulties, the more control he will be able to exert over the concerns that cause him pain. In this endeavor, the therapist can help by listening, remembering, and aiding the patient to learn to deepen his own awareness of himself. The patient is offered the expectation that through increased knowledge and understanding comes increased control over his person and his functioning. Such increased control becomes the cornerstone of therapy.

Actually, this preliminary work orients both the therapist and the patient toward regarding the therapeutic situation as the basis of a joint venture. The expectations of the patient and the functions of the therapist have been outlined, and the psychotherapeutic equivalent of the "working alliance" has been fostered. In psychoanalysis, the working alliance has been defined as "that part of the therapeutic alliance related to the healthy portions of the patient's ego. This involves the reality relationship between doctor and patient".[9] "Therapeutic alliance" is a more inclusive term, bringing into consideration positive transference in addition to the real relationship between the patient and the analyst.[10-12] In this psychotherapeutic milieu, an engrafted intellectual construct built around the depiction and description of the psychotherapeutic situation is offered as a common bond with the patient for the joint therapeutic effort. This forms the nidus for the "therapeutic working compact,"[3] which incorporates elements in the working alliance (reality relationship between doctor and patient) plus the suggestive element inherent in the construct of the psychotherapeutic situation, with its implied promise of relief if the patient cooperates. This added element is necessary because these patients need a more rapid and concrete depiction of the structure of the therapeutic situation to ward off the anxiety that would otherwise accrue from their being subjected to the more abstinent, slowly evolving, gradually structured, analytical sort of situation. The ego of the alcoholic requires nurturing, not judicious neglect.

It has already been noted that many of the so-called autonomous ego functions[13] of the alcoholic patient are impaired in their operations. This is a result of the alcoholic's increasing preoccupation with the drinking itself and the resultant deflection of interest from those functions. The therapist lends his own autonomous functions as a temporary prosthesis[9] for the patient. This might involve supplying help in the recognition of a judgment the patient was making in testing the reality of that judgment, in determining the meaning and meaningfulness of the judgment in the patient's present and past life situations, and in helping the patient to integrate the judgment in a psychologically useful sense. In the same manner, perceptions, observations, ideas, and feelings have to be scrutinized. The patient must be helped to learn the use of the many evaluative activities that are operative prior to making a decision or initiating an action. As the therapist "lends" the alcoholic his ego abilities in areas where the alcoholic's are defective, it is the therapist's ego functions which tend to replace the patient's reliance on alcohol, which, as previously mentioned, has given the alcoholic the illusion of adequate performance.

As can be seen, this approach to the psychotherapy of the alcoholic patient is at marked variance with the traditional analytic method. The rationale for this approach comes from knowledge originally gleaned from psychoanalysis and modified to fit our particular objective in psychotherapy. Thus, in the psychotherapy of the alcoholic, we deal with reality problems, impaired reality functioning, and the altered autonomy of ego functions in a reparative sense first. The "therapeutic working compact" will come in next for repeated scrutiny, and interpretations will be offered to thwart any attempts to infringe upon its viability. Transference interpretations, as a rule, will be avoided. The transference relationship will be interpreted as a last resort in order to maintain the therapeutic working compact. In the interpretation, the therapist will first be described as representing the wished-for parent from the past. The therapist will also be seen as supplying those attributes and attitudes which the parents never supplied but which the patient so desperately missed.

Practically, this means that only those negative transference reactions that threaten the viability of the therapy will be interpreted. The same goes for erotic positive transference features. Transference interpretations are eschewed to avoid bringing genetically earlier determinants into the forefront of the therapy, which emphasizes present functioning. The genetic elements that do emerge are recast into a perspective that highlights our intellectual knowledge regarding individual psychic development (thus, making general the specific element learned, as well as isolating its unique emotional significance). This is done instead of concentrating upon specific libidinal fixations and the actual consequences of regressive tugs. The defense of isolation is being energetically fostered.

Symptoms are noted and respected. They will generally come into the center of the therapeutic arena when ample knowledge of their defensive significance has been understood and the importance of the patient's compromise formations has been absorbed by the therapist. Only symptom formation that seems manifestly deleterious to the patient's well-being and ability to continue therapy will be circumspectly probed (eg, denial). Defenses, and certain character traits, are usually reinforced rather than attacked. For example, reaction formations and some counterphobic activities are strengthened rather than analyzed. In general, an attempt is made to enhance existing defenses,[14,15] with some of the binding element being contributed by the therapist's ego functions, which are temporarily lent to the patient. These ego operations are offered to enable the patient to gain greater recognition of his own inner world, his person, and his environment. They are also essential to help make the therapeutic situation viable, since it is dependent for its stability upon the intactness of these autonomous activities. These autonomous functions focus the communications between patient and therapist and sharpen the patient's ability to grasp his own inner world. The therapeutic approach is both manipulative and seductive. It takes as much advantage as possible of our knowledge of the general psychological background of patients suffering from alcoholism. Their need to be given and cared for is exploited by our detailed explanations, which begin to offer a structure of some stability within which the treatment will be conducted. Suggestion is used in a psychologically sound sense that takes advantage of the basically unstable sense of identity these patients manifest. They are psychologically open, looking for precepts, guidance, information, and general help in learning how to live. They are searching for a parent who can be consistent, fair, and informative and who will employ all his pertinent knowledge in the patients' interest. We take advantage of the neglect and omissions and attempt to supply, in a genetically general rather than specific sense, what we suspect is developmentally lacking. We help build a picture of an inner world which has some psychological fidelity and lend ourselves, especially our attitudes and knowledge, for them to use. We try to make do by offering a synthetic psychic structure that represents them, others, and their new-found psychic world. This provides a consistent generalized reflection through which these essentially unstable and identity-less individuals can view themselves.

Another important observation also helps explain why these patients are so open to change if the therapy is conducted by a reasonable, benign, knowledgeable, and consistent therapist. Almost all alcoholic patients seen had at least one parent who manifestly displayed psychotic behavior. Such behavior was especially pronounced during the early developmental years and exerted a profound and far-reaching effect upon the development of these rather vulnerable individuals.

The significance of the family constellation in the etiology of alcoholism has been stressed by many authors. Knight[16-18] indicated that both parents affect the development and elaboration of the illness. Simmel[19] described mothers who overtly seduced and manipulated their children. When the child, as a result of this marked overstimulation, responded to the seduction with a sexual response of its own, it was unmercifully attacked by the outraged parent. This behavior is similar to that of parents of sexually delinquent children described by Litin et al,[20] Johnson,[21] and Szurek.[22] These workers noted that the delinquent sexual behavior of these children was an acting out of the sexual impulses of their parents. Chafetz[23] felt that "the common thread running through these patients' early relationships was the absence of a warm, giving, meaningful relationship with a mother figure during this early period of development." Ferenczi[24] noted that pathological adults, especially if they have been disturbed in their balance and self-control by some misfortune or by intoxicating drugs, mistake the play of children for the desire of a sexually mature person and allow themselves to be carried away. "The real rape of girls who have hardly grown out of the age of infants, similar sexual acts of mature women with boys, and also enforced homosexual acts, are more frequent occurrences than has hitherto been assumed."[24]

One psychiatrist in training described an alcoholic stepfather who insisted on sleeping in the same bed with his ten-year-old stepson. The other son and mother were banished from the bedroom. The boy developed an anal tear with moderate bleeding which required suturing at a local hospital emergency room. The stepfather attacked the boy for having irregular bowel habits and was reinforced in his verbal and physical abuse by the mother and the spared stepbrother. I had some difficulty convincing the resident that it was necessary to intervene with the mother of this boy (she was the alcoholic patient in treatment) and to help rescue him from the bedroom and the activities of this stepfather.

This type of tale is frequently reported by alcoholic patients about parents. The bizarre actions often take place when the parents are in a state of alcoholic intoxication, at which point there is minimal control of impulses and reality-testing by the ego. In other instances, the strange behavior is an expression of the chronic psychological disturbance of the parent. Chafetz,[23] in enumerating factors contributing to the emotional deprivation of alcoholic patients, listed the fact that as children they had psychotic mothers and that some parents were also severely alcoholic during the patient's early years.

In therapy, the reality of the parents' abnormalities is pointed out and worked over. Since the bizarreness had been part of the developmental reality of the patient's background, the ability to see the parents' disturbed behavior against the background of an average environment may be possible for the first time. This approach, if successful, gives rise to a great sense of relief on the part of the patient. It helps him to see not only the parent, but himself as well—as Shengold[25] noted, "to see and not to be" the parent.

This atypical parental behavior is enmeshed within the family structure. Attempts at clarification evolve into a problem of ferreting out those aspects of the family situation that are pathological in the psychological sense from those that are more consistently normal. This understanding then provides a background against which the symptomatology of the parent can be judged more accurately. The extensive identification with the parents' abnormalities still affects the patient's character and behavior in the present. These pathological identifications represent a bond with the parent and compromise the patient's separate identity. There is special damage to one's sense of identity and a satisfactory integration of disparate aspects of the personality when the attitudes and actions of the parents are contradictory, confused, bizarre, or psychotic.

The therapist, who is placed in the role of an ideal, can be substituted in the patient's mind for the disturbed parental figure so that the possibility for new identifications with a healthy, reality-oriented figure is possible. This is a process that takes place slowly and silently as therapy progresses. It is often responsible for the rather marked changes in behavior that can be observed in the psychotherapy of the alcoholic. Sudden shifts in comportment are frequent. Some patients will precipitously give up drinking. They may start to work more steadily or suddenly become aware of very positive feelings toward their spouse. They become willing to listen to the judgment of the therapist and will readily substitute his attitudes for their own. Many alcoholic patients seem to form easily rapid although shallow and diffuse temporary identifications. These may be based upon the tentative acceptance of the therapist's criteria for reasonable behavior as being consonant with their own newly evolving values. The standards of the therapist are gradually absorbed by the patient, and those of the disturbed parent are reevaluated against the new models held forth by the therapist. The patient, with this therapist's help, learn to reevaluate attitudes that are based on superego identifications and functions that are dependent upon ego tendencies. As internalized elements of the disturbed parent that are represented in both the ego and the superego of the patient are critically evaluated, they can be replaced by features that are now derived from the therapeutic working compact between therapist and patient. This process is frequently expedited by the patient's ease in resorting to imitation and mimicry. The sense of identity in these patients is tarnished and burdened by the pathological parental attitudes, and they have a marked "as if" propensity.[26] They vicariously adopt attitudes of others easily and adeptly. Thus, an attempt is made to exploit this pathological ego tendency therapeutically, but at the same time to foster attitudes based on the therapeutic working compact with the therapist.

In a therapeutic sense, one is first setting oneself up in opposition to the parent by highlighting his or her unrealistic attitudes. The patient will frequently be pleased to have the therapist as an ally who acts as an extension of his ego for reality-testing and who serves as an opponent of his parents. Therapists have continually found themselves in this role in opposition to some of the traditional views of the parent. The difference in this instance is that the focus is on the pathology of the parent. The parent's disturbed behavior is made alien to the rest of the parent's functions. This helps the patient to recognize aspects of the parent's disturbed behavior within himself and then to make this ideation of behavior alien to the rest of his personality. The therapist offers his views as representative of a different reality from the parent's now discredited and objectively faulty perception and depiction of reality. The patient now has the opportunity to compare and choose a view of reality with a freedom heretofore denied him by virtue of the early pathological identifications.

One can trace the vicissitudes of parents' pathology as seen in the alcoholic patient. Frequently, these patients act out in relation to their own children certain trauma inflicted upon them as children. The action is frequently carried out in a fury, during which there may be some subtly altered state of consciousness, so that the patient gives the impression of being momentarily "lost." In this instance, a hypnoid state[27] wards off the patient's awareness of certain drives and affects. This defective ego control permits an "acting out" of primitive impulses. In one instance, the same hairbrush that was used on a patient was saved and used in exactly the same manner on the patient's own child.

Another very frequent manifestation of irrationality that also must be interpreted involves the patient's attacking himself the way he was attacked by a disturbed parent. This is an example of identification with the aggressor,[28] whose actions are internalized and made syntonic. The element of identification with the parent must be pointed out, made alien, and interpreted. Further vicissitudes of the pathology of the parent can then be followed by noting externalizations of elements of behavior onto other figures in the environment, with a quasi-delusional effect. For instance, every superior is seen as a demanding, irrational, tormenting object. This often has little to do with his actual behavior, for, by using primary process mechanisms, especially *pars pro toto*, and displacements, a slight element in the behavior of the superior becomes *the* behavior of the superior. All of this can be profitably traced back through patient to parent. It is also manifestly obvious that elements of distortion of this kind will be perceived by the patient in relation to the person of the therapist. It then becomes clearer why the delineation of the pathology of the parent strengthens in the psychotherapy the entity analogous to the working alliance in analysis, which is the important element in the patient–therapist relationship, in its "real" rather than its "transference" implications. The therapist becomes an understanding ally in dealing with a frequently overwhelming and shattering experience (the experience of the patient with his disturbed parent). The therapist is initially acting like an auxiliary ego and one that is anchored in reality, rather than the parental ego that was rooted in pathology. The therapist thus allies himself with the healthy portion of the patient's ego against the ill parts. This joint effort, involving the highlighting of the pathology of the parent, contributes to a rapid and early welding of the therapeutic working compact. It provides the necessary ingredients for withstanding some of the transference reactions that may arise in the course of therapy and also helps blunt the intensity of the pathological projections onto the therapist of the internalized parental attributes.

After the pathology of the parent is clearly defined as constituting a major problem in the way the patient views his person, one that alters in a most deforming way his sense of self and thus his sense of identity, this part of the therapeutic task can recede. This technique, which alerts the therapist to look for rather typical pathological behavior as an indication of parental disturbance, is a most valuable addition to the therapeutic armamentarium, facilitating the successful psychotherapy of the alcoholic patient.

Thus, basic psychoanalytic information derived from our increased knowledge of the sequence and importance of early development, especially the skewing effect of the severe parental pathology upon this development, provides the background of data through which to view the alcoholic patient.

We know that maturation took place in an environment that would not be considered a generally expectable one and that these patients have needs that were not met during phase-appropriate periods in their development. They are literally bound to their primary objects by virtue of unsatisfied needs and have great difficulty moving on to more appropriate objects. Their frustration tolerance is minimal, as is their ability to bear anxiety. They were not adequately helped to differentiate their wishes from their actions by the imposition of proper parental restraint. Self-control is minimal, pleasure in experiencing feelings, evaluating them, and making decisions in regard to action has to be learned in the present therapeutic situation. The therapist is viewed, and in a way acts, as the wished-for and needed parent, a parent who in reality was too psychologically disturbed to be developmentally helpful and who left the patient with a residue of distorted and fragmented ego functions and a lasting object hunger. As a group, these patients lack a stable or consistent inner psychological structure. Their sense of identity is unjelled, as is any stable sense of self. They eagerly seize upon any suggestive information supplied by the therapist that will provide support for their inner being. They need help in evaluating what they observe in others, and frequently they need to be taught how to evaluate their self-observations as well. It is their openness to suggestion, but virtue of their extensive psychological disturbance and vulnerability, that makes the strongly suggestive approach outlined in this paper such an effective tool for therapy. Suggestions, in the form of information and knowledge, are imparted in an intellectual manner with the object of fostering the defense of isolation.

The therapist supplies a new psychological matrix in the form of intact ego functions that are lent out to the patient to make up for those functions that are found to be developmentally deficient because of parental pathology. In therapy, the parent's deficiencies are clearly highlighted so as to help the patient separate his attitudes, ideas, and functioning from theirs. As the therapist helps in this process, he permits his attitudes, ideas, and methods of functioning to be substituted for those of the degraded and psychologically deformed parent. The readiness and openness to change that these patients demonstrate frequently lead to dramatically effective therapeutic results. These are not, however, because of any real understanding or insight into motivation for either the drinking or for giving it up. The patients are responding to sound suggestions which they may view as a beloved order from a longed-for and needed parent who has been essentially absent in a developmentally helpful sense but is now experienced as present in the form of the therapist.

This technique utilizes insight in the form of increasing knowledge of certain functions of the ego, which may be initially defined and offered by the therapist and finally may be utilized by the patient. The patient is familiarized with his inner life and its differentiation from his external world. He is also supplied with more general information about the norms of development. Insight is thus offered in a more selective sense with less stress on the more traditional transference and resistence. More emphasis is also placed on defining and explicating various ego functions and general developmental knowledge. The main vehicle for change revolves around new identifications with the ideas and attitudes of the therapist, which replace those of the pathological parents.

The next hypothesis follows upon the observation regarding the psychotic parent as a developmental reality in the life of the alcoholic patient. The alcoholic patient, as a child, would in all likelihood respond to an assault by psychotic parents in a manner similar to those patients reported by Fleiss[29] and Shengold.[30,31] They noted that children traumatized and overstimulated by psychotic parents resort to what they called hypnosis and what Dickes[27] defined as a hypnoid state. Thus Dickes, in speaking of the adult hypnoid state, says, "This adult state is often a repetition of a childhood hypnoid state which occurred as a means of warding off intolerable feelings due to overstimulation and abuse."[(p397)] He continues:

> I would venture the opinion that all who suffer from this syndrome to any marked degree have encountered unusual and excessive seductions and beatings. These injurious and devastating traumata, usually inflicted by parents, were carried to such an extreme and intolerable degree as to force these unlucky children to seek refuge in a stupor which can be likened only to the deep trance state of hypnosis.[(397)]

In carefully listening to the reports of many alcoholic patients, one notes their efforts to achieve a comfortable intoxicated (clouded or altered) state. This altered state of awareness is similar to the defensive stupor adopted by the abused child. *It is this state of mind that can be reinstituted by the ingestion of alcohol.* This altered state, of varying depths, is actively sought and can be regularly induced by the ingestion of alcohol. The ingestion of alcohol now magically brings about the hypnoid state. The function of actively inducing this state is to ward off the reexperiencing and remembering of the painful feelings and frightening memories related to early traumatic events. Instead, the defense against these traumas—the hypnoid state—takes over. At the same time, the defense mechanism of denial is fostered and enhanced by fantasies that seek to undo, master, and overcome the early trauma. These fantasies are woven together and structured in both conscious and unconscious forms. These pleasurable fantasies now likened to the alcohol-induced hypnoid state form a significant inducement to drink. A fantasy world based on the denial of the original trauma and maintained by the actively induced hypnoid state is repeatedly sought.

An example of the evocation of the hypnoid state by ingesting alcohol follows. A therapist reported on a young male patient, in his early twenties, who would rush to a neighborhood bar immediately after work. He was aware of a sense of unease as he sat on a bar stool and looked at the bartender. Instead of asking for a drink, he would point to a bottle of bourbon (Old Grandad) and by motioning with his hand indicate that he wanted a drink. After downing this drink, he would immediately indicate his desire to have another of the same, as he paid for the initial drink. The patient described to his therapist the pleasant, peaceful feeling that supervened with the quick dispatch of his refill. He felt at ease, though somewhat foggy and not fully alert: "Not quite with it, a little drowsy but feeling no pain." (Similar expressions have been used by many of the alcoholic patients treated. This is the state they wish to attain and strive to remain in as long as possible.) The other customers in the bar seemed friendly. Once he had succeeded in reaching this pleasant fuzzy state, a state I would define as a self-induced hypnoid state, he wished that time could be suspended, he felt so at ease. As Dickes has noted, the hypnoid defense "is one of the most primitive among the ego's repertory of defenses and perhaps most closely related to denial."[27(p398)]

The patient's father and grandfather were both heavy drinkers. He remembers his father at home, drunk, screaming abuse at him and his two younger siblings. He remembers a younger brother being picked up by his father and flung onto the floor with such force that a leg was broken and had to be placed in a cast. His father was hospitalized after suffering a nervous breakdown and spent some years in a mental institution. He recalls his father screaming in terror, fearful that a prowler in the apartment would attack him with a knife "which he shoved up his ass." His father also felt that his own father had instigated this prowler to attack him. The patient remembers how he feared his father's shouting and cursing and how he dreaded going home after school for fear of what he would find. His father might be drunk and fighting his own father. While the patient was a child, the grandfather lived with the family for some years. His mother was quiet; she would sit at home looking helpless, withdrawn, and apathetic. She never intervened to protect the children. As soon as the patient finished high school, he obtained a job and moved into his own apartment, a short distance from where his mother still lived.

He became aware of being fearful of returning to his own apartment after work and went to a neighborhood bar instead. As he bolted down the liquor, he was aware of the warm feeling in his stomach. He felt protected and safe. The alcohol made him feel comforted and secure. He realized that this was what he had always hoped his mother would do. He remembered thinking, "Dear mother," as he downed the drink.

It became apparent that a number of unconscious fantasies were being acted out in his bar ritual. They represented his attempt, in fantasy at least, to exert control over some area of his life. Thus, choosing to go the bar represented his attempt to set up a different home atmosphere. The bartender, who would respond to his gesture and provide the liquor that brought about the good feeling in his stomach, was supplying the kind of satisfying substance (milk) that symbolized the comfort he wished his mother could have given him. Shortly after swallowing, he would become aware of a pleasant, slightly drowsy feeling, his state of awareness would change, and the sought-after hypnoid state supervened. In fantasy, he was feeling protected by his mother, whose advocacy he evoked magically by pointing and handling and swallowing the liquor. As the hypnoid state induced by the alcohol began to take over, the anxiety he had initially experienced began to dissipate. He was now no longer fearful that he would be screamed at or abused. In fact, he was able magically and silently to bring about this good feeling by having the bartender fill his glass. Thus, the bartender also represented, in unconscious fantasy, a now tractable father who could, without an uproar, help make the patient feel comfortable. By ordering Old Grandad, he was also magically converting his grandfather, whom he also feared, into a now benign, comforting agent magically helping to disspell his fears. As the effect of the alcohol became more apparent and as the self-induced hypnoid state deepened, he felt that his life was a comfortable one in these warm, accepting surroundings. He felt as though he were at home, the way he had always wished home would feel—safe and protected, with parents (bartender) responsive to his every whim and gesture. The hypnoid state made the environment of the bar feel friendly, and these cozy conscious fantasies (surrounded as he was by friends who were, like family, eager to please and satisfy him) took over. This was the state he magically attempted to bring about again and again with alcohol. This actively induced hypnoid state, which he could bring about at will, substituted for the hypnoid state that in all probability had been invoked in childhood to deal with the overwhelming assault of his depraved father and depriving mother. Similar tales were reported by many patients.

For many alcoholic patients, the environs of the local bar, in fantasy, is converted into a warm, cozy home, full of cheer and good feelings—in contrast to the frequently reported stark, strident home atmosphere that, in reality, had prevailed. The bartender or barmaid becomes the good parent offering acceptance and love, all concentrated in the alcoholic product (which can represent milk, feces, urine, or semen in fantasy.) The vessel in which the alcohol is served can, in fantasy, represent breast, penis, bladder, and so forth. Thus, woven about the bar and its occupants and the alcoholic products that are served are many unconscious fantasies, soothing and replacing in a narcissistic way the starkness and despair of the actual home and homelife. This fantasy existence is expedited by inducing the hypnoid state with the ingestion of alcohol.

Freud[32] called masturbation the primary addiction. The ingestion of alcohol leads to an altered state of consciousness which may have an equivalence to the altered state associated to masturbatory climax. Masturbation and alcoholism have been linked:

> It is striking how often we find that the struggle of the alcoholic with himself or with his environment in combatting or indulging the forbidden enjoyment of drinking is an actual repetition of his original fight for or against masturbation.[19]

At the same time, the altered state of the alcoholic may also be invoked as a defense against the awareness of fantasies and memories involving earlier parental assaults and indiscretions.

In the psychotherapy clinic cases, it was ascertained that one psychological consequence of the ingestion of alcohol was the illusion that impaired functions had been restored to optimal activity.[4] Specifically, these were certain autonomous ego functions (self-observation or verbalization) whose intactness remain essential for any psychotherapeutic situation. For the alcoholic, alcohol ingestion, and the supervening altered awareness, promoted the use of fantasy formation as a defense against the recognition of compromised functioning and painful life circumstances. The unwelcome reality in regard to both past and present was denied, while fantasies, which invariably involved the patient's actively overcoming sexual and aggressive obstacles, provided a welcome gratification. In the alcoholic, pleasure in handling his glass of liquor and swallowing it can be substituted for the pleasurable manipulation of his penis. (See Arlow[33] for discussion of the two aspects of masturbation: physical manipulation of the organ involved and the fantasy accompanying this manipulation.)

In this way the construction of fantasies capable of absorbing the interest and satisfying the libidinal longings of the patient were encouraged. An important advantage of alcohol is that it permits the individual to bring about this altered state from outside his own body, and at will. The hypnoid state, then, a necessary defense against experiencing too much pain or anxiety (as related to earlier assaults and seduction), is now brought about in a controlled and magical way by the effects of the ingestion of alcohol. The actively sought hypnoid state helps maintain the repression of the earlier victimization. Secondarily, the process of construction and weaving together these many fantasies can bring its own satisfaction. Interest in the real world and its objects are loosened, and the fantasy life of the individual flourishes.

I have attempted to summarize my added understanding of alcoholism derived from twenty years of supervising the psychotherapy of alcoholic patients in a clinic setting. My knowledge of these patients was enhanced by my psychoanalytic background, which alerted me to the significance and portent of pathogenic developmental pressures. It was through this augmented analytic filter that the supervisory situation was viewed and the evolving techniques for psychotherapy were developed.

References

1. Silber A: Psychotherapy with alcoholics. *J Nerv Ment Dis* 129:477–485, 1959.
2. Silber A: Psychodynamic therapy in alcoholism, in Fox R (ed): *Alcoholism-Behavioral Research Therapeutic Approaches.* New York, Springer, 1967.
3. Silber A: An addendum to the technique of psychotherapy with alcoholics. *J Nerv Ment Dis* 150:423–437, 1970.
4. Silber A: Rationale for the technique of psychotherapy with alcoholics. *Int J Psychoanalytic Psychotherapy* 3:28–47, 1974.
5. Silber A: The alcohol-induced hypnoid state and its analytic corollary. *Int J Psychoanalytic Psychotherapy* 6:253–267, 1977.
6. Freud S: Inhibitions, symptoms and anxiety. London, Hogarth, Stand ed 20:77–175, 1959.
7. Schur M: Symptom formation and character formation. *Int J Psychoanal* 45:147–150, 1964.
8. Loewenstein RM: Ego autonomy and psychoanalytic technique. *Psychoanal Q* 41:1–22, 1972.
9. Dickes R: Severe regressive disruptions of the therapeutic alliance. *J Am Psychoanal Assoc* 15:508–533, 1967.
10. Greenacre P: Certain technical problems in the transference relationship. *J Am Psychoanal Assoc* 7:484–502, 1959.
11. Greenson RR: The working alliance and the transference relationship. *Psychoanal Q* 35:155–181, 1965.
12. Zetzel ER: The concept of transference. *Int J Psychoanal* 37:369–376, 1956.
13. Hartmann H: *Ego Psychology and the Problem of Adaptation.* New York, International Universities Press, 1959.
14. Gill M: (ed): *The Collected Papers of David Rapaport.* New York, Basic Books, 1967.
15. Knight RP: Borderline states. *Bull Menn Clin* 17:1–12, 1953.
16. Knight RP: The dynamics and treatment of chronic alcohol addiction. *Bull Menn Clin* 1:233–250, 1937.
17. Knight RP: Psychodynamics of chronic alcoholism. *J Nerv Ment Dis* 86:538–548, 1937.
18. Knight RP: The psychoanalytic treatment in a sanitarium of chronic addiction to alcohol. *JAMA* 111:1443–1448, 1938.
19. Simmel E: Alcoholism and addiction. *Psychoanal* 17:6–31, 1948.

20. Litin EM, Griffin ME, Johnson AM: Parental influence in unusual sexual behavior in children. *Psychoanal Q* 25:37–55, 1956.
21. Johnson AM: Sanctions for superego lacunae of adolescence, in Eissler MM (ed): *Searchlights on Delinquency*. New York International Universities Press, 1959, pp 225–245.
22. Szurek S: Genesis of psychopathic personality. *Psychiatry* 5:1–6, 1942.
23. Chayfetz ME: Practical and theoretical considerations in the psychotherapy of alcoholism. *Q J Stud Alcohol* 20:281–291, 1959.
24. Ferenczi S: Confusion of tongues between adults and the child, in Balint M (ed): *Final Contributions to the Problems and Methods of Psychoanalysis*. New York, Basic Books, 1955.
25. Shengold L: The parent as sphinx. *J Am Psychoanal Assoc* 11:725–751, 1963.
26. Deutsch H: Some forms of emotional disturbance and their relationship to schizophrenia. *Psychoanal Q* 11:301–321, 1942.
27. Dickes R: The defensive function of an altered state of consciousness: A hypnoid state. *J Am Psychoanal Assoc* 13:356–403, 1965.
28. Freud A: *The Ego and the Mechanisms of Defense*. London, Hogarth, 1937.
29. Fleiss R: *Ego and Body Ego*. New York, International Universities 1961.
30. Shengold L: The effects of overstimulation: Rat people. *Int J Psychoanal* 48:403–415, 1967.
31. Shengold L: More about rats and rat people. *Int J Psychoanal* 52:277–288, 1971.
32. Freud S: *The Origins of Psycho-analysis*, Bonaparte M, Freud A, Kris E (eds). New York, Basic Books, 1954.
33. Arlow J: Masturbation and symptom formation. *J Am Psychoanal Assoc* 1:45–58, 1953.

CHAPTER 15

Office Psychotherapy of Alcoholism

SHELDON ZIMBERG, MD

Physicians, psychiatrists, and other mental health professionals have been ineffectual in the treatment of alcoholics and have lost interest in attempting to treat them. Such a situation is not unexpected, since physicians and other health personnel are exposed only to the medical and psychiatric complications of alcoholism and not to the diagnosis and treatment of the disorder itself. This lack of awareness of successful treatment outcomes supports the myth that this illness is untreatable.

It is generally accepted that psychological factors alone are not sufficient to produce alcoholism in an individual. Sociocultural and physiological factors (probably of genetic origin), along with psychological mechanisms, contribute to alcoholism. This presentation will look at the psychological aspects of the primary alcoholic, develop a paradigm of the psychodynamics of alcoholism as a biopsycho-social model of alcoholism, look at various treatment interventions as they relate to this model, describe the principles and techniques in alcoholism psychotherapy, and report a follow-up study of private psychiatric office treatment based on these principles. A successful psychotherapeutic technique must be based on an understanding of psychological conflict and provide techniques that can establish a successful therapeutic relationship that can lead to resolution of the psychological conflict and improved feeling state and behavioral functioning. The psychotherapy of alcoholism must, in addition, consider the effects of the drug alcohol on the individual, since alcohol itself produces significant mood and behavioral changes as well as addiction. Therefore, modifications of traditional psychotherapeutic interventions is required in the treatment of alcoholism because of the role of alcohol itself in the manifestations of the disease.

SHELDON ZIMBERG • Director of Psychiatry, Joint Diseases, North General Hospital, New York, New York, 10035.

Psychodynamics of the Primary Alcoholic

Blum[1] reviewed the literature on psychoanalytic theories of alcoholism and concluded that psychoanalytic concepts can be applied to the psychodynamic understanding of alcohlism. Oral fixation is thought to be the arrested stage of development in the alcoholic. This fixation accounts for infantile and dependent characteristics such as narcissism, demanding behavior, passivity, and dependence. This fixation occurs after a significant degree of deprivation during early childhood development. Much evidence supports the view that alcoholics were exposed to rejection by one or both parents and that dependency needs are among the major psychological factors that contribute to the development of alcoholism. These issues have been developed and reviewed by Knight,[2] McCord and McCord,[3] Bacon et al,[4] Tahlka,[5] and Blane.[6] Other developmental factors that have been noted to contribute to a conflict with dependency have been overprotection and the forcing of premature responsibility on a child.

The dependency needs of many of the alcoholics the author has treated have been profoundly repressed, with little evidence of overt passivity or dependency traits when the patients were sober. These traits became apparent, however, under the influence of alcohol. While sober, alcoholics in many cases had obsessive compulsive personality traits. They were often perfectionists, had the need to maintain control over their lives, and were completely unaware of even the most intense feelings, particularly anger. These observations were confirmed by an experimental study of drinking to intoxication among a group of alcoholics conducted by Tamerin and Mendelson.[7] Therefore, it is neither appropriate nor useful to look for or characterize an "alcoholic personality." The conflict discussed below forms a psychodynamic constellation which is the key psychological factor in alcoholism and is the core conflict that must be recognized in therapy. This psychodynamic constellation is a common problem among alcoholics, but it does not produce a common personality.

The conflict consists of a lack of self-esteem along with feelings of worthlessness and inadequacy. These feelings are denied and repressed and lead to unconscious needs to be taken care of and accepted (dependency needs). Since these dependency needs cannot be met in reality, they lead to anxiety and compensatory needs for control, power, and achievement. Alcohol tranquilizes the anxiety and, more important, creates pharmacologically induced feelings of power, omnipotence, and invulnerability.

When the alcoholic wakes up after a drinking episode, he experiences guilt and despair because he has not achieved anything more than before he drank and his problems remain. Thus, his feelings of worthlessness are intensified and the conflict continues in a vicious circle, often with a progressive downward spiral.

Alcohol provides an artificial feeling state of power and control that cannot be achieved in reality. The very act of producing this feeling of power at will feeds the alcoholic's grandiose self-image. This intense need for grandiosity can be called "reactive grandiosity."

These observations are supported by the work of McClelland et al,[8] which indicated that (in alcoholics) alcohol produces "ego enhancing" effects and thoughts of power and strength. McCord and McCord[3] conducted longitudinal studies of families in which some of the boys later became alcoholics. They noted that the alcoholics had evidence of heightened unacceptable dependency needs and had feelings of being victimized by society with compensatory grandiosity.

These observations are summarized in Figure 1, which illustrates the psychodynamics of alcoholism. Childhood rejection, overprotection, or premature responsibility leads to an unconscious need for nurturance which cannot be met in reality and results in rejection. The rejection leads to anxiety, which in turn leads to the development of a number of defense mechanisms, particularly denial, and a compensatory need for grandiosity. The grandiosity causes such individuals to try harder and results in inevitable failure. The failures lead to more anxiety, depression, anger, and guilt. These unpleasant affects can be reduced by alcohol, at least for a time, and lead to the pharmacologically induced feelings of power and omnipotence, thus reinforcing the denial and reactive grandiosity.

An individual with such a psychological conflict will become an alcoholic

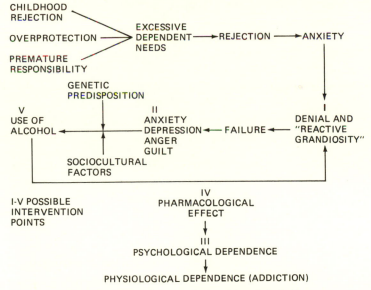

Fig 1. Paradigm of the psychodynamics of alcoholism.

if there is a genetic predisposition to alcoholism and if he lives in a society in which the use of alcohol is sanctioned as a way to feel better or in which there is considerable ambivalence regarding the use of alcohol. In any particular individual, one or more of these etiological factors may predominate and lead to alcoholism.

Treatment of Alcoholism

Alcoholics Anonymous

Alcoholics Anonymous (AA) has been one of the most successful treatment approaches for alcoholism; it is also the model for other successful self-help movements. How does the effectiveness of AA relate to the psychodynamic understanding of alcoholism just presented?

Tiebout[9] described a similar psychodynamic understanding of alcoholism in his paper discussing the process by which an alcoholic becomes involved in Alcoholics Anonymous. The process occurs in four steps: (1) the need to hit bottom, (2) the need to be humble, (3) the need to surrender, and (4) the need for ego reduction. These steps were based on Tiebout's observation of an excessive amount of narcissism in the alcoholic's ego, which gives rise to feelings of omnipotence. The steps in the conversion process are necessary to produce a reduction in this narcissism, which perpetuates the self-destructive behavior and the coexisting denial. Tiebout did not indicate in his paper, however, what happens to the excessive narcissism of the alcoholic's ego. Clearly, the narcissism is sublimated toward the goal of AA to rescue other alcoholics. Thus, the grandiosity becomes fulfilled and socially useful and much of the dependency need is met by the group. AA members recognize that their support of other alcoholics helps them to maintain sobriety. Therefore, the successful development of AA was based on an intuitive understanding of the alcoholic's psychological conflict and needs.

Other Treatment Approaches

Other treatment approaches can be understood by looking at Figure 1 in relation to possible intervention points on this paradigm. Intervention Point I represents the traditional psychoanalytic approach to treating alcoholism. In this case, the therapist attempts to work backwards from the defenses to uncover the underlying psychological conflicts. This approach has failed simply because the pharmacological effects of alcohol are too strong to be altered through insight alone, and the very technique of uncovering therapy produces anxiety, which results in the need to drink.

Intervention Point II represents an area in which mood-altering drugs might reduce the need to use alcohol to reduce dysphoric feelings. Subpopulations of alcoholics who were clinically depressed have been noted in a recent study to have benefited from lithium treatment.[10] Such patients most likely represent secondary alcoholism rather than primary alcoholism.

Intervention Point III represents the use of drugs or other modalities that would alter the effect of alcohol on the brain and result in a reduced craving for alcohol, a lessening of the pleasant effect of alcohol, and/or a reduction in the degree of physiological dependence. With our understanding of the mechanisms of how alcohol affects the brain, we may be able to alter the adverse effects selectively. This area probably represents the future of alcoholism treatment.

Intervention Point IV can interrupt the pleasurable feelings associated with alcohol consumption that become reinforced by repetitive drinking and lead to alcoholism. Lovibond and Caddy[11] applied aversive conditioning with electric shocks to enable alcoholics to discriminate their blood alcohol levels and to maintain low levels characterized by controlled social drinking. They reported considerable success with this approach. Ewing and Rouse[12] reported that, although the alcoholic patients were able to learn to recognize their levels of blood alcohol and develop controlled drinking while in the program, all relapsed into loss-of-control drinking during the 27- to 55-month follow-up period. The literature is replete with equivocal results in various aversive conditioning approaches. However, this still remains an important area for research.

The fifth point of possible intervention represents our current approach to alcoholism psychotherapy and is the basis of the material in this chapter. This method involves eliminating the use of alcohol by directive approaches and helping the alcoholic learn to live without alcohol in the face of stress and unpleasant feelings.

The central problem in the psychotherapy is breaking through the *reactive grandiosity* that produces the massive denial of profound feelings of inferiority and dependency that permit the pattern of self-destructive drinking to continue. The alcoholic destroys, not only himself, but his loved ones without perceiving his lack of control of his behavior pattern. The typical response of an alcoholic without insight into his behavior is, "I can stop drinking any time I want to," despite overwhelming evidence to the contrary. This self-deception must be penetrated if rehabilitation is to succeed.

Sociopsychological Factors Affecting Psychotherapy

During the initial evaluation of the alcoholic, one not only must look for areas of psychological conflict and psychopathology, but must also try to understand the patient's social circumstances. It is necessary to evaluate the family and marital relationships that exist or existed and the employment situation. Information should also be obtained regarding the cultural attitudes toward drinking and drunkenness in the individual's family while he was growing up and how he integrated these attitudes into his drinking behavior.

There must be a determination as to how the individual has handled crises and stress, and whether he has been able to modify or stop destructive drinking behavior spontaneously in the past, and for how long. One must determine the individual's psychological, social, and developmental levels and how he reached them.

The social, familial, and cultural contexts in which problem drinking occurs are significant in determining the most effective treatment and what influences can be brought to bear to convince the alcoholic of his need for help. Coercion is often necessary because of the massive denial and self-deception. Industrial alcoholism programs often use the implied threat of losing one's job unless one enters treatment. Such programs report relatively high rates of success in rehabilitating their alcoholic employees. Such coercion can be viewed as therapeutic leverage in which a small degree of self-awareness is forced upon the alcoholic. Such therapeutic leverage can be useful; however, it cannot in and of itself produce recovery, which can occur only in the treatment process described below. Therapeutic leverage should be sought in the initial evaluation of an alcoholic as a source of increasing motivation for treatment.

All alcoholics are not the same, even though most share the common psychodynamic conflict of dependency and the need for compensatory power and control. Alcoholics exist in differing age groups, socioeconomic circumstances, and cultural groups.[13-16] Approaches with the skid row homeless alcoholic cannot be the same as with the so-called high-bottom executive, or with the individual living in poverty in an urban ghetto.

It should be noted that alcoholism does not occur as an all-or-none phenomenon but has varying degrees in the same individual. Table I shows a scale developed by the author[17] that defines the degrees of alcohol abuse from no problem to the skid row alcoholic at Level 6. Improvement in treatment can be measured by movement upward from Level 6 to Level 1 in this scale.

The Treatment Process

Principles of Treatment

Alcoholism is a chronic illness with a high potential for relapse. As in other chronic disorders, continuous care may be required in some cases. Alcoholics Anonymous is particularly well suited to provide this supportive treatment for

TABLE I. Alcohol Abuse Scale

Level	Characteristics
1. None	Drinks only on occasion, if at all.
2. Minimal	Drinking is not conspicuous, occasional intoxications (up to four per year). No social, family, occupational, health, or legal problems related to drinking.
3. Mild	Intoxication occurring up to once a month, although generally limited to evening or weekends, and/or some impairment in social or family relations or occupational functioning related to drinking. No physical or legal problems related to drinking.
4. Moderate	Frequent intoxications, up to one or two times per week and/or significant impairment in social, family, or occupational functioning. Some suggestive evidence of physical impairment related to drinking such as tremors, frequent accidents, epigastric distress, loss of appetite at times. No history of delirium tremens, cirrhosis, nutritional deficiency, hospitalizations related to drinking, or arrests related to drinking.
5. Severe	Almost constantly drinking (practically every day). History of delirium tremens, liver cirrhosis, chronic brain syndrome, neuritis, nutritional deficiency, or severe disruption in social or family relations. Unable to hold a steady job but able to maintain himself on public assistance. One or more arrests related to drinking (drunk and disorderly).
6. Extreme	All the characteristics of severe impairment plus homelessness and/or inability to maintain himself on public assistance.

an indefinite duration. However, professional intervention during the early stages of treatment is necessary to provide detoxification from alcohol, a thorough psychosocial evaluation, and continued support for alcoholics unwilling or unable to make effective use of AA. After detoxification, alcoholics should *not* be maintained on minor tranquilizers since these may be readily abused. Detoxification can be carried out in many cases on an ambulatory basis. The ambulatory detoxification involves using diazepam (Valium) 5 mg three times a day in decreasing doses over a 7- to 10-day period. The patient should be seen 3 to 4 times during this period to assess the effectiveness of the detoxification. The prescription should not contain more than 21 tablets and should not be renewable. Some patients with more severe manifestations of alcoholism may require inpatient detoxification.

Patients with serious depression or psychoses along with alcoholism should have these conditions treated first. It has often been found that the alcoholism is secondary to these major psychiatric disorders and clears up when the primary disorder is effectively treated. A period of observation of such patients in a hospital setting may be required to make such a differential diagnosis.

Directive counseling during the process of detoxification can enhance an alcoholic's motivation to continue the treatment. Counseling or more intensive psychotherapeutic approaches are necessary after detoxification. Acquainting the alcoholic with the physical effects of alcohol on his body and the effects on his ability to perform his necessary functions should be part of this effort. The deterrent use of disulfiram (Antabuse) is also effective.

Several principles are important in the treatment of an alcoholic individual. The principles apply whether the alcoholic is involved in a therapeutic relationship with a physician, with a mental health professional, or with a paraprofessional alcoholism counselor. First, the drinking itself must be terminated if therapy is to be effective in achieving rehabilitation. A common mistake mental health professional have made is to consider alcoholism a symptom of underlying disorder. Psychological conflict does exist as indicated, but efforts must first be directed to achieve sobriety for the patient through detoxification and the maintenance of sobriety through intensive directive counseling or psychotherapy and the use of disulfiram. A patient who continues to drink will not respond to counseling or psychotherapeutic approaches, and a power struggle will develop between therapist and the drinking patient.

The second principle is the understanding of the *transference* that the alcoholic will establish with the therapist. This transference is very intensive and is characterized by a considerable amount of dependence coupled with hostile, manipulative, and testing behavior. Thus, a great deal of ambivalence will be noted in the transference relationship. The alcoholic will be dependent, but at other times he will be grandiose, believing he can control his drinking as well as his life when the evidence is obviously to the contrary.

The third principle is understanding the *countertransference* that may develop in a therapist in response to the provocative behavior and drinking of the patient as a test of the therapist's continued interest. Because of this type of testing behavior, the treatment of an alcoholic can be felt to be frustrating and unrewarding. The therapist must recognize, however, that he is not omnipotent in regard to the alcoholic's drinking. He cannot, nor can anyone, stop an alcoholic determined to drink. A therapist can only provide the means to assist the alcoholic in achieving sobriety; he cannot force him for long into refraining from drinking. Only the patient's conscious efforts can achieve this. Recognizing this reality, the therapist must impose limits on the behavior of the patient and conditions under which treatment can continue. If the patient cannot meet these conditions, treatment should be discontinued. The door, however, should be left open to renew the efforts to achieve sobriety as the first step in the treatment process. Table II summarizes the basic principles that should be observed in the psychotherapy of alcoholism

TABLE II. Principles of Psychotherapy with Alcoholics

1. Direct intervention in relation to drinking.

2. Transference: intensely ambivalent; testing; denial and grandiosity.

3. Countertransference: intense feelings of frustration and anger; therapist's need for omnipotence.

4. Support and redirection of various defenses rather than attempt to remove.

5. Looking for therapeutic leverage.

6. Therapy carried out in stages designed to achieve control of impulse to drink.

Stages of Treatment

The treatment has been observed to progress through several stages (see Table III). Although the stages can be observed in group therapy and in AA involvement, they are most apparent in individual therapy.

The first stage involves the situation in which the alcoholic *cannot drink*. This situation exists when there is external pressure on the patient to stop drinking such as the threat of loss of job, his spouse's leaving, or the use of disulfiram. In a sense, the alcoholic is forced to stop drinking at least for a short time. His attitudes toward drinking and the denial of drinking as a serious problem have not changed. The alcoholic has stopped drinking not because *he* sees stopping as necessary, but because someone else does. He must be helped by directive counseling to face problems and stress without resorting to alcohol. Involvement of the family in joint sessions with the patient and referral of the family to Al-Anon are helpful in changing family attitudes about the alcoholic family member and in giving the family greater understanding of the illness of alcoholism. During this stage patients should be taught to recognize cues that might lead to drinking so that they can develop alternative copying mechanisms. Forgetting to take a disulfiram tablet can be such a cue, and therefore the use of disulfiram can serve as an early warning system. Often, when the patient has stopped drinking early in treatment, he feels extremely confident about his newly acquired sobriety and experiences a feeling of euphoria. This feeling is a reaction formation to his unconscious lack of control over his drinking, which is now experienced as a certainty of control over his not drinking as well as control over other aspects of his life. Patients should be warned to expect such inappropriate feelings. This situation is by its nature very unstable since there has been neither significant change in the patient's attitude about drinking nor an ego reduction as described by Tiebout.[9] The situation can easily lead to a return to

TABLE III. Stages of Treatment

Stages	Patient Status	Treatment
Stage I	"I can't drink" (need for external control)	Alcohol detoxification Directive psychotherapy Disulfiram AA Family therapy Al-Anon
Stage II	"I won't drink" (internalized control)	Directive psychotherapy Supportive psychotherapy Possible discontinuation of disulfiram AA
Stage III	"I don't have to drink" (conflict resolution)	Psychoanalytically oriented psychotherapy

drinking or, through counseling and/or further Alcoholics Anonymous involvement, to a stage at which the alcoholic won't drink.

This is the stage at which the controls on the compulsion to drink have become internalized and there is no longer a serious conscious conflict about whether or not to drink. At this stage, the individual's attitude toward the necessity of drinking and the deleterious consequences in resuming drinking are apparent; he has experienced a considerable attitudinal change toward drinking. The conflict about drinking is still present, but at an unconscious level. Evidence of the continued existence of this conflict is present in fantasies and dreams. This stage is the level which many Alcoholics Anonymous members have achieved. Discontinuation of disulfiram or its intermittent use only in stressful situations can be considered. Further help in developing alternative coping mechanisms for stress and unpleasant feelings should be provided. This stage represents a reasonably good stage of recovery and is fairly stable, only occasionally leading to a slip after years of sobriety. The reactive grandiosity has now been sublimated (redirected) in the ego-enhancing feelings of control over a previously uncontrollable problem. For active AA members, their work with other alcoholics serves as an additional outlet for the need for grandiosity. At least six months to one year of directive psychotherapy is required to achieve this stage of recovery.

The third stage of recovery involves the situation in which the alcoholic *does not have to drink*. This stage can be achieved only through insight into the individual's personality problems and conflicts and their resolution to a major degree. The habitual use of alcohol at this stage can be understood as a way of dealing with the individual's conflicts. With the resolution of the conflicts, the individual can achieve more adaptive ways of coping with problems internal and external. This stage can be achieved only through psychoanalytically oriented psychotherapy and self-understanding. It is a stable stage as long as the alcoholic refrains from drinking and is relatively easy to maintain. The duration of treatment required to achieve this stage of recovery has in the author's experience been about one or two years after reaching Stage II.

After reaching Stage II or III, some patients enter a situation in which they believe, "I can return to social drinking." Possibly a small percentage of alcoholics can achieve this (see Pattison's discussion[18]), but at our present level of knowledge it is impossible to predict which patient this might be. All alcoholics believe during the initial stages of treatment that they can return to controlled drinking. Alcoholics who have achieved recovery (Stage II or III) in most cases do not desire to resume social drinking because of the risk involved. Recent publicity regarding this issue has raised the question in some recovered alcoholics, but generally they have been persuaded not to take the chance of resuming social drinking. For all practical purposes at the present time, *abstinence* should be the necessary goal in the treatment of all alcoholics. Alcohol is not necessary to life, and it is quite possible to live and even be happy without consuming it. This fact should be part of the attitudinal change an alcoholic experiences during the process of recovery.

Termination of Treatment

The termination of treatment with an alcoholic is critical. If the treatment process is successful, the alcoholic will have established a dependent, trusting relationship with the therapist, and therefore termination will produce anxiety and the possibility of return to drinking. The termination should be based on mutual agreement between the therapist and patient, a termination date determined, and the final period of therapy involved with the issue of termination.

Termination can occur at Stage II or III since both are relatively stable stages regarding control of drinking. A decision has to be made, however, when a patient reaches Stage II, as to whether further treatment to achieve insight into the psychological conflict related to his drinking problem and moving to reach Stage III in treatment is important. This option should be left to the patient. Nonpsychiatric physicians can provide the directive counseling and the prescription disulfiram, where indicated, to help alcoholics reach Stage II. More traditional psychotherapy is required to reach Stage III, and nonpsychiatric physicians and alcoholism counselors might consider referral of such patients to psychotherapists.

Regardless of whether the patient terminates in Stage II or III, the door to return to therapy should be left open. A patient who stops treatment after Stage II may determine after a while that not drinking is not enough to help him deal with his feelings and conflicts and might wish to return for treatment to try to achieve insight into his personality conflicts. A patient terminated after Stage II may have a slip, and a return to treatment should be available. This slip, however, should not be viewed as a treatment failure, but as part of the rehabilitation process that is not yet complete. Patients who slip in Stages II and III generally do not return to continuous uncontrolled drinking because their awareness of their problem is acute and the strength of their control mechanisms is such that the mechanisms can be quickly reinstated. The slip can be looked at as a psychological maladaptation to conflict and anxiety or as a transference reaction, and it is possible to help the patient gain more understanding of his need to drink by analyzing such slips.

This approach to psychotherapy of alcoholics, presented in terms of stages of progression of treatment in relation to varying abilities to control the impulse to drink, provides a framework for a complex and often amorphous treatment process. It provides a goal-directed approach to achievable levels of improvement. Complex therapeutic decisions regarding involvement of the family in treatment, starting or stopping of disulfiram, attendance at AA meetings, use of uncovering techniques, discontinuation of therapy, and other questions can be considered in relation to these fairly preditable stages in the recovery process. It is possible to make predictions of outcome of therapeutic intervention or lack of intervention based on knowledge of the stage of recovery the patient has entered. Therefore, such an awareness can make the complex psychotherapeutic process with alcoholics potentially understandable and subject to a certain degree of predictability.

Report of an Outcome Study

The author analyzed data on 23 alcoholic patients treated in individual psychotherapy during a two-year period in a private psychiatric office setting where the methods described above were utilized. The patients were seen in most cases on a once-a-week basis. In some cases where marital problems were major aspects of the patient's difficulties, joint sessions with spouses were held periodically. All patients received a physical examination and laboratory studies from an internist.

The data obtained for this study came from a review of the charts kept on the patients and follow-up telephone calls on patients who were no longer in treatment.

The results of the study can be seen in Table IV. This table indicates that 14 of the 23 patients treated (61%) were successes. An outcome was considered successful when there was at least 1 year of abstinence from alcohol with functional improvement in other aspects of their lives. Of the 14 patients who achieved a successful outcome, 10 patients achieved a Stage II level of

TABLE IV. Characteristics of Treated Patients

	Successes[a] 14[b]	Early[c] Dropouts 5 (22%)	Failures 4 (17%)
1. Sex			
Male	8	4	2
Female	6	1	2
2. Age			
Average	43	38	41
Range	33–54	22–52	30–51
3. Religion			
Catholic	3	1	1
Protestant	6	2	3
Jewish	4	1	0
Other	1	1	0
4. Marital status			
Married	7	3	1
Divorced	3	1	1
Single	3	1	1
Separated	0	0	1
Widowed	1	0	0
5. Employment			
Employed	11	5	3
Student	1	0	0
Housewife	2	0	1
6. Social class			
Lower middle	1	2	1
Middle	7	1	1
Upper middle	6	2	2
7. Duration of alcohol abuse (years)			
Average	7	6	5
Range	3–17	2–12	2–10
8. Level of alcohol abuse			
4	8	3	2
5	6	2	2

Continued

TABLE IV. (Continued)

	Successes[a] 14[b]	Early[c] Dropouts 5 (22%)	Failures 4 (17%)
9. Use of disulfiram			
Yes	13	2	4
No	1	3	0
Complications	2	0	0
10. Type of Detoxification			
Hospital	3	0	1
Ambulatory	9	5	3
None	2	0	0
11. Use of Alcoholics Anonymous			
Yes	10	2	1
No	4	3	3
12. Previous Treatment			
None	6	3	2
Psychiatric	7	2	2
Alcoholism	1	0	0

[a] One year or more of abstinence with improvement in other aspects of their lives.
[b] Stage II–10; Stage III–4
[c] Six sessions or less.

recovery (internalized controls over the impulse to drink) and 4 achieved a Stage III level of recovery (conflict resolution).

In the study, 5 patients (22%) dropped out of therapy early (6 sessions or less) and 4 patients (17%) were failures. If we consider the outcome of the 18 patients who remained in therapy, 14 (78%) had successful results.

There were 14 males and 9 females. The average age was 44 with a range of 22–54. The average duration of their alcoholism was 8 years with a range of 2–17 years. The severity of their alcoholism was 13 of the patients at Level 4 on the Alcohol Abuse Scale (see Table I) and 10 and Level 5.

Additional demographic characteristics of this treatment population indicated that 11 patients were married, 6 divorced or separated, 5 single, and 1 widowed; 5 were Catholic, 11 Protestant, 5 Jewish, 1 Moslem, and another with no religious affiliation; all of the patients were middle-class individuals, with 19 employed, 1 a student, and 3 housewives.

History of the treatment population indicated that 11 had no previous treatment for their alcoholism, 11 had previous psychiatric treatment which was unsuccessful, and 1 had previous alcoholism treatment which was unsuccessful.

When first seen for treatment, most of the patients required detoxification from alcohol, with only 2 being sober on initial contact. Of the 21 requiring detoxification, 17 (81%) were successfully detoxified on an ambulatory basis; 4 (19%) required in-hospital detoxification after failure of ambulatory detoxification.

Regarding Alcoholics Anonymous attendance, 13 participated in AA and 10 did not. Among the patients who dropped out and those who failed in therapy, 3 used AA and 6 did not. Although the numbers are too small to determine statistical significance, it is suggested that attendance at AA is associated with a successful outcome.

Disulfiram was used with 19 of the 23 patients and with 13 of the 14 patients who had successful outcomes. There were 2 patients who had complications from the use of disulfiram which required its discontinuation. One patient developed a toxic hepatitis and another developed an organic brain syndrome. These conditions cleared up after the disulfiram was stopped.

Organic Brain Damage in Alcoholics

A CT scan study conducted by Lusins *et al*[19] of alcoholics without psychiatric disorder, drug abuse, dementia, or neurological disorder found 58% of 50 patients with cerebral atrophy. The atrophy was not correlated with neuropsychological deficits, age, age of onset of drinking, or severity of alcoholism. The only correlation was in the duration of problem drinking, 8.7 years without atrophy and 13.3 years with atrophy.

In private practice, three patients who were not responding to the psychotherapy described recently were found to have cerebral atrophy on CT scan. The role of organic brain damage in unresponsive alcoholics is suggested by this finding in a small number of patients. CT scan studies should be done in patients who have drinking histories of more than 10 years in duration or who are unresponsive to psychotherapy. Other nonverbal approaches may be more appropriate for such brain-damaged alcoholics.

Summary

Alcoholism can be treated psychotherapeutically in individual or group therapy. The underlying psychodynamics consists of conflict with excessive dependent needs leading to the defenses of denial and reactive grandiosity. The use of alcohol serves to reinforce these defenses. Certain principles are necessary for the successful psychotherapeutic treatment of alcoholism: (1) efforts must first be directed at producing abstinence from alcohol; (2) there must be an understanding of the transference and countertransference aspects of the treatment process by the therapist. The treatment process has been observed to progress through fairly distinct stages, consisting of the patient's ability to maintain controls on the compulsion to drink. In treating the alcoholic, one must determine first if the alcoholic has coexisting physical or serious psychiatric disorders that will affect the treatment process. In addition, the social, family, and economic circumstances of the patient must be understood and utilized to provide therapeutic leverage that will enhance the effectiveness of treatment.

A report of patients treated in individual psychotherapy over a two-year period in a private psychiatric office setting was presented. The results indicated a 61% success rate in the total population and 78% successful results in those patients who remained in treatment beyond six sessions. Therefore, alcoholism was found to be eminently treatable in a psychiatric office setting, contrary to the common experience of most psychiatrists.

Patients who have long drinking histories and are found to be unresponsive to this psychotherapeutic approach may have brain damage as determined by CT scan.

References

1. Blum EM: Psychoanalytic views of alcoholism: A review. *QJ Stud Alcohol* 27:259–299, 1966.
2. Knight RP: The psychodynamics of chronic alcoholism. *J Nerv Ment Dis* 8:538–543, 1937.
3. McCord W, McCord W: *Origins of Alcoholism.* Stanford, Stanford University Press, 1960.
4. Bacon MK, Barry H, Child IL: A cross-cultural study of drinking: II. Relation to other features of culture. *Q J Stud Alcohol* 3:29–48, 1965.
5. Tahlka V: *The Alcoholic Personality.* Helsinki, Finnish Foundation for Alcohol Studies, 1966.
6. Blane HT: *The Personality of the Alcoholic: Guises of Dependency.* New York, Harper & Row, 1968.
7. Tamerin JS, Mendelson JH: The Psychodynamics of chronic inebriation: Observations of alcoholics during the process of drinking in the experimental group setting. *Am J Psychiatry* 125:886–899, 1969.
8. McClelland DC, Davis, WN, Kalin R, *et al: The Drinking Man.* New York, Free Press, 1972.
9. Tiebout HM: Alcoholics Anonymous: An experiment of nature. *Q J Stud Alcohol* 22:52–68, 1961.
10. Merry J, Reynolds CM, Baily J, Coppen A: Prophylactic treatment of alcoholism by lithium carbonate. *Lancet* 2:481–482, 1976.
11. Lovibond SH, Caddy G: Discriminated aversive control of alcoholics drinking behavior. *Behavior Therapy* 1:437–474, 1970.
12. Ewing JA, Rouse BA: Failure of an experimental treatment program to inculcate controlled drinking in alcoholics. *Br J Addict* 71:123–134, 1976.
13. Kissin B, Platz A, Su WH: Social and psychological factors in the treatment of chronic alcoholism. *J Psychiatr Res* 8:13–27, 1970.
14. Mindlin DF: The characteristics of alcoholics as related to therapeutic outcome. *Q J Stud Alcohol* 20:604–619, 1959.
15. Zimberg S: The elderly alcoholic. *The Gerontologist* 14:221–224, 1974.
16. Zimberg S, Lipscomb H, David EB: Sociopsychiatric treatment of alcoholism in an urban ghetto. *Am J Psychiatry* 127:1670–1674, 1971.

17. Zimberg S: Evaluation of alcoholism treatment in Harlem. *Q J Stud Alcohol* 35:550–557, 1974.

18. Pattison EM: Abstinence criteria: A critique of abstinence criteria in the treatment of alcoholism. *Int J Soc Psych* 14:268–276, 1968.

19. Lusins J, Zimberg S, Smokler H, Gurley K: Alcoholism and cerebral atrophy: A study of 50 patients with CT scan and psychological testing. *Alcoholism: Clin Exp Res* 4:406–411, 1980.

Index